DOOMSDAY

DOOMSDAY

50 VISIONS OF THE END OF THE WORLD

NIGEL CAWTHORNE

Capella

CONTENTS

Published by Arcturus Publishing Limited

For Bookmart Limited
Registered number 2372865
Trading as Bookmart Limited
Blaby Road, Wigston, Leicester LE18 4SE

This edition printed in 2004

©2004 Arcturus Publishing Limited

British Library Cataloguing-in-Publication Data: a catalogue record for this book is available from the British Library

Arcturus Publishing Limited 26/27 Bickels Yard, 151–153 Bermondsey Street, London SE1 3HA

ISBN 1-84193-238-8
Jacket and book design by Alex Ingr

Printed in China

INTRODUCTION

THE sixteenth-century French astrologer Nostradamus had no problem foreseeing the end of the world. The Antichrist would be born in the east, he said, following which event the yellow people of east Asia would join forces with the Muslims to invade Europe. In a war that would last from 1999 to 2026, the Western nations would be destroyed. All opponents would be put to death or taken into slavery and that would be that.

In identifying this threat to humanity, however, Nostradamus was limiting his field of view: catastrophic warfare is not the only threat to life on this planet. Since the Renaissance, the human race has developed many more varied and interesting ways to spark the apocalypse. Modern science has also drawn our attention to numerous other threats to our fragile planet.

Throughout history humankind has withstood numerous catastrophes. It has been conservatively estimated that the two world wars of the last century caused the deaths of some 187 million people, through the hostilities themselves and also in the persecution, disease, disruption and famine that accompanied the conflict. Seven centuries before, Genghis Khan killed 20 million people, a tenth of the population of the world at the time. The Black Death swept across Europe in the 14th century killing between a third and a half of the population. Somehow, however, humanity survived. So how realistic is it that humankind will wipe itself out or be wiped out in the foreseeable future?

Well, here's the bad news. In 1983, the physicist Brandon Carter made a speech to the Royal Society in London, in which he laid out what has become known as the 'Doomsday argument'. Carter was a pioneer of the so-called anthropic principle in science, which maintains that the laws of physics seem to have been tailor-made for human life to exist. Any slight change in the basic laws that govern the universe and we would not be here in the first place. It seems that we live in the only possible universe that we could live in – which may go some way to explaining why we can understand it.

At the time, Carter was studying the possibility that life might exist elsewhere in the universe and he began to wonder, if a civilisation like ours had sprung up on a similar planet orbiting a star like our Sun, how long it would last. He quickly concluded that, even though our Sun would keep shining for another six billion years, human life would have ceased to exist on this planet long before then.

The argument runs as follows: there is no reason for use to assume that we are living at some special time in the history of humanity, so there is no reason to think that we are among the first or the last of humankind to exist. More than likely we are somewhere in the middle.

We know with some degree of certainty that some 60 billion *Homo sapiens* have lived on this planet. For most of their existence, humans were hunter-gatherers and it is unlikely that the world could sustain a population of more than ten million. When agriculture came along around 8,000 BC, the population began to expand, until by Roman times there were around 300 million. By the middle of the 19th century there were a billion. Now there are six billion.

So if we are around halfway through the roll call of humanity, another 60 billion will come after us. Even if we kept our population growth down to replacement rate – that is, with each woman having, on average, 2.1 children (the extra 0.1 compensates for children who do not reach reproductive age) – then we have just ten generations to go. The current fertility rate is around 2.7.

Doomsday is coming: of that there is little doubt. The only question is whether the demise of humankind and the Earth itself will be as a result of humanity's own actions, or whether cosmic forces, far beyond our understanding, much less control, will take our fate out of our own hands and place it at the mercy of the laws of physics.

CHAPTER I
WAR

One Man's War

DURING WORLD WAR II, Hitler maintained that the Aryan race was defending itself against an international conspiracy that he claimed had been organised by the Jews, and asserting its natural right to rule over the racially inferior Slavic peoples to the east. But despite the Holocaust and the appalling treatment meted out to the people in the territories Germany occupied, World War II was not a race war. It was a war of one man's ambition, an ambition which took the world to the brink of global annihilation. We may not be so lucky next time.

Whether World War II would have happened without Hitler is a matter of philosophical debate; there is, however, no doubting the fact that he was its chief architect. Born in Austria, the son of a brutal drunken customs officer, Hitler had a troubled childhood. His idolised mother died of cancer when he was 20, and his 'artist's talents' turned out to be not so great as he had fondly imagined. Failing as an artist, he became a down-and-out in Vienna, where he nurtured

megalomaniac fantasies of revenge on the world, and more sinisterly, on the Jews, whom he blamed not only for his personal misfortunes, but those of Europe as a whole.

At the outbreak of World War I, Hitler was in Munich, where he had gone to avoid being conscripted into the Austrian army, and joined the German army instead. Wounded and gassed, he proved a brave soldier, winning the Iron Cross First Class in 1918, but he was never promoted beyond the rank of corporal.

Germany's surrender in 1918 left the country in political turmoil. In 1919, Hitler joined the German Worker's Party, which became the National Socialist German Workers' Party – or Nazi Party – in August 1920. Based in Munich, it attracted former servicemen who felt that the front-line troops had not lost the war on the battlefield, but had been 'stabbed in the back' by Communist agitators and Jews at home, none of whom had Germany's interests at heart. As the party's propaganda chief at the time, Hitler also played on the discontent caused by the punitive nature of the Treaty of Versailles that had ended the war. This stripped Germany of its colonies, redrew its borders, restricted its military and forced it to pay reparations.

With the help of Ernst Röhm, an army staff officer, Hitler took over the Nazi

Party in July 1921. Hitler's hypnotic oratory soon drew a following. He viciously denounced Communists and Jews, while Röhm organised a private army of storm troopers named the *Sturmabteilung*, the SA, better-known as the Brownshirts, to police meetings and attack political opponents.

In November 1923, Hitler made his first attempt to gain power, staging a coup against the Bavarian government generally referred to as the Munich Beer Hall Putsch. When the putsch failed, Hitler was arrested, tried, convicted of treason and sentenced to five years in prison. In Landsberg prison, he wrote *Mein Kampf* – 'My Struggle' – in which he extolled the virtues of racial purity and the will to power, and denounced Communists, liberals, Jews and foreign capitalists. Germany was destined to become the world's dominant power, he said. It would take revenge for its defeat in World War I, unite the German-speaking peoples now living in other countries and expand to the east, finding *Lebensraum*, or living space, in central Europe and Russia. This was to be achieved by war.

Released after just nine months, Hitler recruited World War I air ace Herman Göring, strong-arm man Heinrich Himmler and master propagandist Josef Goebbels to the cause. The worldwide economic collapse of 1929 brought chaos to the streets that was exploited by the Nazi stormtroopers. In the 1932 elections, the Nazis were the biggest party in the Reichstag and in January 1933, the German president, ageing war hero Paul von Hindenburg, appointed Hitler as Reich Chancellor.

The following month the Reichstag was burned down in a fire, which was probably started by a Dutch Communist Marinus van der Lubbe acting on his own, although Hitler was quick to use it as an excuse to outlaw the Communist Party and arrest its leaders. He took dictatorial powers, outlawed all other political parties, purged Jews and brought all branches of government under the direct control of the Nazi Party. The only possible source of opposition to Hitler's rule now came from within the Nazi Party itself. So on 30 June 1934 – the Night of the Long Knives – he had Ernst Röhm and hundreds of other early followers murdered and the postion of the SA was taken over by the *Schutzstaffel* or SS, under Himmler, who were loyal only to Hitler himself.

When Hindenburg died in August 1934, Hitler took over the presidency, naming himself *Führer* of what he called the Third Reich. (The First Reich was the German-led Holy Roman Empire from 800 to 1806; the Second Reich the German Empire from unification in 1871 to defeat in World War I in 1918.) Political enemies, Jews, homosexuals, intellectuals, trade unionists and radical members of the clergy were arrested by the new Nazi secret police force, the Gestapo, and sent to concentration camps set up by the SS. Hitler set about building a 'master race', stripping Jews who remained at large of their citizenship, killing or forcibly sterilising mental defectives and others he felt were inferior, and beginning a selective breeding programme for his blonde, blue-eyed elite, the SS. Meanwhile, in defiance of the Versailles Treaty, he set up an air force – the *Luftwaffe* – started building tanks and sent troops into the demilitarised Rhineland.

In 1936, he formed the Rome-Berlin

Nazi Party rally, Berlin, 9 September 1938. Mass gatherings of the Party faithful like this one were essential to building the Führer myth.

'Axis' with Italy's Fascist dictator Benito Mussolini, and signed a pact with the militarist government in Japan. In 1938, he annexed his homeland Austria and demanded that Czechoslovakia hand over the Sudetenland, a border region where the inhabitants spoke German. Unprepared for war, Britain and France agreed to the dismemberment of Czechoslovakia at the Munich Conference in September. However, Hitler soon swallowed up the rest of Czechoslovakia and began making more territorial demands.

After concluding a non-aggression pact with the Soviet Union on 23 August 1939, Hitler invaded Poland on 1 September. Poland's allies Britain and France declared war, but could offer little practical military help, and Poland was quickly overrun.

Hitler then seized Denmark and Norway. His fast-moving mechanised forces overran the Low Countries and France in a matter of weeks, but his plans to invade the United Kingdom had to be shelved when the *Luftwaffe* failed to gain control of the skies in the Battle of Britain.

Despite this setback, Hitler felt he could do no wrong. In June 1941, he tore up the non-aggression pact and invaded the Soviet Union. Although his army won spectacular victories in the field, it failed to take Moscow before the Russian winter set in. The Red Army regrouped and revised its tactics, and in the winter of 1942–43 defeated the Germans at Stalingrad. Meanwhile British troops had decisively beaten Hitler's seemingly invincible mechanised forces in the deserts of North Africa.

By now Hitler had another powerful enemy to face: in December 1941, the Japanese had attacked the US Pacific Fleet at its base in Pearl Harbor, Hawaii, beginning a war in the Pacific. Hitler, displaying the curious loyalty to an ally he would later show to Mussolini, promptly declared war on the United States.

In occupied Europe, Hitler's pathological hatred of Jews led directly to the 'Final Solution', the plan to rid Europe of Jews permanently. In the ensuing Holocaust, six million Jews – along with gypsies, homosexuals, Slavs and other people Hitler regarded as *untermenschen* – subhumans – were murdered in death camps, worked to death in labour camps or simply died from maltreatment and disease.

By 1943, the war had turned against Germany. On the Eastern Front, the Soviet army was pushing the Germans out of Russia. Sicily had been invaded, Mussolini had fallen and Allied forces were pushing their way up the Italian peninsula, and British and American bombers were pounding German cities every night.

On 6 June 1944, Allied troops landed on the coast of Normandy. Believing himself to be invincible, Hitler had now taken the conduct of the war into his own hands and persisted in making disastrous military blunders. A plot was hatched among a number of his senior officers and on 20 July 1944 a bomb went off under a table where he was working. It failed to kill him. Those responsible were rounded up, tortured and executed horribly.

Once the Allies had broken out of the Normandy beachhead, it was clear that the war was lost. But Hitler now set about extracting vengeance with new terror weapons. First was the V-1, a pilotless jet plane carrying an explosive warhead. These were launched against London, where they killed civilians, rather than against the military staging posts along the south coast. These weapons were soon followed by the V-2, a ballistic missile which could deliver a massive warhead over 220 miles. There were other V weapons, including a huge gun capable of shelling London from the Pas de Calais, which was spotted and destroyed before it could go into action. The 'V' in these designations stand for *Vergeltung* – or Vengeance. They had no purpose other than to punish the Allies for winning the war.

A short-lived counter-offensive in the Ardennes in December 1944 failed as Hitler no longer had the manpower or the industrial might to resist the forces ranged against him. He kept on promising his men new Vengeance weapons that would turn the tide. There is speculation that Germany was developing an atomic bomb, along with long range bombers and missiles that could deliver it to the eastern seaboard of the United States. Hitler believed that the US and the Western Allies would capitulate in the face of such an attack, allowing him to turn Germany's full strength against the Soviets.

However, by that time, America's own

atomic bomb programme was near completion. If a bomb had been dropped on New York or Washington, the US would certainly have responded with an atomic attack on Germany. When the US dropped atomic bombs on Hiroshima and Nagasaki, the Japanese had no way to respond and were forced to surrender. But an atomic exchange between Germany and America could quickly have escalated, given a sufficiency of fissile material, into an all-out atomic war, which would have devastated much of Europe and North America.

Hitler showed no compunction in sacrificing the German people. As the Russians and the Allies closed in on Berlin, Hitler organised a defence to the last man. Germany, he believed, deserved to be destroyed because it had failed to live up to his great vision for it. But his own courage failed him and he committed suicide.

There is no doubt that, given the weapons, Hitler would have continued the war, whatever the cost. Even after his own generals had lost faith in him, they were unable to stop him. Since the days of Hitler, technology has moved on apace. In the current era of weapons of mass destruction, one such individual could easily destroy all of humankind. History is littered with men who, given modern military technology, would have finished off the human race. Armed only with a sword and a small group of followers, Genghis Khan succeeded in killing around 20 million people. While this may not compare with the 35 to 60 million deaths for which Hitler was responsible,

There is no doubt that, given the weapons, Hitler would have continued the war, whatever the cost

it was around a tenth of the population of the world at the time, and Genghis Khan, it must be borne in mind, barely ventured out of Asia.

Leaving aside the number of Soviet citizens he sacrificed during World War II, Soviet dictator Josef Stalin killed at least 50 million of his own people. He ordered the building of the Soviet atomic bomb and would certainly not have hesitated to use it.

In the late 1970s, Pol Pot oversaw the complete collapse of civilisation in Cambodia, forcing the urban population out into the countryside where they starved or were murdered in a demented attempt to build a socialist peasant society. Pol Pot was responsible for the death of 1.7 million people – over 20 per cent of the population of Cambodia – before a Vietnamese invasion put a stop to him.

By the time Ivan the Terrible died in 1584, parts of Russia had become so depopulated by his murderous rule that countless acres of farmland had been reclaimed by the forests.

It seems there is no shortage of people prepared to kill any number of people and inflict any amount of damage to hang on to power or to advance their own deranged ideologies. There also seems no shortage of people prepared to follow them: even Hitler, while not directly elected to power, gained more votes than any of the more moderate parties in the Reichstag. There are plenty more like him out there all too ready to push the button and bring us all to our doom.

Religious War

SINCE THE ATTACK on the Twin Towers and the Pentagon on 11 September 2001, and the US-led invasions of Afghanistan and Iraq, many in the West have feared that the world is embarking on a struggle to the death between Islam and Christianity – or, at least, between the Muslim world and the secular Western world. This view would be endorsed by a number of Islamic radicals who have declared a 'jihad' or holy war against the West.

Jihad is a religious duty imposed on Muslims to spread Islam by waging war. Those who die in the struggle are considered martyrs and are guaranteed an esteemed place in heaven. However, jihad is divided into two categories, the greater and the lesser. The greater involves doing battle against the devil in your own heart and resisting temptation. The lesser jihad is the defence of Islam, which can be done with the pen and the tongue, as well as the sword. Even if the jihad involves violence, this must be defensive and the rules are strict. Muhammad said: 'In avenging injuries inflicted on us, do not harm non-belligerents in their homes, spare the weakness of women, do not injure infants at the breast, nor those who are sick. Do not destroy the houses of those who offer no resistance, and do not destroy their means of subsistence, neither their fruit trees, nor their palms.'

The Koran also forbids jihad being undertaken to convert others because there 'cannot be compulsion in religion'. The jihad code is supposed to show special consideration to the 'People of the Book' – Jews and Christians: if they embraced Islam or agreed to submit to Islamic rulers by paying poll and land taxes, they would be entitled to the status of a 'protected' community within the House of Islam.

However, throughout Islamic history, in wars against other Muslim states as well as non-Muslim ones – even if political in nature – the word jihad has been used to rally support and denigrate opponents. This was especially true in the 18th and 19th centuries with the Wahhabis in the Arabian Peninsula and the Mahdi in the Sudan. Usman dan Fodio declared a jihad to set up the Sokoto caliphate in what is now northern Nigeria, and the followers of Ahmad Barelewi committed themselves to holy war in the Northwest Frontier Province (now Pakistan), as did the Naqshbandiya Sufis in the Caucasus and China.

In the 20th century, the concept of jihad transformed into an ideological weapon to combat Western influences in the Middle East. This began at the height of British colonialism, when Muslim intellectuals in Egypt and Pakistan blamed the decline of Muslim nations on the Western idea of separating politics and religion. Hassan al-Banna's Muslim Brotherhood in Egypt and Syed Abul Ala Maududi's Jamaat Islami believed that the power of the Muslim world would only be restored when religion and the state were reunited, and society was ruled with a strict adherence to traditional Islamic law – that is, *Shari'ah* law. *Shari'ah* literally means 'the path leading to the watering place'. Jihad was seen as a way of of ending the foreign occupation of Muslim lands.

Even when this was achieved with the collapse of the British Empire after World War II, some hardliners were far from satisfied with the secular governments that replaced the colonial authorities. In the 1950s, Sayed Qutb, a leading member of the Muslim Brotherhood declared that all non-Muslims were infidels – even the 'People of the Book' – and predicted a clash of civilisations between the Islamic world and the West. He was executed in 1966 by Egypt's secular ruler Gamal Abdel Nasser. However, Qutb's writings became influential throughout the Arab world, especially after Israel's victory in the Six Day War in 1967, and the Ayatollah Khomeini developed a Persian version which led to the establishment of an Islamic Republic in Iran in 1979.

Al-Banna, Maududi and Qutb were also the main sources of inspiration for the Arabs who fought alongside the Afghan mujahideen against the Soviets in the 1980s. One of them was Abdullah Azzam, who had fought with the PLO in the 1970s but fell out with the Palestinian leadership because of its secularism. He had studied Islamic law at Cairo's Al-Azhar University, where he met the family of Sayed Qutb. He then went on to teach in Saudi Arabia, where one of his students was Osama bin Laden.

When the Soviets invaded Afghanistan in 1979 to prevent the Marxist government being overthrown, Abdullah Azzam seized the opportunity to test his revolutionary ideas. One of the first Arabs to join the Afghan mujahideen, he was dubbed the 'Emir of Jihad'. With Osama bin Laden, he set up a base in Peshawar, where they recruited Arabs to join the 'holy war'. Azzam maintained in books and magazines that it was the moral duty of every Muslim to undertake jihad and he toured the world encouraging Muslims to join the fight.

The fundamentalist Wahhabi school of Islam practised in Saudia Arabia had become the natural home of radical Islamist scholars, including Ayman al-Zawahiri, the leader of Egypt's Islamic Jihad, an extremist offshoot of the Muslim Brotherhood, who had been jailed in Egypt for his part in the assassination of President Anwar Sadat in 1981. The House of Saud being criticised for its pro-Western stance, the ruling family seized upon the Soviet invasion of Afghanistan as a cause which could deflect Islamist criticism and rally support. They threw their political and financial weight behind the Afghan jihad, which was also backed by Pakistan and bankrolled by the United States as part of the Cold War against the Soviet 'Evil Empire'. Meanwhile, Pakistan nurtured its own jihad movements, which could be used in its territorial dispute with India over Kashmir.

While the Saudis were careful to limit the jihad to Afghanistan, and Azzam urged Arab fighters to return home after the Soviets had withdrawn, al-Zawahiri argued that 'Afghanistan should be a platform for the liberation of the entire Muslim world'. Azzam was killed by a car bomb in Peshwar in 1989 and al-Zawahiri's ideas prevailed. A 'mentality of jihad' had been established.

Al-Zawahiri's hardline cause was strengthened by the 1991 Gulf war. Iraq under Saddam Hussein's Ba'athist rule was a determinedly secular state, but the international coalition's efforts to free

Kuwait from Iraqi occupation was seen as a Western invasion of Muslim land and the idea of jihad emerged in the Iraqi propaganda campaign.

The war also brought US troops to Saudi Arabia. Bin Laden, who had dedicated ten years of his life to the liberation of Muslim territory from foreign occupation, was outraged to see land he regarded as sacred occupied by 'infidel' soldiers, even though he himself had been backed by the US in Afghanistan.

Although al-Zawahiri is seen as Osama bin Laden's number two after Islamic Jihad and al-Qaeda forged a coalition in the late 1990s, some maintain that he is the senior figure. They had been together on a video threatening retaliation against the US after the arrest of the Egyptian Sheikh Omar Abdel Rahman in connection with the 1993 World Trade Center bombing and al-Zawahiri is thought to have been behind the massacre of foreign tourists at Luxor in 1997. With bin Laden, he signed the 1998 *fatwa* calling for attacks against US citizens. He was behind the embassy bombings in Africa that year and he is thought to be the 'operational brains' behind the 11 September attacks on the United States.

More recently he has called for the overthrow of Pakistani leader, General Pervez Musharraf, and for Islamic fighters to turn Iraq into a graveyard for US troops. He also accuses America of carrying out a new 'crusade' against Islam and Muslims, under the guise of fighting global terror.

Al-Zawahiri argued that 'Afghanistan should be a platform for the liberation of the entire Muslim world'

'The crusaders and the Jews only understand the language of murder and bloodshed,' he said on a video aired by the Qatar-based satellite TV news channel al-Jazeera on 21 May 2003, 'and are only convinced by coffins, destroyed interests, burning towers and a shattered economy.'

He went on to tell the Iraqi people, 'we have defeated those crusaders several times before and kicked them out of our countries. Know that you are not alone in your battle… The mujahidin in Palestine, Afghanistan, Chechnya and even in the heart of America and the West are making the crusaders taste all forms of death. The next few days will reveal to you news that will gladden your hearts, God willing.'

'Crusader' and 'crusades' are interesting word to use in this context as, in the aftermath of 11 September, George W. Bush, described his war against global terrorism as a 'crusade', although he quickly dropped it from his vocabulary after it was pointed out that this would only serve to inflame Muslims. The struggle between the Islamic world and the West has a long history.

The original crusades began in 1071 when the Seljuk Turks defeated the Byzantines, whose Orthodox Christian empire centred on Constantinople (now Istanbul), and took over the Holy Land, cutting the pilgrimage routes. The Byzantines asked for help from Pope Urban II, who declared the First Crusade, promising that those who went to free

Jerusalem from the 'infidel' would earn salvation in the life to come. Jerusalem had, in fact, been in Muslim hands since 638, when it was captured by Islamic forces under Caliph Umar, but Christian and Jewish pilgrims had been tolerated until 1010, when the Egyptian caliph al-Hakim ordered the destruction of Christian shrines.

In 1099, Jerusalem fell to the crusaders who were not nearly so tolerant. They slaughtered its Jewish and Muslim inhabitants and established the Kingdom of Jerusalem as one of four crusader states. These crusader states would not last long, however. One of them, Edessa, fell to the Seljuk ruler Zangi in 1144, prompting Pope Eugenius to declare the Second Crusade, which ended in humiliation when Christian forces under Emperor Conrad III of Germany and King Louis VII of France were forced to withdraw from their siege of Damascus.

In 1187, Saladin captured Jerusalem and the other European strongholds. Pope Gregory VIII called the Third Crusade. In 1191, Richard I of England – the Lion-Heart – and Phillip II Augustus of France captured the port of Acre and slaughtered its inhabitants, but they failed to take Jerusalem. Instead, Richard, a pragmatic king, and an admirer of Saladin's chivalrous, if ruthless, approach to warfare, negotiated a treaty giving Christian pilgrims access to the holy shrines.

The Fourth Crusade, called by Pope Innocent III in 1198, ended up with the

In the aftermath of 11 September, George W. Bush described his war against global terrorism as a 'crusade'

sacking of Constantinople. Although it established Latin rule in the city for the next 60 years, it ended any further co-operation between the Roman and Orthodox Churches.

The so-called Children's Crusade of 1212 resulted only in thousands of children being lost or sold into slavery, and the Fifth Crusade landed in Egypt in 1219, but was prevented by floods from reaching Cairo. On the Sixth Crusade in 1229, Emperor Frederick II of Germany negotiated a treaty returning Jerusalem to European control for 10 years.

After Jerusalem was sacked in 1244 by Kharezmian Turks retreating from the Mongols, Louis IX of France launched the Seventh Crusade in 1248 which again foundered in Egypt. The Eighth Crusade only got as far as Tunis, where Louis and most of his army died of disease. In 1268 the Egyptian Mameluks captured Antioch and slaughtered its inhabitants, and Acre, the crusaders' last outpost on the mainland, fell in 1291.

However, these largely ineffectual attempts by the European nations to secure the Christian shrines in the Holy Land were only one side of the story. Christian Europe had withstood the onslaught of Islam for centuries beforehand. After Islam had swept across Christianised North Africa, Muslim armies had invaded the Iberian Peninsula in the eighth century. They overran Spain and crossed the Pyrenees into France, their advance only being halted by Charles Martel at the Battle of Tours in 732. The Christians did not reconquer the whole of the peninsula until they finally retook Granada in 1492.

Meanwhile, Europe's eastern flank was under attack. The Turkish army of the Ottoman sultan Murad I won the first Battle of Kosovo in Serbia in 1389, encircling the crumbling Byzantine Empire. Constantinople – soon to be called Istanbul – fell to Mehmed II the Conqueror in 1452, ending the Byzantine Empire. Süleyman I – called 'the Magnificent' in Europe and 'the Lawgiver' by the Ottomans – went on to extend the Ottoman Empire through Greece, the Balkans and Hungary, reaching the gates of Vienna in 1529. The siege failed because of the problems of supplying such a large army so far from its base in Istanbul. The Ottomans reached Vienna once more in 1683, when a combination of a solid defence and the timely arrival of the Polish army under John Sobieski forced their withdrawal. Although the Ottoman star was now waning, it was not until 1832 that they finally withdrew from their last European outpost in Greece.

Looking even further back, it is possible to see the roots of the conflict between Europe and the Middle East in the wars between Greece and the Persian Empire in the fifth century BC. After the Persians had tried repeatedly to invade Greece, Alexander the Great struck back, conquering the Persian Empire and taking over much of what would become the Muslim world. He marched his victorious armies as far as modern Pakistan. He would have conquered the Arabian peninsula if he had not died in Babylon at the age of 32 in 323 BC. He had already occupied Egypt and had well-laid plans to take over the rest of North Africa.

It is unlikely that a conflict with such deep roots can ever be resolved. There is also a long history of groups involved in this struggle that have used terror tactics to further their aim, perhaps the most famous of whom were the Assassins. This sect was founded by Hasan-e Sabbah who died in 1124, in Daylam, Iran. Sabbah was the leader of the Nizari Isma'ilites, a religious-political Islamic sect which existed from the eleventh to the thirteenth century, the time of the crusades. In its early years, it considered murdering its enemies a religious duty.

The cult's Arabic name means 'hashish smoker', referring to the Assassins' alleged practice of taking hashish to induce ecstatic visions of paradise before setting out to face martyrdom. The historical existence of this practice is in doubt. Marco Polo and other Europeans who travelled to the east told stories of the gardens of paradise into which the drugged devotees were introduced to receive a foretaste of eternal bliss, but these are not confirmed by any known Isma'ilite source.

In 1094, with some Persian allies, Hasan-e Sabbah, seized the hill fortress of Alamut in Daylam. Opposing the growing empire of the Seljuk Turks, he established a loose but cohesive state, defending it by sending Assassins into enemy camps and cities to murder the generals and statesmen who opposed him. They often lost their own lives in the process. Sabbah's deadly tactics were not confined to his enemies: when one of his sons was accused of murder and another of drunkenness, he had both of them executed.

The cult's most devoted follower was Rashid ad-Din as-Sinan who died in 1192. He was leader of the Syrian branch

of the Assassins at the time of the Third Crusade and operated independently of the headquarters of the cult in Alamut. His headquarters were a fortress at Masyaf, in northern Syria, and he was known to Westerners as the Old Man of the Mountain. Feared for his practice of sending his followers to murder his enemies, he made several attempts on the life of Saladin, an Ayyubid leader who opposed the Isma'ili Shi'i sect.

The Assassins' power came to an end when the Mongols invaded Persia. One by one their castles fell until, in 1256, Alamut was overrun. The Syrian fortresses were gradually subjugated by the Mameluk sultan Baybars I, who installed Mameluk governors.

Now considered a minor heresy, cult followers are still found in Iran, Persia and Central Asia, although the largest groups are to be found in India and Pakistan, where they are known as Khojas and owe allegiance to the Aga Khan. However, their role has been taken over by al-Qaeda, Islamic Jihad, Hamas, Chechhyn Nationalists and other groups who employ suicide bombers.

As these people have no fear for their own lives, they make a formidable foe. If the world becomes polarised between the Islamic and the secular world, it is hard to imagine that such groups would have any hesitation in using nuclear weapons, if they could get their hands on them. Although Pakistan has a pro-Western government, it is home to some of the most passionately anti-Western groups. It already has nuclear weapons and the means of delivering them. There have been several attempts by suicide

The fall of Constantinople during the Fourth Crusade, 1204. Although a Christian city, Constantinople was nevertheless sacked by Christian crusaders.

bombers to kill President Musharraf, and a coup in Pakistan by hard-line Islamists could deliver these weapons into the hands of bin Laden and al-Zawahiri. As it is, the 'father' of Pakistan's nuclear bomb, Abdul Qadeer Khan has admitted selling nuclear technology to Iran, Libya and North Korea – and offering it to Saddam Hussein.

A nuclear war against suicide bombers would be unwinnable. Those eager for martyrdom and the pleasures of paradise would have no hesitation in blowing the whole world up. And, on present showing, the West seems to possess neither the strategy nor the diplomatic skills to stop them. The 'clash of civilisations', in the idiotic modern phrase, is likely to lead to the extinction of both the Western and Islamic worlds.

Nuclear Holocaust

EVEN THOUGH the Cold War is over, both the US and Russia still have massive nuclear arsenals. The strategy is now minimal deterrence. However, at its core lies the old ideas of MAD – mutually assured destruction – which existed for most of the post-war superpower confrontation.

The main plank of MAD lies in a second-strike capability. This means that in the event your enemy wipes out the bulk of your nuclear arsenal in a sneak attack, you still have the capability of inflicting unacceptable damage on his cities. This is why the US Navy, the Royal Navy and even the Russian Navy keep submarines armed with nuclear missiles at sea: they are hard to detect and almost impossible to destroy. If just one submarine survived a nuclear attack, it could take out New York, London or Moscow in retaliation.

However, MAD is in itself a Doomsday Machine. Once a nuclear attack had started, everything would be thrown into the fray, engulfing all of humanity in the holocaust. Clearly, humankind survived the threat of nuclear destruction which hung over it during the Cold War for over 40 years, but it was a close-run thing.

The nearest the world came to the brink was during the Cuban Missile Crisis of 1962, when Soviet nuclear weapons were deployed on the Caribbean island of Cuba, just 90 miles from the continental United States. The world teetered on the edge of all-out nuclear war for six days until eventually the Soviets pulled their missiles out of Cuba in exchange for the US, secretly, removing its missiles from Turkey. The US president at the time, John F. Kennedy, calculated that the chance of nuclear war during the Cuban Missile Crisis was 'somewhere between one out of three and even'.

The crisis had come about through a simple misunderstanding. The US had announced that it was no longer targeting Soviet cities, instead concentrating on military targets in the USSR. This was meant as a conciliatory gesture, but in the USSR it was perceived as a threat: plainly, the US missiles were much more accurate than their own, if they could pinpoint military targets rather than hitting large areas such as cities. Consequently, the Soviets sought to move their missiles closer to the USA, so

that they, too, could pinpoint military targets.

Kennedy's Secretary of Defense Robert McNamara said later that 'we came within a hairbreadth of nuclear war without realising it'. Kennedy's biographer, the Pulitzer Prize-winning historian Arthur Schlesinger added: 'Fortunately, Kennedy and [Soviet premier Nikita] Khrushchev were leaders of restraint and sobriety; otherwise, we probably wouldn't be here today.'

Nuclear Errors

There were at least 130 accidents involving nuclear weapons during the Cold War. Nuclear bombers crashed at Thule in Greenland and Palomares in Spain, spreading radiation over a large area. A 10-megaton nuclear bomb was dropped by accident near Kirkland Air Force Base, due to a faulty release mechanism; fortunately, it did not explode. Then in January 1984, a computer error in a control console at Warren Air Force Base in Wyoming made it appear as if a nuclear missile was going to launch itself. The USAF insists that there was no danger, but they took the precaution of parking an armoured car on the silo doors to prevent them opening. And there is the continuing danger that someone in charge of launching the missiles will become mentally unstable or lose control due to the abuse of drugs. Five per cent of the staff – around 5,000 people – are removed from nuclear weapons duty each year.

One mistake could have caused a nuclear exchange. In the worst case scenario, a nuclear war would have killed some 1,600 million people and injured 930 million more – putting out of action around 86 per cent of the population of the industrialised nations and 46 per cent of the Third World. There would be so many dead that it would be impossible to bury them. The cities would be full of rotting corpses. The injured would go untended as surviving doctors would be overwhelmed. Medicine would run out, and there would be no electricity to power any hospital that survived – and no fuel to keep the ill and dying warm.

Industrial and agricultural production would grind to a virtual halt, water and sewage systems would be destroyed, and there would be economic chaos, unstoppable epidemics and mass starvation. In six months over three-quarters of the world's population would be dead. It is unlikely that humankind could ever recover from such a body blow.

Given this prognosis, most countries had long since given up on any plan to protect their populations. Civil defence was, if anything, seen as provocative, indicating that a nation was preparing to go to war. In his book *The Limits of Civil Defence in the USA, Switzerland, Britain and the Soviet Union* published in 1987, defence analyst Lawrence J. Vale concludes: 'While civil defence in Britain and the United States has rarely advanced beyond the periodic articulation of paper plans, Switzerland and the USSR have attempted to put such plans into operation. Yet none of these four states has succeeded in giving full effect to the stated rationales for its programme, let alone succeeded in providing full protection against the effects of nuclear attack. All four states have been forced to confront both the technical and the political limits of civil defence. Even Switzerland, with its near-comprehensive network of blast shelters built to exacting

government specifications, cannot claim to provide an adequate measure of protection against direct attack on its cities. The Swiss freely admit to the impossibility of protecting the civilian population within a mile-and-a-half of a one-megaton detonation.'

But then, who was threatening to bomb the Swiss anyway?

Until 1982, Britain had a plan to evacuate almost two-thirds of the population – some 30 million people, as well as a more limited plan for moving around 12 million people away from primary target areas. But Margaret Thatcher's government decided that the best policy was to continue to encourage people to stay in their homes in the event of a nuclear war even though, according to government estimates, this would result in an additional 13 million deaths.

One of the reasons the government wanted people to stay put was that they did not want refugees clogging the road when troops were being deployed: nothing must be allowed to hamper the war effort. A Greater London Council risk study published in 1986 said: 'The government would have good reasons for not passing on any warning it received to the public... [as] between 35 and 38 per cent of Londoners intend to leave the city when a world war seems imminent.'

The strategy of deterrence meant that the government had to show that, not only did it have nuclear weapons, it was also prepared to use them, even if that meant the virtual annihilation of its own people. This meant that troops would have to be deployed to quell the massive protests that would also certainly occur once nuclear war was imminent.

Keeping people at home also meant that, as an attack would surely target the cities, the maximum number of people would be killed on the first day. They would be better off that way, as those not killed in the blast could not be helped. What remained of the health service simply would not have the resources to help people suffering from the resulting burns, injuries and radiation sickness. For this reason, the National Health Service during the 1980s was deliberately decentralised so that a disproportionate amount of its resources were out of the cities and away from likely targets. The only provision the government made for those dying slowly in the cities was to stockpile heroin to ease their pain.

After an attack, areas affected by high levels of fall-out would be designated Z Zones, where the dying would be left to their own devices. No attempt would be made to feed or nurse them and unburied bodies would simply be left to rot. Even the smallest nuclear attack envisaged by defence planners would leave more than half the population in these zones, and 97 per cent of Londoners were expected to perish.

By allowing those in the cities to be wiped out, those in the countryside would have a better chance of surviving in the subsistence economy that would follow a nuclear war, as the remaining tillable land would certainly not be able to sustain large numbers of refugees from the cities as well as country dwellers.

In a notorious UK government pamphlet entitled *Protect and Survive*, people in the cities who survived the blast and the subsequent fire storms were told to stay indoors to shelter from the lethal fall-out that would rain from the skies for the following two weeks. Somehow

they were expected to make their almost certainly bomb-damaged houses secure against the radioactive dust that had been hurled into the sky in the mushroom clouds of the nuclear impacts.

Those who survived the fall-out would almost certainly be struck down by one of the many epidemic diseases that would sweep the population centres after a nuclear strike. Decaying bodies and the vomiting and diarrhoea brought on by the radiation would taint the water supply, spreading typhus, cholera and dysentery. Even then, if survivors fled the cities to try and escape these diseases, they would be stopped by the military. Troops would have orders to shoot them if necessary, along with those judged to be terminally ill from radiation sickness. Anyone exhibiting any signs of disease or radiation sickness would be interned in a concentration camp – where they would not be fed – until they died. The diagnosis would be made, not by a doctor, but by a non-commissioned officer, putting the power of life and death into the hands of corporals.

Even the unaffected population would not receive rations from the nation's stockpiles for two weeks after the attack, thus ensuring that the sick and the weak, the very young and the very old would die off, leaving those who were healthy and could fend for themselves with the maximum chance of survival.

Government defence analysts estimated that the population of the UK would fall to ten million in the weeks following the attack. As babies born subsequently would have the odds stacked against them, the population would go

An ominous beauty: the 'mushroom cloud' of an atomic bomb test, 1952, one of the most enduring images of the twentieth century.

on declining. It was thought that it would stabilise at around six million – provided there was enough uncontaminated land to sustain farming, the radiation given off by the nuclear blast had not irreparably damaged the ozone layer and the dust thrown up into the upper atmosphere had not plunged the world into a nuclear winter.

The government itself, key civil servants and much of the military would be safe in underground bunkers or in the countryside. A five-tier emergency bureaucracy was put in place, so that government control could continue seamlessly into the devastated post-war era.

The British government's plan was hopelessly optimistic. It assumed that a nuclear war would be over in six hours. But once a nuclear war had been unleashed, government officials and military staff safe in their underground bunkers would have little reason to stop simply because their own and their enemies' countries were devastated. At the height of the Cold War the stockpile of weapons was such that they could go on lobbing nuclear missiles at each other for months. With their friends and families dead, submarine commanders in particular would have every reason to continue to exact revenge from what remained of humankind.

Realising that material in this sensitive area inevitably leaked, planners deliberately wrote ludicrously cheerful reports. Over the years, they even managed to whittle down the likely power of the expected strike. In 1960, when for

In a nuclear emergency troops would have to shoot survivors to maintain order

the first and only time the government told local authorities the likely extent of the threat they faced, it was estimated that the UK would be hit by nuclear explosives totalling, at the very least, 150 megatons. By 1982, however, when the government planned the civil defence exercise Operation Hard Rock, the estimate was that Britain would be hit by just 48 megatons of nuclear explosives. Even that is 3,000 times the power of the bombs dropped on Hiroshima and Nagasaki.

Experts outside government said that 200 megatons was the minimum the British people could expect. One suspects that even the military planners could not face the awful truth.

In that case, the general public could hardly be expected to cope. When the BBC tried to portray the grim reality in *The War Game* in 1965, the TV film was banned after Home Office psychologists predicted that, if it was aired, it would precipitate 'a wave of 20,000 suicides'.

Although humankind breathed a collective sigh of relief when the Cold War ended, this was premature. The threat of nuclear war is very far from over. The US and Russia still have enormous stockpiles of nuclear arms. Many elderly Russians look back to the certainties of life under Communism with nostalgia, while many young people say that they would have joined in the Bolshevik Revolution in 1917, if they had had the chance. In the US President George W. Bush is an open advocate of the first use of nuclear missiles, even against countries which do not possess them, while in January 2004, President of the USSR Vladimir Putin, an ex-officer of the KGB who has been, one might say, equivocal in his embrace of democracy, ordered the first military exercise involving nuclear weapons in Russia since the demise of the Soviet Union. Is the Cold War about to break out again?

Terrorist Bomb

IN 1991, THE SOVIET UNION broke up into its constituent parts. This left the world's second largest nuclear arsenal divided among fledgling nation states. Thousands of atomic warheads and hundreds of tons of plutonium were abandoned in far-flung places in the hands of nuclear scientists who did not get paid for months on end, and soldiers who had to grow their own potatoes and forage for food. Organised crime quickly permeated every facet of the former Soviet society. Ex-Communist officials led the stampede to embrace capitalism with a vengeance: everything was for sale. This meant that after the end of the Cold War, the world was not the safer place it may have been supposed, but an infinitely more dangerous one. Instead of two relatively stable superpowers standing eyeball to eyeball, aware that a war would mean their own destruction, every crackpot terrorist or tin-pot terror state had access to nuclear weapons – if they could pay for them.

While Russia let other former Soviet republics go their own way, it tried to hold on to the Caucasian state of Chechnya, but the Chechens themselves had other ideas. In 1994 the Chechen warlord Dzokar Dudayev, a former Soviet nuclear-bomber general, seized control of the state. He claimed he had stolen two nuclear warheads when the Soviet army had withdrawn two years before and threatened to sell them to Libya's Colonel Qaddafi unless the Americans recognised Chechnya as an independent country.

This threat was all too credible and it put Washington in a bind. It did not want to annoy the Russian President, Boris Yeltsin, by recognising Chechnya, but it could not risk allowing nuclear weapons to fall into the hands of the mercurial Qaddafi. Stalling for time, Washington asked Dudayev for more details. Dudayev said that the Americans were welcome to send a team to inspect the weapons, provided they did not tell the Russians.

The Americans knew that Yeltsin would be outraged if he discovered that they were sending agents into Chechnya behind his back. On the other hand, there was the terrible possibility that Dudayev was telling the truth. Weeks of stormy meetings followed in Washington. Eventually, it was decided that they had to send an inspection team. But the Russians were secretly informed. To Washington's surprise, they were happy the Americans were sending in inspectors: they also believed that the threat was credible as the Kremlin had no idea where most of its nuclear weapons were.

Many of them had been lost in transit in the confusion that came during the Soviet pull-out of former Warsaw Pact satellite countries after the fall of the

Berlin Wall in 1989. Then when the nuclear stockpile was being withdrawn from newly independent states such as Kazakhstan, the railway system broke down and thousands of freight cars went missing every day, some of which were carrying nuclear weapons.

It turned out that Dudayev was bluffing. When the Americans confirmed that he did not have any nuclear weapons, Yeltsin sent the Russian Army into Chechnya, beginning the Chechen war which over the next two years would cost 100,000 Chechen lives and which continues to this day.

This incident underlined the fact that nuclear weapons could easily fall into the hands of someone prepared to sell them to Libya or another hostile state. With each nuclear warhead worth hundreds of millions of pounds, there would be no shortage of buyers, and neither would there be a problem getting them out of the country: in 1992, Major General Vladimir Rodinov had turned his top secret nuclear bomber unit into an international freight and charter service.

In 1991, Greenpeace even tried to borrow a warhead. They had contacted a lieutenant whose unit was guarding a warhead storage site near Berlin, who assured them that no one would even miss one warhead. The lieutenant originally demanded £200,000, but settled for the movie rights to the operation. Greenpeace planned to exhibit the warhead at a press conference, then hand it back. Everything was arranged, however, in August 1991, during the short-lived hardliners' coup against Soviet leader Mikhail Gorbachev, the lieutenant disappeared.

11 September, 2001: passenger jets hijacked by Islamic militants are crashed into New York's World Trade Center, symbol of American economic might across the world.

In November 1993, two workmen stole two multi-megaton warheads and stashed them in their garage. Three days later, the warheads – each big enough to take out London – were found and the men arrested. But nuclear warheads are big and bulky and weigh several hundred pounds. Although they are easy enough to manhandle, they are not ideal for smuggling. Uranium, plutonium and other fissile material, on the other hand, can be carried onto a plane in a bag, or concealed in a car as it crosses a border. One foolhardly smuggler just popped a pellet of radioactive caesium in his pocket, but died of radiation poisoning before he could find a buyer.

By 1994, there were around five cases a week of nuclear smuggling – and those were just the ones that were caught. Hungarian border guards seized uranium bound for Austria in a fruit jar; Bulgarian police found capsules of radioactive materials on a bus bound for Turkey, and the Turkish police arrested an Azeri national with 750 grams of enriched uranium for sale – and seven Turkish nationals with nearly twelve pounds of the stuff.

Nuclear material appears everywhere: four Indian villagers were caught selling 2.5 kilograms of raw uranium; an Estonian was found with three kilograms of uranium 238 buried under his garage, and nine pounds of the more dangerous uranium 235 was found in St Petersburg and twelve members of the Russian mafia were arrested.

On 10 August 1994, a Lufthansa flight from Moscow touched down in Munich with 363 grams of weapons-grade plutonium on board, belonging to a Colombian doctor-cum-arms dealer by the name of Justiniano Torres Benítez, and was just a sample of the eleven kilos accomplices had smuggled out of the closed city of Tomsk. Unfortunately for Benítez, the buyers he had found in Germany were undercover agents.

The German police had already been alerted to the trade in plutonium. In May that year, they had found six grams of weapons-grade plutonium 239 quite by accident when they raided the home of suspected counterfeiter Adolf Jaekle, who had stored the lethal bomb-making material in his garage. Inhaling just one speck of plutonium dust is fatal. The police did not even know what the stuff was when they came across it, but fortunately, none of them tasted it to see if it was drugs.

Highly enriched uranium 235 was found in the sleepy Bavarian town of Landshut in July, then in December 1994, 2.72 kilograms of uranium 235, 87.7 per cent enriched, was found in the back of a car in Prague. When the smugglers were rounded up, police found among them a Czech nuclear physicist. They also discovered that the shipment was only part of a larger cache, ten kilos in all – enough to obliterate Manchester. It was on sale for $800 a gram. The client had originally been the North Koreans, but they pulled out when they found what they needed cheaper elsewhere. Some Spaniards moved in, but they would only pay in counterfeit dollars and a Nigerian sale was scuppered when they wanted to swap the uranium for drugs.

Eventually German middlemen found a buyer who wanted five kilos a month. The smugglers agreed to supply a ton. When they were caught they refused to say who the buyer was, but authorities believed it was destined for a company called Nordex, which had been set up in Vienna by the KGB to generate hard cur-

rency and was run by former KGB agent Grigori Loutchansky, once described by American intelligence as 'the most dangerous man in the world'. The CIA tied Nordex to four tonnes of beryllium – a metal used to intensify the nuclear reaction inside atomic bombs – found in a bank vault in Lithuania. Nordex was also implicated in an attempt to sell Scud missiles to Iran, and had ties with the media magnate Robert Maxwell, who died in a mysterious yachting accident in 1991.

In 1993, Loutchansky bailed out the Ukrainian government, getting the heating oil it needed for the winter by bartering sugar, steel and fertiliser. He was so well connected that he was introduced to President Clinton in Washington later that year. The Ukrainian deal turned out to be a scam. The Ukraine's prime minister fled with Loutchansky's help, and $25 million. No one knows how much Loutchansky made on the deal. In 1994, Loutchansky was refused permission to enter Canada and Britain. His application for Austrian citizenship was rejected and an invitation to dinner at the White House was withdrawn. But as a Jew, Loutchansky could not be refused Israeli citizenship, even though it is thought that he has sold nuclear materials to both Iran and Iraq.

In 1994, the Americans discovered over half a ton of uranium 235 – enough to make ten bombs – in an unguarded vault in the three-year-old Republic of Kazakhstan. The uranium had once belonged to a secret programme of the Soviet Navy, and was enriched to 90 per cent, perfect for making bombs. Aware that the cache was dangerous, the Kazakh government had tried to give it to the Russians, but they refused to take it. So they tried to sell it. When American agents first saw the cache, the uranium was in canisters with its destination written in Cyrillic on the side. It said Tehran. The Americans promptly made a better offer.

Moving the uranium was going to be difficult: not only was the radiation from the uranium lethal, it had been mixed with beryllium which, if inhaled, causes the lungs to seize up. A team from the nuclear laboratory at Oak Ridge, Tennessee was sent. In special air-tight radiation suits, they opened the canisters one by one, and weighed and repackaged the contents, to be sure that the cargo would not accidentally reach 'critical mass', triggering an explosion. This took six weeks. Two huge C-5 planes then flew the uranium back to Tennessee non-stop.

Two weeks later another two tons of uranium were found and the operation began all over again.

Not only is the world awash with the radioactive material needed to build atomic bombs, there is also no shortage of the necessary expertise. During the first Gulf War, Saddam Hussein's top nuclear physicist defected, bringing the news that the Iraqis were building an atomic bomb, using old American blueprints declassified in 1949. A 7,500-man team of physicists and engineers were working on the project. The main problem was enriching the uranium: they had, however, perfected a magnetic method that the Americans had abandoned during World War II.

Bombing during the Gulf War dam-

One foolhardly smuggler just popped a pellet of radioactive caesium in his pocket; he died of radiation poisoning before he could find a buyer

aged, but did not destroy, the facilities. When United Nations weapons inspectors were allowed into Iraq after the Gulf War, Saddam Hussein's nuclear weapons programme played cat and mouse with them, until in 1995 a defector revealed where the enrichment plants were and the UN closed them down.

By then the routes to smuggle nuclear materials out of the former Soviet Union were already well established: eight tons of Russian zirconium, for example, another metal used in atomic bombs, was found in a Customs house in Queens, New York, and there is good evidence that there is more out there.

In 1996, when General Alexandr Lebed was secretary of Russia's National Security Council, he checked on the 132 nuclear 'suitcases' the Russians were supposed to have. He could only find 48: 84 were missing! Each suitcase had a yield of several kilotons – enough to make a 'decent boom', Lebed told a press conference. These nuclear suitcases are the perfect terrorist weapon. They could be shipped in the cargo hold of an airline, or carried on as hand luggage. The American authorities are terrified that they are going to turn up in an American city. What to do if one appears is regularly rehearsed by the emergency services, and a top-secret tracking agency, the Z Division, has been set up in an ultra-secure building at the Livermore Laboratory in California, from where US intelligence analysts try to piece together where missing Soviet nuclear hardware can be so it can be intercepted and retrieved. So far they have been lucky.

Not all nuclear deals are made by renegades and mafiosi: in 1995, Victor Mikhailov, the Minister of Atomic Energy of the Russian Federation, negotiated the sale of two nuclear reactors to Iran, claiming that they could not in any way be used to produce atomic bombs. However, hidden in one clause was the promise to also provide a centrifuge of the type used to enrich uranium, and in a secret protocol, Mikhailov agreed to build a breeder reactor, which would allow the Iranians to produce weapons-grade plutonium, to help them open their own uranium mines and to train their nuclear physicists. The Americans found out about it and, when President Clinton visited Moscow to celebrate the fiftieth anniversary of the end of World War II, he protested to Boris Yeltsin. The centrifuge and breeder reactor were dropped from the contract. Mikhailov claimed that they had only been included in the first place so they could be dropped when America found out about them. Otherwise the Americans would have objected to the sale of the reactors and pressured the Russians to drop the whole deal. As it is, Tehran got its two reactors and is looking elsewhere for a uranium-enriching centrifuge.

While still an international pariah due to apartheid, South Africa developed nuclear weapons. Israel has them. Both Pakistan and India have developed them, along with missiles to deliver them, while confronting each other over the future of Kashmir. Communist China has a large arsenal and North Korea makes belliger-

ent noises over its nuclear capability.

While it is unlikely that al-Qaeda or other terrorist organisations could build a missile system to deliver a warhead, they would not need to. They do not even need to build a purpose-built nuclear suitcase, or buy one of the ones that has gone missing. Once you have gathered enough fissile material you could set off an atomic explosion in an apartment: dropping one chunk of uranium-235 onto another chunk to produce a critical mass would do it. If a suicide bomber had knocked together two lumps of enriched uranium the size of grapefruit in the area where the twin towers of the World Trade Center once stood, three square miles of southern Manhattan would have been flattened, including the whole of Wall Street, and hundreds of thousands of people would have been killed in the blast. Every city in the world is vulnerable to such an attack. Terrorists would only have to take out New York, London, Frankfurt and Tokyo to damage the world's financial system beyond repair.

Even a small nuclear skirmish would risk the danger of a 'nuclear winter'. Scientists believe that the detonation of even a fairly small number of nuclear warheads would throw up so much debris into the atmosphere that the light of the Sun would be blocked out, plunging the Earth into prolonged semi-darkness, and restricting or completely stopping photosynthesis. Crops would die causing mass starvation and the freezing temperatures would make life difficult, if not impossible, for those who survived. It has not yet been established how long such conditions would last.

War Between East and West

NOSTRADAMUS WARNED that the danger lay in the east, not just from the world of Islam but from the 'yellow people' of Asia. Even in his time, it was not hard to see China as a sleeping giant.

China is roughly the size of the United States and slightly smaller than the whole of Europe put together – yet it is home to a quarter of the Earth's population. The beginnings of Chinese civilisation seem to predate those of the Mesopotamia and the Indus Valley and the Chinese can boast the world's longest-running continuous civilisation. They are responsible for the invention of paper, printing, gunpowder, spectacles. But throughout its long history China has been under an almost constant state of siege, and has good reason to resent foreigners. The Great Wall of China was begun in the fourth century BC, to protect the Chinese from the nomadic tribes of the northern steppes.

The Shang dynasty was overthrown by the Chou, a subject people of the Chous, in 1111 BC. The Chou were then overthrown by the Ch'in, a vassal state, in the second century BC. The Han quickly took over, but their four centuries in control were characterised by the arbitrary excesses of a multitude of warlords, and by frequent invasions by non-Chinese from the north. The Sui dynasty fought off the Turks, then the Tang took over in 618, whose decline was marked by militarism and warfare. The Sung dynasty that followed again fought the Turks, and had to move its capital south to protect it from invaders. Then in 1279 the Mongols, under Kublai Khan – Genghis's grandson – took over with the Yüan dynasty. When the Ming dynasty re-established Chinese rule in 1368, anti-foreign feeling was running high and China virtually closed itself off until 1644, when the Manchurians took over, establishing the Manchu or Ch'ing dynasty. This isolation had weakened China, and there would be no shortage of foreign powers to take advantage of this weakness for commercial gain.

At the beginning of the nineteenth century, British traders began selling opium illegally in China. When the Chinese government seized their shipments in Canton in 1839, the British government intervened, quickly defeating the Chinese. In the treaties ending the first Opium War, the Chinese were forced to pay huge reparations, and to cede five ports to the British. Other countries soon demanded similar cessions. In 1856 the British and French found new excuses to go to war against China, winning further privileges. When the Chinese government refused to ratify new treaties, the British and French captured Beijing – then Peking – and in 1860 forced them to sign. The United States and Russia imposed treaties of their own, and the Japanese got in on the act after winning the Sino-Japanese War of 1895. Meanwhile, the Taiping Rebellion had been put down by an army equipped by the West commanded by the American adventurer Frederick Townsend Ward and, later, by Charles 'Chinese' Gordon (the future Gordon of Khartoum), leaving 20 million dead.

In 1900, the Boxer Rebellion turned

Chinese Red Guards reading from the little red book of 'Thoughts of Chairman Mao' before starting their day.

on foreign interference in China and the Dowager Empress Tz'u-his ordered all foreigners to be killed. An international force fought its way through to Peking to relieve the besieged diplomatic compound, and as foreign troops looted the city, the Chinese were forced into making more humiliating concessions and paying further reparations to the foreign powers who were ravaging them.

After the fall of the Manchus, China entered a long period of civil war with the competing sides backed by foreign powers, a civil war interrupted by the brutal invasion of the Japanese in 1937. After the defeat of the Japanese in 1945, the Civil War continued until the Soviet-backed Communists achieved victory in 1949. Even then, backed by the US, the old nationalist government under Chiang Kai-shek held on to the island of Taiwan, and retained China's seat on the Security Council of the United Nations until 1971. The United States refused to recognise the Communist government in Peking until 1979, while Britain and Portugal held on to their concessions in Hong Kong and Macao until 1997 and 1999 respectively.

Looking at the history of China, it is hard not to sympathise, to an extent, with the Chinese distrust of foreigners. They even felt themselves to be in danger of invasion during the Korean War, when US General Douglas MacArthur led UN troops up to the Chinese border in October 1950. After the Red Army intervened, MacArthur was relieved of his command and the war ended in a stalemate in 1953 at the 38th parallel where it had begun three years previously.

Despite the fact that China's Communist leaders retain a tight grip on the country politically, economic reforms have given China a growth rate that topped nine per cent in 2003, while the rest of the industrial world could only manage between zero and three per cent. Many predict that China will become the economic giant of the twenty-first century and is set to outstrip both the United States and the European Union in output.

China became a nuclear power in 1967 and left no doubt that it could deliver a nuclear warhead anywhere in the world when it put a man into space in 2003. Every Chinese citizen who reaches the age of 18 has to serve three years in the army, or four years in the navy or air force. This gives China the world's largest military with over three million men under arms. If China decided to take its revenge on the rest of the world for the abuses of the past, it would be unstoppable.

China has also shown itself very susceptible to a demagogue. The leader of the Taiping Rebellion, Hung Hsiu-ch'uan, was a Christian convert who claimed to have met God who told him his mission was to expel the Manchu – that is Manchurian – rulers from China. As leader of a sect called the Society of God Worshippers, Hung proclaimed a new dynasty, the Taiping Tien-kuo – the Heavenly Kingdom of Great Peace – with himself as Tien Wang or Heavenly King. After capturing the city of Yung-an, he built an army of over a million men and women – who were allowed no intimate contact with each other, even between married couples, while Hung indulged himself with a large harem.

In 1853, the rebels captured China's southern capital Nanking. When his minister of state Yang Hsiu-ch'ing challenged his absolute authority, he was murdered. Hung also turned a deaf ear to his general and depended on divine guidance instead. He refused to stockpile supplies in case of a siege, saying that God would provide. Refusing to flee when the besieged city was overrun, he committed suicide on 1 June 1864. When Nanking finally fell on 19 July, over 100,000 of Hung's followers preferred death to capture.

Another demagogue, Mao Zedong, was even more successful. From a small base in the Ching-Kang mountains in 1927, he fought his political opponents, the government of China and the invading Japanese, emerging as absolute ruler of China in 1949, a state of affairs which continued almost unchallenged until his death in 1976. Mao had a simple and compelling philosophy: 'Political power grows out of the barrel of a gun'. The year after he took over he showed no compunction in throwing his army into the war against the United States and its allies who were fighting under the banner of the United Nations in Korea. He also backed the North Vietnamese against the Americans during the Vietnam war, even though Vietnam was a traditional enemy of China. He meddled in Cambodia and Laos, launched several confrontations with the Soviet Union after the Sino-Soviet split in 1956 and ordered an incursion into Vietnam in 1978 after the Americans had withdrawn.

He positively relished the idea of nuclear warfare, saying that, although 'half mankind would die, the other half would remain, while imperialism would be razed to the ground and the world would become Socialist'. Unfortunately, the half that became Socialist would not be safe in his hands. In the economic chaos caused by his 'Great Leap Forward' in 1958 some seven million people died, and more died in the 1966 'Cultural Revolution' when Red Guards took to the streets and mobs killed those marked out as 'class enemies'.

After Mao died in 1976, those in power remained every bit as ruthless. Anyone opposing Communist rule found themselves in labour camps, exiled or executed. When tens of thousands of students gathered to protest in Tiananmen Square in Beijing in June 1989, between 1,500 and 3,000 were killed when the old men who ruled the country sent in the Red Army armed with tanks.

Despite the fact that the leadership has now been handed over to a younger generation, there is no sign of political change. The Communist Party apparatus is still in place. At any time it could be used to let another Mao, Stalin, Pol Pot or worse rise to power who would be a danger to the West, his own people and the world.

Global Class War

SINCE THE INDUSTRIAL REVOLUTION, the nations of Europe and North America have grown richer, while those of sub-Saharan Africa and South America have grown poorer. And the economic gulf between the two is increasing.

Throughout the twentieth century, barriers were erected to limit migration from poorer countries to richer ones, barriers which in the twenty-first century show no signs of coming down; on the contrary. Although drought and famine sometimes touch the consciences of TV viewers in the First World, with a consequent outpouring of charity, the rich nations show little real desire to help out their poorer brethren. While aid may be sent to starving people in refugee camps in Ethiopia or elsewhere, if they get on boats or planes and attempt to enter countries where food is abundant, they are condemned as 'economic migrants' and sent back, just as the populations of politically stable nations are quite happy to see political refugees being returned to face imprisonment, torture and death.

Ultimately, this callous *de facto* division of the world into rich and poor must cause resentment. Through movies and TV, the poor people of the Third World see how well people in Europe and North America live – indeed they see an impossibly glamorised version of it, which must make it all the more appealing. And, not unreasonably, they want some of the goodies too.

Although patrols along the US–Mexican border in Arizona return as many as 22,000 illegal immigrants a month, there is no way the US authorities can effectively police the border. Vigilante groups are taking over and, as a result, immigrants are getting killed. But even this shows no sign of stemming the flow. Immigrants escaping poverty, not just in Mexico but throughout Central and South America, make their way to the southern border of the United States in ever-increasing numbers, lured by the riches on the other side. And like the vigilantes, the men involved in the lucrative business of smuggling the illegals across are increasingly resorting to violence.

The confrontation between North and South in the Americas is not helped by the fact that this border also represents a racial, religious and cultural divide. Those to the north are traditionally of northern European, Protestant stock, who now speak English. To the south, the people are of mixed southern European and Indian stock, Catholic and speak Spanish or Portuguese. The fact that the Hispanic population living in the United States is growing rapidly does not help: immigrants who have established themselves in a new country are often the most vociferous opponents of fresh waves of immigration, even when the new immigrants share a similar background.

The Cuban missile crisis of 1962 was informed by Spanish-speaking resentment of the English-speaking North. The Cuban revolutionary Che Guevara, who bore a bitter hatred of the United States, was delighted by the armed confrontation. Although he was an Argentinian, not a Cuban, he said of the Cuban people: 'This people you see today tell you that even if they should disappear from the face of the earth because an atomic war is unleashed in their name… they would feel completely happy and fulfilled' – not that the Cuban people themselves were consulted on the matter. Both Guevara and the Cuban leader Fidel Castro were outraged when Soviet leader Nikita Khrushchev appeared to back down and removed the missiles. Guevara told the British Communist newspaper *The Daily Worker* (now the *Morning Star*): 'If the rockets had remained, we would have used them all and directed them against the very heart of the United States, including New York.'

Further to the south, the resentment runs just as deep. The year after the 11 September attacks on New York's Twin Towers and the Pentagon, tens of thousands of Osama bin Laden masks appeared at the Rio carnival.

Europe is also under siege. It has an eastern border that it porous and people from as far away as Bangladesh and China pay smugglers to bring them overland. Smugglers also ply the Mediterranean, bringing migrants from Africa and the Middle East. Australia, which is essentially a Western nation stuck in the southern hemisphere, attracts migrants from all over Asia. If the poor of Africa and Asia marched on fortress Europe, there would be no stopping them – any more than if they all got in small boats and headed for Australia.

The more the rich nations resist, the more the resentment will grow among the poor. So far, the rich nations have held the whip hand politically by dividing poorer nations against themselves. At the World Trade Organisation's meeting at Cancun, Mexico, in 2003,

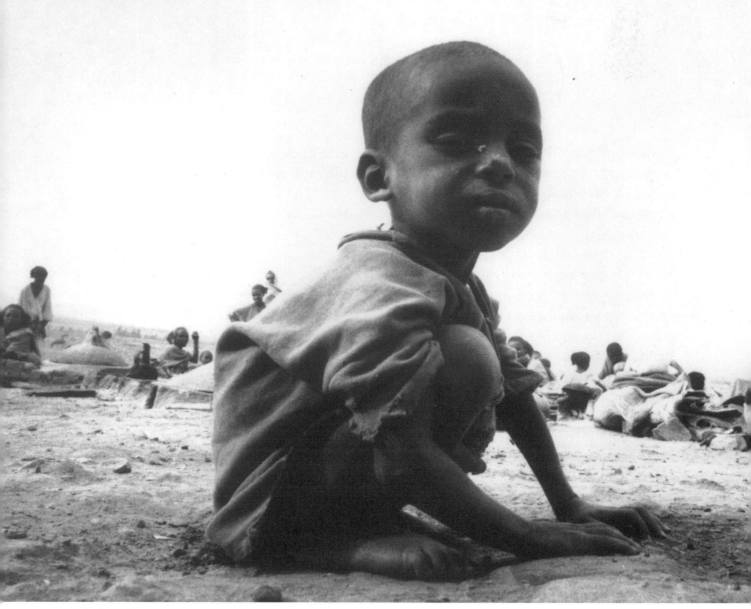

The face of hunger. While millions of people across the 'Third World' starve, their governments spend huge percentages of their revenues on repayment of debts to multi-billionaire Western corporations.

however, agreement was blocked by the concerted effort of the poorer nations, for once showing that they could work together.

If the rich and poor nations will no longer talk to each other, the result will be a world divided along the Rio Grande, the Dnieper and the Torres Strait. Any confrontation across that line could prove disastrous. As the birth rate among the poorer nations is higher, they could eventually overwhelm the rich nations by sheer weight of numbers. What is more, most of the world's remaining raw materials are in the poorer nations, as is much of its under-exploited agricultural land. On the other hand, most of the world's weapons are

in the hands of the rich, so the outcome of a conflict between the rich and poor nations is unclear.

Certainly both would be losers. The world has now become so inter-dependent economically that the rich could not survive without the poor – any more than the poor could survive without the rich: a globalisation of the class war would probably spell doom for all of us.

It has to be said the prospects are not good. The Third World has abundant agricultural land and a surplus of cheap labour with farming skills, but the US and the EU persist in subsidising their own farmers, allowing them to price the produce of the Third World out of the market. With trade deals stacked so much in favour of the rich nations, is it any wonder that poor farmers stop growing coffee or cocoa and start planting opium, coca or khat? Many in the First World, however, see the growing use of drugs in more simplistic terms as a symptom of a moral collapse, and call for an increase in pressure in the 'War on Drugs' – a fatuous term, as a glance at the pharmaceutical industry quickly shows; also, drugs do not fall into that category of things upon which war can be declared. This in its turn increases the tension between the 'First' and 'Third' Worlds. How much longer before it spills over into a real war?

Race War

WHEN CHARLES MANSON and his group of hippie followers, the Family, embarked on a series of senseless murders in California in 1969, they did so in the belief that this would spark a race war between black people and white people. Manson thought that this would be the war preceding the end of world history referred to in the Book of Revelation. Manson was sure about this: the Beatles had told him all about it.

Manson was born 'No Name Maddox', the son of a 16-year-old prostitute who could not even remember the day she gave birth. He inherited the name Manson from a man his mother was briefly married to. When he was six, Manson's mother was jailed for robbing

a gas station. From then on he was despatched to a series of orphanages and reformatories where he was often treated brutally.

Jailed for stealing cars, pimping and passing forged cheques, he was repeatedly raped by other prisoners, many of whom were black, which left him with a lifelong racial chip on his shoulder. To survive he became cunning and manipulative, and learnt techniques of mind control from Scientology.

Released in 1967, he found himself in San Francisco during the 'summer of love'.

'Pretty little girls were running around every place with no panties or bras and asking for love,' he said. 'Grass and hallucinatory drugs were being handed to you on the streets. It was a convict's dream after being locked up for seven solid years.'

Already mentally unstable, Manson aggravated his condition by taking LSD and supported himself by busking in Haight-Ashbury. At the time, young people were turning against 'straight' society and Manson found himself the height of fashion. The manipulative powers he had learned in jail also worked on the long-haired flower children of California: his hypnotic stare, unconventional lifestyle and the strange meaningless phrases he babbled made him the perfect hippie guru.

He became involved in a millennial outfit known as the Process Church of the Final Judgement, which preached that a spree of motiveless killings would hasten the Day of Judgment and took as its commandment 'Thou shalt kill'. Its leader, Winchester-educated Robert De Grimston believed not just in human sacrifices, but that life should be one long murderous rite, with black people in particular as a target.

When the Process Church moved to Los Angeles, Manson followed, intending to establish himself as a rock star there. Along the way, he picked up a harem of vulnerable young women, introduced them to LSD and had sex with them, often in skilfully choreographed orgies. A number of docile young males also joined the 'Family' which numbered between 30 and 35 at any one time. The inner circle included Patricia Krenwinkel, who quit being a legal clerk to join Manson; 19-year-old high-school-dropout Leslie Van Houten; 20-year-old Linda Kasabian who left her husband and two children and stole $5,000 from a friend to join the Family; librarian Mary Brunner; preacher's daughter Ruth Ann Moorehouse and Susan Atkins, a 21-year-old topless dancer who had been involved in San Francisco's fashionable First Church of Satan, which had boasted Sammy Davis Jr and Jayne Mansfield as members. The men in the commune included former high school football star Charles 'Tex' Watson and Bobby Beausoleil, protégé of underground filmmaker Kenneth Anger, who went on to write the best-selling *Hollywood Babylon*.

The Family lived on a ranch in the desert that was part of an old movie set where early westerns had been shot. They supported themselves by collecting discarded food from supermarkets, 'borrowing' credit cards and 'liberating' cars. Meanwhile Manson was courted by the likes of Dennis Wilson of the Beach Boys, and John Phillips of the Mamas and the Papas.

Susan Atkins convinced Manson that his name was no accident, and that Man-son, or Man-son, meant Son of Man, or Christ. Manson also saw himself as the Devil and 'the Beast of the bottomless pit' who would bring salvation after the apocalypse – that is, the forthcoming war between blacks and whites.

When the Beatles' 'white album' came out in 1968, Manson believed it was full of messages. The track 'Sexy Sadie' referred to Susan Atkins, whose real name was Sadie. 'Blackbird' was a call for black people to revolt and 'Revolution 9' meant Revelation, chapter nine, which talked of the war at the end of time and the coming of Appollyon, the Exterminating Angel. Although illiterate, Manson knew his Bible.

Unaware that a helter skelter was a British funfair ride, Manson believed the track 'Helter Skelter' referred to the inevitable race war, when the blacks would rise up and wipe out the 'Piggies' – the name of another track. 'Piggies' in Family-speak were the police, authority figures, the rich and the famous. Throughout this cataclysm, Manson would wait in safety in the desert. Manson believed that black people would win this war. He also believed that they were intellectually inferior, so it would then be an easy matter for him to take over afterwards. To provoke this Armageddon, Manson turned to the Process Church's solution – random acts of violence.

The first victim was West Coast musician Gary Hinman. Manson sent Mary Brunner, Susan Atkins and Bob Beausoleil to Hinman's house, where Beausoleil stabbed Hinman twice in the chest and left him to bleed to death. Devil-worshipper Susan Atkins dipped her finger in Hinman's blood and wrote 'political piggie' in blood on the wall.

She also drew a cat's paw, a crude version of the logo of the Black separatist movement, the Black Panthers, hoping they would get the blame.

When Hinman's body was discovered four days later, the Los Angeles Sheriff's Office found Beausoleil's fingerprints in the house, and they also found the knife that killed Hinman and a T-shirt drenched in Hinman's blood in Beausoleil's car. Beausoleil was convicted of murder and went to jail – but without implicating Atkins or Manson.

On 8 August 1969, Manson took his death squad to the remote home of Terry Melcher, Doris Day's son and a big wheel in the music industry. It was at 10050 Cielo Drive in the Hollywood Hills. Melcher had moved, but this did not matter to Manson, as any new occupants were plainly also 'piggies'. He sent Tex Watson, Susan Atkins, Patricia Krenwinkel and Linda Kasabian into the house – though Kasabian lost her nerve and stayed outside.

The new tenant was movie director Roman Polanski. He was away in London filming, but his wife, movie star Sharon Tate, who was eight months pregnant, was at home, along with coffee heiress Abigail Folger, her boyfriend the Polish writer Voytek Frykowski and celebrity hairdresser Jay Sebring.

After cutting the telephone wires, Watson, Atkins and Krenwinkel made their way down the driveway where they met 18-year-old Steven Parent, who had been visiting the caretaker. Watson pumped four bullets into his chest.

Breaking in through a window, Manson's disciples found Voytek Frykowski asleep on the couch. Waking to find a .22 in his face, he asked what they wanted.

'I am the Devil,' replied Watson. 'I am here to do the Devil's business. Give me your money.'

Atkins found Sharon Tate and the others talking in a bedroom. They were told that the house was being robbed and no harm would come to them. But Sebring made a lunge for the gun. Watson shot him in the armpit, then stabbed him four times.

Frykowski then attacked Watson, who hit him with the pistol butt. He staggered to the door, screaming for help. In a frenzy, the girls stabbed Frykowski 51 times. Abigail Folger made a break for it, but Krenwinkel caught up with her halfway across the lawn and Watson stabbed her to death. Sharon Tate begged for the life of her unborn child. But, while Krenwinkel held her down, Atkins stabbed her 16 times. Watson then mutilated the lifeless bodies. The killers spread an American flag across the couch and wrote the word 'pig' on the front door in Sharon Tate's blood.

'I felt so elated,' Susan Atkins told Manson back at the ranch. 'Tired but at peace with the world. I knew this was just the beginning of helter skelter. Now the world would listen.'

Later that night, Manson went to inspect their handiwork. He got high on marijuana as he read the reports of the murders in the newspapers. To celebrate, he had an orgy with his female followers.

Two days later, Manson, Watson, Kasabian, Krenwinkel and Atkins set out again, this time accompanied by Leslie Van Houten and Steven 'Clem' Grogan. Manson randomly selected a house in the Silver Lake area of Los Angeles. It belonged to 44-year-old grocery store-owner Leno LaBianca and his 38-year-old wife Rosemary, who ran a fashionable dress shop. They awoke to find Manson holding a gun in their faces. He tied them up and told them they would not be harmed. Returning to the car, Manson sent Tex Watson, Leslie Van Houten and Patricia Krenwinkel back into the LaBiancas' house. He said that he was going to the house next door to murder its occupants. Instead, he drove home.

Meanwhile Watson dragged Leno LaBianca into the living room and stabbed him four times with a kitchen knife, which he then left sticking out of the unfortunate LaBianca's throat. With his own knife, Watson stabbed LaBianca more eight times in the stomach, leaving him to bleed to death. Then Watson and Krenwinkel stabbed the helpless Mrs LaBianca 41 times while chanting a murderous mantra. Watson carved the word 'War' on Leno LaBianca's abdomen and they used their victims' blood to write the revolutionary slogans 'Death to pigs' and 'Rise' on the living room wall and 'Healter [sic] Skelter' on the door of the refrigerator. The killers then took a shower together, had something to eat and went home.

When it became clear to them that their senseless slaughter had not set off 'helter skelter', the great revolutionary race war, as they had hoped, the Family began to break up. After a number of false starts 24 Family members, including Manson himself, were arrested. Kitty Lutesinger, who was five months pregnant with Bobby Beausoleil's child, told the police that she had heard Manson order Beausoleil and Atkins to go to Gary Hinman's house. She had also heard Family members talking about a man being stabbed in the legs. This was not Hinman, who had no wounds on the legs; it

could, however, have been Frykowski.

Susan Atkins admitted to being at Hinman's house when he was murdered, but denied killing him. Confronted with testimony from a cellmate, however, to whom she had bragged about the killings, Atkins told the Grand Jury what had really happened at 10050 Cielo Drive on the night of 8 August, placing the blame squarely on Manson. He admitted his connection with the Process Church, whose views on random violence, Armageddon and a race war were on the record.

The Manson trial began on 15 June 1970. It lasted for nine-and-a-half months, the longest murder trial in America at that time. And it was unique. Never before had someone been charged with mass murder by proxy: Manson had not actually done any of the killings himself.

He managed to persuade Susan Atkins to retract her earlier statements saying that he had ordered the slaying, but did himself no favours when he carved a swastika on his forehead and threaten to cut the judge's head off.

Manson's strategy of letting his acolytes take the rap failed. Linda Kasabian took the stand as a witness for the prosecution and Tex Watson testified that Manson had told him to go to Cielo Drive and 'kill everyone in the house as gruesomely as possible'. Manson was reduced to taunting the jury that they would be killed in the murderous race war he had stirred up. Manson and his followers were convicted and sentenced to death, but the death penalty was abolished in California before the sentence could be carried out. He remains in jail to this day.

Manson and the Process Church were

not the only people who believed in race war. The Ku Klux Klan have always had it on their agenda, and the Black Panther Party armed themselves for a revolutionary confrontation, but a series of shoot-outs in the early 1970s effectively ended their activities.

To this day, the Nation of Islam – popularly known as the Black Muslims – preach that the white man is the devil and must be exterminated. The organisation was founded in Detroit in 1930 by street peddler Wali Fard, who called himself 'The Great Mahdi'. He taught that black men should give up drinking, narcotic addiction, fornication, gluttony and lying – vulgarities taught them by the white man – and prepare themselves for Armageddon where the forces of good – black people – would conquer the forces of evil – the whites.

Many survivalists in America have taken the same line. Believing that black street crime in the deprived inner cities threatened to turn into open warfare, they armed themselves and took to the hills. There are also those who believe that a race war is underway, pointing out that in the state of Texas, for example, there are more black people in jail than in school.

Even in England, whose high proportion of inter-racial couples have made mixed race children the fastest growing ethnic group, there are more Afro-Caribbean men in jail than in university. In 2000, a young Nazi tried to spark a race war by planting a nail bomb in Brixton market – though he was surprised to see many white peo-

To this day, the Nation of Islam, – the Black Muslims – preach that the white man is the devil and must be exterminated

ple were shopping there. Fortunately no one was killed, though 40 people, including a 23-month-old baby, were injured. He was caught after leaving a second bomb in the Admiral Duncan, an Old Compton Street pub used by gay men, which killed three people, including a pregnant woman.

Many wars have a racial element to them: the United States' expansion across the Great Plains and the dispossession of the American Indians can be seen as a race war. In the former Yugoslavia in the 1990s, the world heard for the first time the hideous euphemism 'ethnic cleansing', a term roughly equivalent to 'genocide'. The Yugoslavian conflict also had a religious element dating back to roughly the time of the Crusades: while the Serbs are largely Orthodox Christians, the Croats are Roman Catholics and the Bosnians are Muslims – as were the Albanians whom the Serbs tried to 'cleanse' from Kosovo by murder and expulsion. However, in recent memory, there has been one singularly chilling example of what happens when neighbour turns on neighbour simply on the grounds of race – Rwanda.

Of the eight million people living in Rwanda in 1990, 14 per cent were Tutsi and 85 per cent Hutu. The other one per cent was Twa hunter-gatherers, formerly known as pygmies. In 1890, the Germans seized Rwanda as part of German East Africa. They allied themselves with the Tutsis who were tall, slim and looked more 'European' than the Hutus,

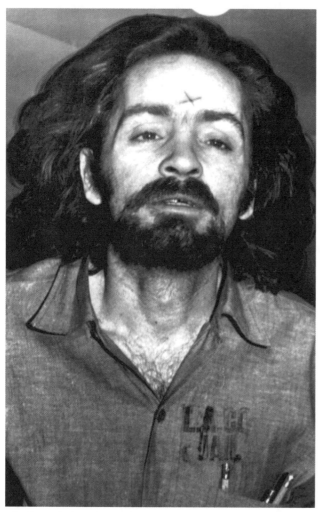

The drugs don't work: Charles Manson, hippie guru and Beatles fan is led into court to be charged with mass murder by proxy.

a shorter race with broad noses and stubby fingers. According to folklore, the Tutsis had originally come from Ethiopia. Though this is probably untrue, the Catholic Church argued that, as Ethiopians, they would once have been Christians, so the first duty of Catholic missionaries was to reclaim the Tutsi for Christianity.

In 1916, the Belgians took over the country, again favouring the now well-educated Tutsi, while the Hutu were pressed into a typically Belgian slave-labour system that was only abolished in 1927. In the late 1950s, the Hutu began to call for independence. Seeing which

way the wind was blowing, the Belgians quickly changed sides. The Tutsi king was assassinated while visiting Burundi, while an uprising in the north left 15,000 Tutsis dead, and thousands more refugees in neighbouring Uganda, Zaire, Tanzania and Burundi.

A Hutu named Gregoire Kayibanda became the first president of an independent Rwanda in 1962. Maintained in power by the Belgian army, he retained the system of identity cards introduced by the Belgians in the 1930s which specified whether the holder was a Tutsi, Hutu or Twa, an ethnic designation that could only be changed if you paid a huge bribe.

Tutsis were dubbed *inyenzis* or cockroaches and removed from all positions of authority. Then in 1963, the Hutu turned on the Tutsis, massacring 20,000 and sending another 100,000 fleeing into Burundi.

In 1973, General Juvenal Habyarimana came to power, promising an end to ethnic strife, but he was soon declaring that not only Tutsis would be excluded from power, but also any Hutus who had been 'infected' by the Tutsis. Meanwhile, he ruled the country with an iron hand – and an army that he increased from 5,000 to 35,000 men.

Despite massacres, and the exile of hundreds of thousands of Tutsis, the population of Rwanda swelled from three million in 1962 to eight million in 1990, leading to a shortage of land. Hutus who had occupied the land of exiled Tutsis, feared the return of the *inyenzi*, and Habyarimana decreed that Tutsi refugees in neighbouring countries would have to stay there because Rwanda was full up.

However, the exiled Tutsis had not

been sitting on their hands. In Uganda, they had joined the National Resistance Army, which overthrew the regime of Tito Okello who, in turn, had ousted Milton Obote. In 1986, Tutsi ex-NRA officers formed the Rwandan Patriotic Front. In 1990, the 1,500-strong RPF invaded.

Habyarimana's army outnumbered the RPF by over 20 to one, but they were inexperienced and poorly motivated. It was only the intervention of firstly Zaire, and then France, that kept Habyarimana from being routed. As peace talks dragged on, Rwandans alienated by the corruption of the Habyarimana regime seized the opportunity to form new political parties. Outmanoeuvred politically, Habyarimana began organising a murderous militia called the *interahamwe*, meaning 'those who stand together'.

Although Habyarimana distanced himself from the *interahamwe*, it killed over 2,000 of his political opponents. The killers were pardoned. The judicious use of murder coupled with executive clemency meant that Habyarimana could maintain the appearance of democratic government, even allowing other parties into the administration, with no danger of losing power. Meanwhile Habyarimana's cronies – the *Azaku* – ran everything in the country, including drugs, prostitution and protection rackets.

With the peace talks getting nowhere, the RPF renewed its attack on the Rwandan capital Kigali, but Habyarimana was saved by the arrival of French troops. Habyarimana and the RPF were now forced back to the negotiating table, where a power-sharing deal was agreed. A 600-man RPF battalion was to be stationed in Kigali to protect Tutsi politicians, while the French-trained Presidential Guard –

essentially Habyarimana's hit squad – was to be disbanded. But Habyarimana stalled and the World Bank pulled the plug. The *interahamwe* took to the streets, setting up its own road blocks in downtown Kigali to harass and rob Tutsis, while a radio station owned by Habyarimana's in-laws, who had grown rich under his rule, began pumping out anti-Tutsi propaganda.

Fearing Rwanda would destabilise the whole region, neighbouring heads of state summoned Habyarimana to a meeting in Tanzania. On the way home, the Mystère Falcon given to Habyarimana by President Mitterrand was blasted out of the sky by three heat-seeking missiles and the president's charred remains landed in the gardens of his splendid new Presidential palace. The missiles that shot him out of the sky were French-made too. To maintain their influence in Francophone Africa, the French had been playing a double game. They had been supplying and training the RPF as well as Habyarimana's army and the *interahamwe*.

Despite all the high-tech hardware supplied to both sides by the French, the Rwandan murder weapon of choice was the *panga* – a small machete imported from China that Rwandan peasants used as an all-purpose farm implement and carried around like a third arm. Those who could not afford a *panga* simply hammered nails into a piece of wood to make a club called a *mazu*.

The radio station belonging to the family of Agathe Habyarimana, the president's widow, told all able-bodied Hutu to go out and kill every Tutsi they could find. If they did not, the station warned, the RPF aimed to restore the Tutsi monarchy and purge the Hutu: it was a case of kill or be killed. Helpfully, the radio station even broadcast tips on the best ways of killing the *inyenzi*.

The Presidential Guard distributed weapons and ready-prepared death lists, and the killing began within an hour of Habyarimana's death. The first to die were not Tutsis. They were moderate Hutus who had opposed Habyarimana's corrupt administration, among them Joseph Kavaruganda, president of the constitutional court. Meanwhile, Agathe Habyarimana and 15 members of her family were on a flight to Paris, where they would stay as guests of President Mitterrand.

Early on the morning of 7 April 1994, the Presidential Guard came to the residence of Agathe Uwilingiyamana, Rwanda's 41-year-old acting prime minister. She escaped and found sanctuary at the United Nations Development Programme, where ten Belgian soldiers were assigned to protect her. When the Presidential Guard arrived and ordered them to disarm, however, having no mandate to resist, they had no choice but to obey. Mrs Uwilingiyamana tried to flee again, but was gunned down and her bloodstained body left in the road. Meanwhile the Presidential Guard took the Belgian soldiers, tortured them mercilessly, then executed them.

Fearing another Somalia, the United Nations ordered its 2,500 troops in Rwanda to return to barracks. Even when a young Rwandan woman was hacked to death by machete in full view of the UN troops, they did not inter-

vene. Their Canadian commander General Dallaire said that his men could have taken out the Presidential Guard, the gendarmerie and the worst of the *interahamwe* within 48 hours, saving hundreds of thousands of lives, but he was ordered by the UN secretary general in New York not to do so. General Dallaire could not even save 250 Tutsis and six priests who were trapped in St Andrew's College in Kigali. They were slaughtered.

The telephone lines were cut to prevent the world hearing what was going on. Electricity and water supplies also failed. Drunken *interahamwe* youths, rampaged around the streets tossing grenades into buildings. Banks were looted; fire trucks vandalised. Even in hospital, the sick and wounded were murdered in their beds.

With all foreign embassies closed and their staff evacuated, the killing of Tutsis began in earnest. In one day alone, 40,000 corpses floated down the Kagera River into Lake Victoria. Many of the bloated bodies seen in the swirling waters of the Rusumo Falls were women and children. Some had been decapitated; others had drowned themselves, rather than face the raging *interahamwe*.

Even a month after the killing had begun, when it was clear that an organised campaign of genocide was underway the rest of the world had not the faintest idea how to stop it. In all, it is estimated that between 800,000 and one million died, one third of them children, before the RPF finally took over on 4 July.

It was a case of kill or be killed; helpfully, the radio station broadcast tips on the best ways of killing Tutsis

In the city of Cyangugu, fewer than 8,000 of the 55,000 Tutsis survived. The local Prefect had organised the slaughter; the Tutsis were herded into the local football stadium where fragmentation grenades were lobbed at them. There were eleven mass graves in the city. In the rural area the slaughter was worse: of the 450,000 Tutsis in country districts of the Prefecture of Cyangugu only a handful remained.

One Tutsi woman admitted killing her wounded stepmother and two of her friends with a nail-studded club. The *interahamwe* forced her to do it, she said. If she did not, she knew her own life and those of her children would be forfeit. Some people went mad with guilt and grief.

More than 30,000 Tutsis packed into the Roman Catholic centre at Kabgayi were slaughtered. The Hutu priest of the Eglise Sainte Family in Kigali offered sanctuary to 8,000 Tutsis, but this was no more than a cynical ploy to round them up. The *interahamwe* took people from the church at will and hacked them to death individually, or machine-gunned large groups, leaving any survivors to starve or die from disease.

Hutu politicians blamed the RPF who had resumed fighting after the death of President Habyarimana. This meant the government soldiers were too busy fighting the rebels to prevent the atrocities, they said. They also justified the killing by comparing it to the fight against apartheid. The Tutsis, they said, wanted to control everything like the whites had in South Africa. Although the RPF were in truth responsible for atrocities of their own, when they finally took over, they installed a provisional government consisting of two Hutus and one Tutsi.

With the war lost, the Hutu government fled, taking with them the entire contents of Rwanda's exchequer. They were making a strategic withdrawal, they said, and they intended to return and finish the job, an intention frustrated by the fall of President Mobutu in Zaire. While many senior figures have found safe haven in Europe and America, over 100,000 suspects were held in prison for years before facing trial. But with the justice system overwhelmed, another 800,000 were left at large to face trial in front of their local villages. With only a small police force to keep order, this led to another outbreak of ethnic murder as the accused sought to eliminate survivors of the genocide who might testify against them.

Sadly, Rwanda is not the only country in Africa riven by tribal rivalries. In Zimbabwe, for example, the Ndebele are persecuted by Robert Mugabe of the majority Shona tribe: in South Africa, the Zulus traditionally support the Inkatha Freedom Party, while the other Bantu people support the African National Congress. In both countries, there are also substantial white minorities to ratchet the racial tension up another notch.

A global confrontation between black and white would be the ultimate race-war nightmare. It would catastrophically destabilise America, for example, where although white people are in the overwhelming majority, there is a high proportion of black people in the armed forces, as the services were seen as a way for people from deprived backgrounds to secure a good education, free healthcare and a well-paid occupation. European countries with substantial ethnic minorities could be similarly undermined and the remaining white settlers in Africa would become targets for ethnic cleansing.

Although most of the world's arms are unquestionably held by nations with white majorities, there are many more non-white people in the world, and with the US and European nations divided against themselves, the outcome of any racial confrontation could not be predicted. The only certainty is that humankind as a whole would be the loser and a race war between black and white would have the potential to so damage humankind's sense of itself as to send the species into a terminal decline.

Biological Warfare

THE USE OF BIOLOGICAL AGENTS in warfare stretches back into antiquity. As far back as 400 BC, Scythian archers were in the habit of infecting their arrows by dipping them in blood mixed with manure or slurry from decomposing corpses. By 300 BC, Greek, Persian and Roman literature talks of polluting enemies' wells by dropping the corpses of dead animals in them and, at the Battle of Eurymedon in 190 BC, Hannibal defeated the fleet of King Eumenes II of Pergamon by hurling pots full of venomous snakes onto the enemy ships.

The Holy Roman emperor Frederick Barbarossa used the bodies of dead soldiers to poison wells during the Battle of Tortona in 1155. Then in 1347, the Golden Horde hurled the bodies of plague victims over the walls into Caffa, causing the Black Death which ravaged Europe for the next three centuries. But humankind had not learnt its lesson and the same tactic was used again in 1710 when Russian forces were besieging the Swedes in the Estonian city of Reval.

In the French and Indian Wars of 1754–1763, the British introduced biological warfare to North America by distributing blankets infected with smallpox to Native Americans who had no resistance, with genocidal consequences. It is thought that the British used the same tactic during the American War of Independence causing a major smallpox epidemic among the American forces who had occupied Montreal, affecting about half of the 10,000 soldiers. The Americans retreated in chaos after burying their dead in mass graves, leaving Canada to the British. The Americans themselves adopted the same tactic during the Civil War. In 1863 a Confederate surgeon was charged with attempting to distribute clothes infected with yellow fever in the North.

During World War I, the Germans developed anthrax, cholera and glanders – a disease of horses that sometimes affects humans – along with wheat fungi to employ as biological weapons. There are allegations that the Germans spread plague in St Petersburg, infected mules in Mesopotamia with glanders and tried to do the same with the French cavalry.

In 1925, the Geneva Protocol outlawed the use of chemical and biological weapons, but it provided no means of verification to ensure compliance, and during World War II both sides continued research. The British tested anthrax bombs on the island of Gruinard off the coast of Scotland, leaving it uninhabitable for 50 years, and stockpiled cattle-cake laced with anthrax. The US also stockpiled anthrax and botulinum toxin in case the Germans made first use of biological warfare. And the Japanese operated a secret biological warfare facility in Manchuria, where they exposed Chinese prisoners to anthrax, plague, syphilis and other biological agents.

Although biological warfare was not used during the war, there were fears that it might in any coming conflict between the Communist world and the West. Between 1951 and 1954 benign biological agents were released off the west and east coasts of the US to determine how vulnerable American cities were. A similar test was performed on the New York subway in 1966. The British government admitted in mid-1998 that more than a million people were sprayed from the air in secret germ warfare tests during the 1970s. The strain used was a harmless e-coli bacterium together with bacillus globigii. Some 150 miles of coastline and areas up to 30 miles inland were exposed.

In 1972, the Biological Weapons convention was signed by over 100 countries, including the five permanent members of the Security Council. Again this did not end their use. The Soviet Union is thought to have deployed 'yellow rain' – trichothecene mycotoxins – in Communist campaigns in Laos, Cambodia and Afghanistan. In 1979, an accidental release of anthrax from a weapons facility in Sverdlovsk killed at least 66 people.

Officially, samples of smallpox are held only in Atlanta and the Vector Laboratory in Moscow

The Russians denied this until 1992, when they also admitted killing the Bulgarian defector Georgi Markov in London in 1968 by injecting ricin into his leg using the tip of an umbrella.

The chief scientist of the Sverdlovsk biological weapons facility, Kanatjan Alibekov, admitted working on an 'improved' smallpox weapon there. After defecting to the US, he expressed the fear that badly paid ex-Soviet scientists had sold smallpox to rogue states involved in illicit biological weapons production. Officially, samples of the virus are held only at the Center for Disease Control and Prevention in Atlanta and the Vector Laboratory in Moscow, but Alibekov believes that other states – including China, Cuba, Indian, Iran, Pakistan and Yugoslavia – had retained stocks.

And accidents do happen. In 1973, smallpox virus was released by a laboratory in London, killing two. A woman died in a similar accident in London in 1978 and a deadly epidemic was only prevented because most laboratory staff had been immunised against smallpox in their youth. Now that there is no longer a national vaccination programme, there would be nothing to prevent it spreading. There was another near miss in 1985 when workers at the same establishment found smallpox ampoules in a biscuit tin in a fridge. Although dated 1952, they were still deadly.

In Iraq, Saddam Hussein continued developing biological weapons. After the first Gulf War in 1991, he admitted hav-

ing bombs, Scud missiles, 122mm rockets and artillery shells armed with botulinum toxin, anthrax and aflatoxin, which causes cancer and liver disease. He also had aircraft fitted with spray tanks that could drop 2,000 litres of biological toxin over the target. However, they were not used during the first Gulf War, or the second, and it seems that they had long been decommissioned by the time of the US invasion of Iraq.

While it is thought that 17 countries around the world run biological weapons programmes, the main threat comes from terrorists. In September and October 1984, followers of the Bhagwan Shree Rajineesh spread salmonella in local salad bars near the cult's headquarters in Oregon, affecting 751 people. The attack was a misguided attempt to alter the outcome of a local election in order to secure planning permission for the cult's expanding commune. In 1995, two members of a Minnesota militia group were convicted of possession of ricin for use against local government officials. And in 1996, an Ohio man was able to obtain bubonic plague cultures through the post.

The Aum Shinrikyo 'Supreme Truth' cult in Japan, that released sarin nerve gas on the Tokyo subway, killing 12 and hospitalising 5,000, was also experimenting with biological agents including botulinum toxin, anthrax and Q fever – a deadly form of pneumonia isolated in Australia in 1935. Their aim was to herald the end of the world.

During 1998 and 1999, there were numerous hoaxes in the US involving anthrax. The Center for Disease Control and Prevention took these threats seri-

Be prepared: soldiers on exercises test anti-biological warfare equipment.

ously and did a study, which showed that the intentional release of anthrax by a terrorist in any major US city would have an economic impact of up to $26 billion per 100,000 people infected.

Another exercise called 'Dark Winter' in July 2001 simulated a covert smallpox attack on the US. It assumed that terrorists hit just three shopping malls in different states. The result, it was estimated, would be that three million people would be infected and one million would die. This was altogether too optimistic. The following year, the BBC broadcast the docu-drama *Smallpox 2002, Silent Weapon*. Its premise was an attack on New York by a single, suicidal fanatic. The result: 60 million dead. President Bush ordered a copy as part of his effort to get $6 billion from Congress to improve the US's defences against bio-terrorism.

But even the BBC's scenario might be optimistic, if one imagines, for example, an attack on a Third World country with no access to vaccines, or an attack on a busy airport. Smallpox has an incubation period of 12 days before the first symptoms appear. By that time, those infected would have travelled around the world infecting others. By then it would be too late for any effective quarantine. With numerous countries around the world affected, health services would collapse and a global pandemic would ensue.

We know that there are people out there willing to make such attacks. After 11 September 2001, there were 23 cases of bio-terrorist anthrax attacks in the US. In the front line were postal workers in New Jersey and Washington, D.C., and media companies in New York and Florida. The Senate building also had to be shut down after a suspected attack using 'weapons grade' anthrax. In all, 32,000 were exposed. According to the FBI, all that is needed to produce weapons grade anthrax is $2,500-worth of equipment in the garage or attic. There is simply no way that the authorities can guard against an attack from a single disaffected individual that would cause a global catastrophe.

In January 2003, a small quantity of ricin – tiny amounts of which can kill and to which there is no known antidote – was found in a flat occupied by six Algeriansin North London. This was being manufactured on the premises from castor oil beans, a process that takes almost no equipment at all. Ricin was used again in an attack on the US

Senate in January 2004 and a package was sent to President Bush.

Then there are strains of mutant microbes held in places such as Porton Down Biological Warfare laboratory in Wiltshire, for which no vaccines are available. Even diseases that we thought we had beaten could turn deadly again: there are already 5,000 germs that have developed a resistance to penicillin, largely due to the indiscriminate and unrestricted use of antibiotics, fed in their hundreds to cattle and sheep, and freely available over the counter in many countries, such as Spain. The 'biological bullet', it seems, is one we are loading into the gun ourselves.

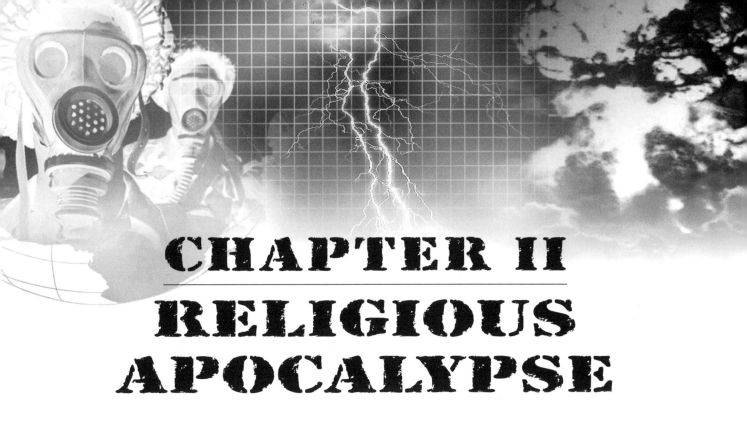

CHAPTER II
RELIGIOUS APOCALYPSE

The Christian Apocalypse

NEARLY TWO CENTURIES after the Book of Daniel was written, Jesus and his disciples clearly believed that the end of the world its authors predicted was on its way. In the Gospel according to Mark, Jesus warns of war, earthquakes, famines and persecutions, and says that 'the sun will be darkened, the moon will not give her light [and] the stars will come falling from the skies'.

It seems that the coming of the end is being held up by 'the evil one' – Belial or Satan – so that he can subvert the faithful and maintain his power on Earth. Indeed, the end did not come during Christ's lifetime. God did not arrive to judge who was righteous and should live forever, and who was not. As a result, Jesus was executed by the Romans.

Even so, the Day of Judgment is not far off. Jesus tells some of his disciples: 'There are some of those standing here who will not taste death before they have seen the kingdom of God already come in power...' and also that '...you may know that the end is near, at the very door. I tell you this: the present generation will live to see it all.' In the Gospels, the Acts of the Apostles and the Epistles, Jesus repeatedly appears as the judge of the world, either standing alongside God or in place of him.

John the Baptist had already warned that Jesus had 'his shovel... already in his hand and he will winnow his threshing-floor; the wheat he will gather into his granary, but he will burn the chaff on a fire that can never go out'.

Jesus also warned that, when the time came: 'Whoever then will acknowledge me before men, I will acknowledge him before my Father in heaven; and whoever disowns me before men, I will disown him before my Father in heaven.'

In Matthew he said: 'When the Son of Man comes in his glory and all the angels with him, he will sit in state on the throne, with all the nations gathered before him. He will separate men into two groups, as a shepherd separates the sheep from the goats.'

The righteous on his right will have 'my Father's blessing' and 'enter and possess the kingdom that has been ready for you since the world was made', while those on his left would be condemned to the 'eternal fire'. Elsewhere he promised that 'all whose deeds are evil... will be thrown into the blazing furnace, the place of wailing and grinding of teeth. And then the righteous will shine as brightly as the Sun in the kingdom of their Father.'

Then, some 60 years after the death of Jesus – around AD 95–96 – the Book of Revelation was written, which spelt out in detail what would happen when the world came to an end. The book begins by stating: 'This is the revelation given by God to Jesus... He made it known by sending his angel his servant John...'

This John is not thought by Biblical scholars to be the same as the John who wrote the fourth Gospel and three of the Epistles. He received his revelation on the island of Patmos in the Aegean and warns that 'the hour of fulfilment is near'.

He describes the risen Jesus as a transcendent being of inconceivable majesty, who wants to send messages to his various churches. With the heavenly choir assembled, the Lamb of God begins opening the seven seals of the book. The breaking of the first four seals bring forth the Four Horsemen of the Apocalypse, bringing with the traditional litany of war, famine, pestilence and death by wild beasts. When the fifth seal is opened, those slaughtered for being true to God's word were dressed in white robes and told to rest while a tally of those killed in Christ's service was made.

Then when the sixth seal was opened 'there was a violent earthquake; the Sun turned black as a funeral pall and the Moon all red as blood; the stars fell to the Earth, like figs shaken down by a gale; the sky vanished, as a scroll is rolled up, and every mountain and island was moved from its place'. A lot of these things will become very familiar during the course of this book. Seals were then attached to the foreheads of the 144,000 righteous 'who alone from the world had been ransomed. These are men who did not defile themselves with women, for they have kept themselves chaste.' Some may see this as too high a price to pay.

After that the seventh seal was broken and an angel took a censer, filled it from the fire on the golden altar set up before God's throne and threw it down to Earth, where there were 'peals of thunder, lightning and earthquake'.

Seven angels appeared with trumpets. When the first blew his trumpet, hail and fire mingled with blood was hurled down on the Earth and a third of the trees along with all the grass was burnt.

The second angel blew his trumpet and a third of the sea was turned into blood, killing a third of the sea creatures and sinking a third of the ships.

After the third trumpet, a star fell from heaven, polluting a third of the rivers and springs and many died of poisoning. The fourth turned out a third of the sunlight. At the fifth trumpet, another star fell, opening the abyss. Smoke came out, darkening the sky, along with locusts the size of horses with stings like scorpions, which were allowed to torment those without seals on their foreheads for five months.

The sixth trumpet released 200 million cavalry who killed a third of humankind. They unleashed plagues of fire, smoke and sulphur, and rode on horses whose tails were poisonous snails.

The seventh trumpet was sounded, announcing that the 'sovereignty of the world has passed to our Lord and his Christ, and he shall reign for ever and ever'. God's temple in heaven is opened and in it is seen the Ark of the Covenant, accompanied by thunder, lightning, hail and more earthquakes.

Then 'a woman robed with the Sun... who is about to give birth' appeared in heaven. The woman is Israel and her baby is the Christian Church. Satan menaces her in the form of a great red dragon with seven heads and ten horns. With his tail he knocks a third of the stars – traditional symbols of order – down onto the Earth. When the baby is born the dragon tries to devour it. But God snatches the child, while the woman finds refuge in the wilderness for 1,260 days.

War then breaks out in heaven. The Archangel Michael – who appears in the Book of Daniel as the patron saint of Israel – and his band of angels fight Satan, casting him and his angels down to Earth. There, Satan begins pursuing the woman who had given birth, going to war with the rest of her offspring. In this he is assisted by two beasts that seem to be a conglomeration of those that appear in the Book of Daniel. These appear to represent the Roman Empire and 'the false prophet'. Later these were seen as the Antichrist – the letters of whose name have the numerical value 666 – and the Roman church. The beast is assisted by seven angels and is ridden by the Whore of Babylon, who drinks the blood of the righteous.

A scene from Revelations XVII 3-5 showing St John and the Apocalypse. Engraving by Albrecht Dürer.

Then Christ makes his Second Coming, as a fierce sword-wielding warrior at the head of an army of angels, who defeats Satan at the battle of Armageddon. The beast and his accomplices are thrown alive into a lake of fire, while their human allies – the kings and their armies – are killed by a sword that comes out of Christ's mouth. Thus ends the Roman Empire.

An angel then comes down from heaven, chains up Satan and seals him in the abyss for a thousand years. Then comes the first resurrection, when the martyrs who remained true to the word of God and refused to worship Satan reign over the world with Christ for a thousand years. Satan is then released. He seduces the nations of the world and, along with the forces of Gog and Magog, makes war on God's people again. Fire comes down from heaven and consumes them, while the Devil in flung back into the lake of fire where he is tormented forever.

The Last Judgment now begins. The books are opened. The sea gives up its dead, along with those in the keeping of Death and Hades. Each is judged on the record of their deeds and those whose names are not found among the 'roll of the living' are flung into the lake of fire along with Death and Hades. Heaven and Earth then disappear and the New Jerusalem descends. This is a city of great perfection and beauty where there is no day and night, and the righteous share the bliss of angels.

There is another version of the apocalypse in the New Testament. It appears in the Second Letter of Peter, written, like John's Revelation, around AD 90. In it, early Christians are reminded that God had already destroyed the world once by the flood. After the world had been repopulated by Noah's progeny, God had warned humankind against its wicked ways once more by destroying the cities

'Look eagerly for the coming of the Day of God and work to hasten it,' says Peter, 'that day will set the heavens ablaze'

of Sodom and Gomorrah by fire, though Lot was saved because he was a good man. And that is what God had in store for us at the end of the world.

This time, Peter warns, God will punish those who 'follow their abominable lusts'. Even angels who had sinned will not be spared and will be consigned to the pits of hell.

'Look eagerly for the coming of the Day of God and work to hasten it,' says Peter, 'that day will set the heavens ablaze until they fall apart, and will melt the elements in flames. But we have his promise, and look forward to new heavens and a new Earth, the home of justice.'

While much of the imagery of John's Revelation comes from The Book of Daniel, Peter introduces a new concept – the destruction of the Earth by fire. This does not make an appearance in the Old Testament and appears to have been borrowed from the Greek Stoics, who thought that the world was periodically destroyed by a purifying fire, or from the Zoroastrians, who thought that, at the last judgement, all the metal in the mountains would melt and stream over the Earth, destroying all that was evil and preserving those who were good. First-century Christians would have had contact with both Stoics and Zoroastrians and it is this idea that the world will end in a conflagration that has proved the most enduring.

The Jewish Apocalypse

A NUMBER OF VERSIONS of the Apocalypse are presented in the writings from Judea of the third and second centuries BC, but only one found its way into the Hebrew Bible and the Christian Old Testament. It dates from an early persecution of the Jews.

After the death of Alexander the Great in 323 BC, his empire was divided up among his Macedonian generals. At first, Judea fell under the control of the dynasty of Ptolemy, who ruled Egypt and, like other Macedonian and Greek rulers of the time, did not interfere with local religions. In the second century BC, a descendent of Seleucus, the Macedonian officer who took over Syria and Iran, seized Judea. And in 169 BC, the Seleucid monarch Antiochus IV Epiphanes entered the Temple in Jerusalem and plundered it. In 167 BC, he pillaged the city itself, killing the men and taking the women and children into slavery. An altar to the Syrian god Baal Shamen, whose worship involved the sacrifice of pigs, was set up in the temple. The Jewish religion was outlawed and the Jews were forced to worship pagan gods. Many refused and were killed. But three brothers who took the name Maccabee – which means 'Hammer' or 'Hammerer' in Hebrew – led a revolt which drove out Antiochus IV. They liberated the temple in 164 BC, reconsecrated it to the worship of Yahweh and returned their religious rights to the Jews.

The Jewish version of the Apocalypse appears in the Book of Daniel, notably in chapters two and seven. These were written, probably by more than one author, between 169 and 165 BC, during the period of oppression by Antiochus. The book purports to tell the story of a righteous Jew named Daniel, who served in the court of the sixth-century king of Babylon, Nebuchadnezzar. In chapter two, Nebuchadnezzar has a prophetic dream and he challenges his courtiers, on pain of death, to tell him what his dream was and what it meant. Daniel rose to the challenge. He told the king that he had dreamt of a huge and fearsome idol. Its head was made from gold, its chest and arms of silver, its belly and thighs of bronze, its legs of iron and its feet part iron, part clay. In the dream he saw a stone being hewn from a mountain – 'not by human hand'. It hit the feet of the idol and smashed them. The rest of the idol then shattered into fragments which 'were swept away like chaff before the wind... until no trace remained'. The stone that had struck the idol then 'grew into a great mountain filling the whole Earth'.

Having got that much right, Daniel proceeded to interpret the dream. The idol's golden head, he said, was Nebuchadnezzar himself. The silver chest and arms represented a kingdom which would follow his, but be inferior to it. The bronze belly and thighs represented a third kingdom, which would have sovereignty over the whole world. The legs of iron were a fourth kingdom which was doomed – 'as iron shatters and destroys all things, it shall break and shatter the whole earth'. What Daniel is

foreseeing here is the coming of Alexander the Great, who shattered the Persian Empire that was to succeed Nebuchadnezzar's kingdom.

The feet that were part clay and part iron were a new divided kingdom, which was partly strong and partly brittle. The men in it would be mixed by intermarriage, making alliances unstable – 'as iron does not mix with clay'. Before he died, Alexander married his generals off to Persian princesses. The shattering of the legs represents the shattering of Alexander's empire that led, ultimately, to the rivalry between the Seleucids and the Ptolemies and the resulting subjugation of Judea.

'In the period of those kings, the God of heaven will establish a kingdom that will never be destroyed,' says Daniel, 'that kingdom will never pass to other people; it shall shatter and make an end to all these kingdoms, while it shall itself endure forever. This is the meaning of your vision of the stone being hewn from a mountain, not by human hand, and then shattering the iron, the bronze, the clay, the silver and the gold. The almighty God has made known to your majesty what is to be hereafter.'

Clearly, after the current Seleucid and Ptolemaic kingdoms have been destroyed, the kingdom of God will fill up the whole Earth, like the stone.

In chapter seven, Daniel himself has a series of visions in which he sees 'a great sea churned up by the four winds of heaven'. Four huge beasts emerged from it. The angel who interprets the dream for Daniel tells him that these four beasts represent the four kingdoms, as in chapter two. The first is a lion with eagle's wings. When the wings are plucked from him he stands on two feet like a man. The second is a flesh-eating bear. The third is a leopard with four wings on its back and four heads.

'Next in my visions of the night, I saw a fourth beast, dreadful and grisly, exceedingly strong, with great iron teeth and bronze claws. It crunched and devoured, and trampled underfoot all that was left. It differed from all the beasts which preceded it in having ten horns.' (The ten-horned beast traditionally represents Alexander.) 'While considering the horns, I saw another horn, a little one, spring up among them... and in that horn were the eyes of a man, and a mouth that spoke proud words.' This is thought to be Antiochus IV.

Then 'thrones were set in place and one ancient in years took his seat, his robe was white as snow and the hair of his head like cleanest wool. Flames were his throne and its wheels blazing fire; and a flowing river of fire streamed out before him. Thousands upon thousands served him and myriads upon myriads attended his presence. The court sat, and the books were opened.'

The 'one ancient in years' is clearly God and he begins to deliver the final judgement. Antiochus IV is naturally condemned, while all righteous Jews – 'everyone who is written in the book' – will be saved. Remarkably, 'many of those who sleep in the dust of the earth will wake, some to everlasting life and some to the reproach of eternal abhorrence'.

This is clearly a departure from the traditional Jewish belief in Sheol – the 'pit' or 'land of oblivion' inhabited after

King Nebuchadnezzar II (-562 BC), king of Babylon watching Shadrach, Mesach and Abednego in the fire, from the Book of Daniel in the Old Testament, circa 600 BC.

death by the righteous and wicked alike. Here the good – like those killed by Antiochus for remaining faithful to Yahweh – would be rewarded after death, while the bad – those who had abandoned their faith for the rewards offered by the Seleucid kingdom – would suffer 'eternal abhorrence'.

At the end of the vision Daniel is told to 'keep the words secret and seal the book till the time of the end'. Many are still waiting.

The Muslim Apocalypse

THE MUSLIM VIEW of the Apocalypse owes much to the Book of Revelation and to Daniel. Curiously, there is no mention of Daniel in the Koran – though ideas such as Abraham being the friend of God and there being a seal on prophecy are carried over. The Archangels Gabriel and Michael also make an appearance in both books, though Gabriel takes a more central role in Islam where he is both the angel of revelation and Muhammad's frequent counsellor, perhaps even dictating verses of the Koran to him and explaining their meaning.

The Muslim world certainly knew of Daniel. In fact, the first historical reference to Daniel occurs in AD 638, six years after the death of Muhammad, when Muslims conquered Susa, modern-day Shush in Iran. There they were shown

Daniel's remains. Muslim soldiers took a seal in the form of a signet ring showing a man between two lions from the body, but their commander Caliph Umar told them to return it, and ordered that Daniel's body be buried. At Daniel's tomb in Shushtar, there was also a book, which was taken to Umar, who became the first Arab to read it. He also had it translated and copied. This book was said to tell of 'what will occur of civil disorders'.

According to the Koran, Jesus – who is regarded as a prophet in Islam – will return, though his 'second coming' will be one of the signs that the end times are approaching, rather than the end in itself. As in the Book of Daniel, the Koran talks of horned animals, and makes references to Alexander the Great and his conquest of the Persian Empire – using the metaphor of a dam that holds back the forces of Gog and Magog bursting, engulfing the world in war.

Just as in Revelation, the Koran speaks of trumpets sounding, and the appearance of an Antichrist, a false prophet and a beast. As the end approaches, people scatter like moths. Mountains are plucked like tufts of wool and turned into sand. The Earth is shaken and turned to powder. The heavens are split and rolled back. Stars are scattered. Seas boil over and the sun goes dark.

On the Day of Resurrection, Allah resurrects all humans, body and soul. He then proceeds to judge them. The righteous are sent to paradise – a peaceful, sheltered, well-watered garden where they are adorned with gold and pearls and silk, and recline on cushioned couches, though they never grow tired. They will eat fruit and drink a musk-perfumed wine, which will make them neither sick nor intoxicated. And they will enjoy the pleasure of the *houri* (from the Arabic *hur*, plural of *huriya*, a dark-eyed woman'), or 'wives' who are constantly being returned to their pure and virginal state. Although the Koran says that women can gain entrance to paradise, it describes no pleasures for women equivalent to those provided by the *houri*.

For unbelievers, the day of decision will be the day of doom. They will be sent to hell where they will wear 'garments of fire'. To slake their thirst they will be given molten metal or pus that melts the contents of their stomachs. To cool them, boiling water will be poured over their heads and their skin will melt.

According to the Hadith, a record of the sayings of the Prophet Muhammad, the end of the world is heralded by the arrival of the Mahdi – the 'rightly guided one' – who will destroy the Antichrist and, as caliph, bring in a period of peace and justice, fulfilling the mission of Muhammad. Just as Muhammad is the last prophet, the Mahdi is the last Imam.

Over the centuries there have been a number of Muslims who have claimed to be the Mahdi. The best-known, in the West at least, was Muhammad Ahmad, whose forces killed General Gordon at Khartoum in 1885. He ruled a vast theocratic state from Omdurman in the Sudan and sought to drive out the British, along with their Egyptian allies, and the Turks, whose Ottoman Empire still held writ in the area. However, just six months after the death of Gordon, Muhammad Ahmad contracted typhus at the age of 41 and died. His successor Abdullahi ruled until 1898, when the British, under General Kitchener, took their revenge, taking Omdurman and snuffing

General Gordon's last stand at Khartoum, February 1884, against the forces of the Sudanese leader Muhammad Ahmad al-Mahdi. The Mahdi believed he was the herald of the end of the world.

out the Mahdiyyah, as the Sudanese Mahdist state had become known.

Another important Madhi was Muhammad ibn 'Abd al-Wahhab (1703–1792), who led a puritanical Muslim movement in central Arabia. The Saud family adopted Wahhabism and led Wahhabi armies into battle, taking over Arabia as far north at the Euphrates. In 1808, they took the sacred cities of Mecca and Medina. Indian Muslims were near to conversion to Wahhabism and it had many followers in Egypt, North Africa and even Turkey. But after a series of reverses, the first Wahhabi empire was crushed by the Ottomans in 1818.

The Saud managed to cling onto power in Arabia and the sect revived. Eventually the Sauds were driven out by the Rashids, who crushed the second Wahhabi empire in 1891. In 1902, Abdul-Aziz ibn Saud returned from exile in Kuwait, seizing Riyadh, the Wahhabi capital. Finding himself facing the Ottomans again, in 1915, ibn Saud made a treaty with the British. Following the collapse of the Ottoman Empire in the World War I, ibn Saud drove out the Rashids and in 1932 the Kingdom of Saudi Arabia was founded. With the rise of the House of Saud, Wahhabism flourished again.

In Saudi Arabia in 1979, a man named Muhammad – born Abd Allah al-Qahtani – again claimed to be the Madhi. With several hundred followers, he attempted to occupy the Grand Mosque in Mecca. He was gunned down by state security forces, unconvinced by his claims. It was also mooted that Ayatollah Khomeini, who ran an oppressive Islamic state in Iran from 1979 to 1989 was the Madhi, although he never openly claimed the title. A video released in 2003 raised the question of whether Osama bin Laden is the Mahdi. He was pictured standing by a black board with 'awaited enlightened one' – a clear reference to the Mahdi – written in Arabic on it. Since 2001, he has been signing himself Osama bin Muhammad bin Laden. According to the Hadith, the Mahdi must have the same name as the Prophet.

Many of the things that bin Laden has done have an apocalyptic feel to them

Other requirements are that he is descended from the Prophet via Muhammad's daughter Fatima; that he will have a distinctive forehead and prominent nose; that he will be extremely generous and altruistic; that he will arise in Arabia and be compelled by popular acclamation in Mecca to lead the Muslims; that he will withstand attack by an army from Syria, which will be swallowed up by the desert; that he will fill the earth with justice and equity; and that he will reign for five, seven or nine years, perhaps as co-ruler with Jesus, after which the last trumpet will sound and the final judgement will ensue.

Many of the things that bin Laden has done have an apocalyptic feel to them. And it is the Mahdi's job to kill the infidel. If bin Laden makes the claim that he is the Mahdi and many in the Muslim world believe him, the possibility that we are in fact living in the end of days seems a little less far-fetched than it otherwise might.

12

The Hindu Apocalypse

'I AM BECOME DEATH, the destroyer of worlds.' These are the words J. Robert Oppenheimer, the father of the atomic bomb, famously quoted from the Hindu holy book, the *Bhagavad Gita*, on 16

July 1945, when he saw the first bomb explode at a test at Alamogordo, New Mexico. In the passage, the god Vishnu is explaining his powers to the book's hero and says: 'If the radiance of a thousand suns were to burst at once into the sky, that would be the splendour of the mighty one.' In Oppenheimer's view, this perfectly described the fireball he had seen thrown up by the world's first man-made atomic explosion.

However, in Hinduism it is Shiva, rather than Vishnu, who is cast as the destroyer. In the ancient sacred Hindu texts, the *Upanishads*, it is said of Shiva: 'At the time of the end, he annihilates all worlds.' But this is only one of his three faces. He is also the creator and is worshipped as the *linga*, the phallus. He is also the preserver. Shiva is generally depicted with a blue neck, intended to show his holding poison thrown up by the churning of the oceans in his throat to protect humankind. The River Ganges trickles to Earth through his hair, which in his role as destroyer of the world is matted and wild.

His third eye gives him inner vision, but when its power is turned outwards it brings fiery destruction. He has a garland of skulls around his neck and is sometimes shown carrying a club with a skull on the end.

His consort Shakti is the embodiment of Shiva's power. In his manifestation as the destroyer, Shakti becomes the four-armed goddess Kali. Like him, she has dishevelled hair and wears a garland of human heads. She is naked except for this and a belt of severed hands. She is depicted as a hideous, black-faced hag, smeared with blood, with bared teeth and a protruding tongue, while in her four hands she holds a sword, a shield, the severed hand of a giant and a noose.

According to mythology, Kali leads Shiva in a wild dance in the cremation grounds, which threatens to destroy the cosmos. Kali is hell-bent on this destruction, but Shiva finally subdues her. However, in the Tantric tradition, Kali is depicted dancing on the ithyphallic corpse of Shiva, so he is in no position to restrain her.

Kali is said to have developed a taste for blood when she tried to kill the demon Raktavija. The problem with attacking Raktavija was that a thousand new demons were created each time a drop of his blood fell to the earth. So Kali stabbed him with a spear and drank his blood before it could touch the ground. The worship of Kali demands blood sacrifice. In the past humans were sacrificed to her, but in modern times a goat has been substituted. At the height of her cult in the 18th and 19th centuries, so many goats were sacrificed day and night that rivers of blood cascaded down the steps of her temple at Bindhachal, near Mirzapur on the Ganges, and supplicants from all over India would make their pilgrimage there. Within the temple walls they would flagellate themselves into ecstasy.

But Kali's terrible influence spread far outside the confines of the temple. Her adherents from the Indus to Bengal formed themselves into a murderous secret society called the Thuggee, or Thugs, who terrorised the travellers of India for hundreds of years. They strangled travellers on the road and stole their possessions. They did not, however, consider themselves thieves. Each murder was carried out according to a rigid ritual and the victim was considered a sacrifice to Kali herself. The Thuggee believed that

Statue of the Hindu goddess Shakti, in her guise as Kali, goddess of motherhood and death.

tection of rajas and rich men, both Muslim and Hindu, while the lower castes were too terrified to complain as they could all too easily become victims. The Thuggee worked in bands and, each year at the end of the rainy season, they would make a pilgrimage to Bindhachal where they handed over a share of their booty to the priests of Kali. In return, they would be assigned an area to work in the following year. They would be told what fees would be expected and what rituals they had to perform. They would then be blessed with the protection of Kali and sent about their murderous business.

The Thuggee went about their work in absolute secrecy. First, they would seek out a group of travellers, preferably of their own caste. They would befriend them and join their caravan, then, when the omens were right, they would strangle them, according to a strict ritual. The murderer would use a *rumal*, a yellow handkerchief with a silver rupee tied in the middle as a garrotte, and shove his knee deep in the victim's back to hasten their demise. The body was then cut with ritual gashes and buried or thrown down a well. Any of the victim's possessions that had no value were burnt. The rest, along with any personable children, were taken as the Thuggee swiftly moved on, leaving no trace of their crime other than a secret sign that could only be read by other Thuggee.

The profits raised on the goods were not the motive for their killings, the Thuggee maintained. They considered themselves honourable and honest, and would never stoop to common thieving. The killing was done for Kali. Any material benefits accruing to the murderer were rewards given by Kali. She had

when Kali had strangled another demon, Rukt Bij-dana, at the dawn of the world, two men had been formed from the sweat of her brow and they – and their sons and their sons' sons – had been sent forth into the world to strangle.

The Thuggee enjoyed the secret pro-

been merciful enough to provide the assassin with a living while he continued the sacred slaughter.

The son of a Thuggee would follow his father into the craft. He would begin as a scout, then become a grave digger. After that he graduated to becoming assistant strangler, then a strangler himself. A boy's first murder was celebrated as a rite of passage, like puberty or circumcision. There would be elaborate ceremonials involving the sacred pickaxe or *kussee* carried by every gang. The *kussee* was thought of as a tooth from the mouth of Kali, and was essential to the sanctification of Thuggee murders.

The Thuggee had a secret language and other rites and rituals that surrounded the murders. There were special sacred groves where their murders were carried out and they would bury their victims in a circular pit with the corpses packed tightly around a central core of earth. This prevented jackals digging up the bodies and the murders being discovered. After each murder, the Thuggee would consume a lump of consecrated yellow sugar – or *goor*, which they believed altered them. Once a man has tasted the *goor*, they said, he would become a Thuggee for life.

When the British first came to India, they tolerated the Thuggee. It was a local custom and should be respected, the old India hands said. The Indians themselves rarely complained about it, being generally far too frightened: the Thuggee permeated all levels of society and any complaint would surely get back to them.

When Thuggee were prosecuted, they would almost always be acquitted. Local judges too were intimidated. The Thuggee could strike at any place, any time, and no one felt safe from the wrath of Kali. It was estimated that, at their height, the Thuggee killed up to 40,000 people a year. At some times of the year, the chances of completing a journey safely were just one in three. In 1830, one gang murdered 108 people in just three months and individual Thuggee boasted more than a thousand victims. The gangs themselves had up to 300 members.

But the British continued to tolerate the Thuggee. In 1802, the British Army celebrated the signing of the Treaty of Amiens with a parade, led by military bands, outside the temple of Kali. In 1827, when three Thuggee turned informer and four others were charged with murder, a British circuit judge dismissed the case and charged the informers with giving false evidence. They were sentenced to five days riding backwards on donkeys around the city of Jubbulpore, followed by five years in jail.

All that changed in 1830 when Lord William Bentinck was appointed Governor-General. With reforming zeal, he was determined to put an end to what he called 'the most dreadful and extraordinary secret society in the history of the human race'. He made Captain William Sleeman Superintendent for the Suppression of Thugs and gave him 50 mounted irregulars and 40 sepoy infantrymen. Establishing his headquarters in Saugor, Sleeman initiated an intelligence operation aimed at building up a complete picture of the history, rituals, customs and practice of the Thuggee. He traced their activities on a ten-foot map, the most detailed ever made of India up to that time.

Sleeman was ruthless in his suppression of the Thuggee. Convicted Thugs were branded and tattooed with the words 'Convict Thug' on the shoulder or 'Thug' on their lower eyelids, then hanged. Those willing to give information on other Thuggee would be spared, though they would never be freed. Sleeman argued that 'like tigers, their thirst for blood would never be appeased'. This manner of proceeding was very effective: to save their lives, many Thuggee were prepared to speak out and yielded more and more information. Sleeman found Thuggee everywhere. They worked as the trusted servants of Europeans and as senior officials to the Indian princes, with many serving in the Indian Army and several working for British Intelligence.

Arrested Thuggee felt no remorse for what they had done. Killing had brought them a sense of elation rather than guilt and they were proud to have followed in the footsteps of their fathers and grandfathers. One man who had personally killed 931 victims explained to Sleeman the joy of befriending and outsmarting travellers, who were constantly on their guard against the Thuggee, then suddenly killing them. When Sleeman accused him of thieving, he said: 'Thieving? Never. If a banker's treasure were before me and entrusted to my care, though in hunger and dying I would spurn to steal. But let a banker go on a journey and I would certainly murder him.'

However, the Thuggee began to believe that their goddess Kali was losing the battle with Sleeman's Christian god, for which they blamed themselves. Having always

Despite her hideous face, Kali is known for her erotic allure; her cult is on the rise again

believed that their powers were supernatural and they had an occult partnership with the tiger – 'Those who escaped the tigers fell into the hands of the Thugs and those who escaped the Thugs were devoured by tigers,' said one – they now began to believe that Devi – the mother goddess of whom Kali is the ferocious form – had withdrawn her protection. 'We have sadly neglected her worship,' was one Thuggee's explanation for this withdrawal.

They were also overwhelmed by the power of the British. They told Sleeman: 'Before the sound of your drums, sorcerers, witches and demons take flight. How can Thuggee stand?'

Sleeman went on to track down the patrons and bankers who backed the Thuggee, the 'capitalists of murder', as he called them. Some did not require much persuading that investing in the Thuggee was not a very safe bet any more. One banker in Omrautee withdrew his funds and invested them instead in the East India Company, which had just secured a monopoly of the opium trade in China.

By 1841, the Thuggee had been virtually eradicated. Several thousand Thuggee had been tried and hundreds hanged. The rest were imprisoned or transported to penal settlements on the Andaman Islands. The less blood-thirsty were held in Jubbulpore and were taught weaving, carpet-making, carpentry and bricklaying. Later, a walled village was built near the jail, where they lived with their wives and families. Until the end of the century, foreign visitors would come and peer over the wall at what Sleeman hoped were the last members of this terrible sect. Thuggee, however, is not quite dead. In 1970, a bus driver and his father were accused of sacrificing a ten-year-old boy to Kali. Villagers claimed that they felt giddy after eating a sacred chapatti which the accused had distributed after they had worshipped the goddess.

Despite her hideous face, Kali is known for her erotic allure and is seen by feminists as a symbol of female empowerment and sexual liberation, so her cult is on the rise again. According to Hindu eschatology, we are currently living in the age of Kali, or the age of darkness. In it, virtue and religion will disappear and the world will be ruled by unjust men until it is overtaken by chaos. Then Kalki, the tenth and final avatar, or incarnation, of Vishnu will appear on a white horse, with an unsheathed sword blazing like a comet in his hand. The horse will stamp on the earth with its right foot, causing the tortoise that supports the world to drop it into the deep. Vishnu will then return the world to its pristine state.

The revival of the cult of Kali would hasten this end. There is no reason why the Thuggee should not see themselves as the Hindu equivalent of al Qaeda. If they penetrated the highest levels of society, as they did in their heyday, they could be a real danger, not just to the subcontinent, but to the whole world: after all, India now has the atomic bomb.

CHAPTER III
PLAGUE

13

AIDS

AIDS came as a big surprise to science. It arrived at a time when medical science thought it was winning the war against contagious diseases. Smallpox had been wiped out. Diptheria, polio, yellow fever, rubella, tuberculosis, measles, malaria and other diseases spread by the mosquito were in retreat. Then along came an entirely new disease, which was deadly and medical science had no adequate protection against. Palliatives have been developed, but millions have died. AIDS is propagated by a virus and, as with all viral diseases, there is a danger that the virus will mutate into an even more deadly form.

The first cases of AIDS – Acquired Immunodeficiency Syndrome – were identified in Los Angeles in 1981, just one the year after the World Health Organisation had announced that small-pox had been eradicated. Smallpox had been a killer since at least the time of the ancient Egyptians, whose mummified bodies showed signs of the disease, but a

campaign of inoculation had proven so successful that since 1977 there has been no case outside the laboratory.

Initially, AIDS seemed to be limited to homosexual men and intravenous drug users. But then it began spreading into the wider community, and by 2003, it was thought that 33 million people were infected worldwide and over 14 million had died. These figures, ghastly though they may be, pale when compared with the 30 million people who died in the worldwide influenza epidemic of 1918-1919, the worst outbreak of flu in the 20th century and the most deadly pandemic in human history, and it overtook the world at lightning speed.

Spanish Flu

The Spanish flu, so-called because it was mistakenly believed to have originated in northern Spain, had seemed harmless enough when it first appeared in early March 1918 at Camp Funston, Kansas. Many of those affected in Kansas were American troops, who were sent to fight in France in the closing stages of World War I shortly after the outbreak of flu, and they took the virus with them. It spread quickly and by July 1918 the virus had reached as far as Poland. Initially the disease it produced was comparatively mild, and most of those affected seemed to shrug it off in a matter of a few days. By August 1918, however, the virus seems to have mutated into a more lethal variety, killing its victims within two days. It was also more contagious. Six days after the first case of influenza was reported at Camp Devens, Massachusetts, there were 6,674 on the sick list.

When World War I ended in November, troops returning home carried the virus around the world. At the height of the epidemic, New York suffered 851 deaths on a single day. In the US, 550,000 people died – nearly ten times the number America had lost in the war. India is thought to have lost 12.5 million. Entire Inuit villages were wiped out and the casualty rate on some islands in the South Seas hit 20 per cent. The final global death toll dwarfed the 8.5 million soldiers and 13 million civilians who died as a result of World War I.

Fortunately the epidemic died down quickly. Flu has been around for a long time, with the first clear description of an outbreak appearing in 1610. Since then humankind has built up an immunity. The problem with AIDS is not only that it has not been around long enough

AIDS virus. Illustration of a T-lymphocyte white blood cell, infected with HIV viruses, amongst red blood cells. HIV (human immunodeficiency virus) is the cause of AIDS (acquired immune deficiency syndrome).

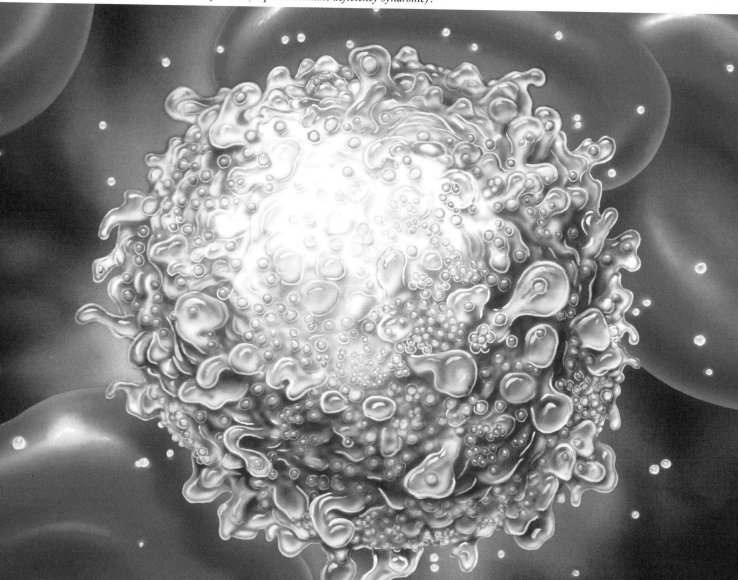

for humankind in general to have built up any immunity – though it has been reported that some Kenyan prostitutes have developed some resistance – but that it attacks the very immune system that protects us from other diseases.

SIV in chimps

Two years after the first cases of AIDS were reported, the Human Immunodeficiency Virus, HIV, which caused it, was isolated. HIV seems to be related to SIV – Simian Immunodeficiency Virus – found in monkeys and it is thought to have jumped species. The early outbreaks in the United States have been traced back to 'patient zero' – Canadian flight attendant Gaetan Dugas, who travelled widely in his job, inadvertently transmitting the disease. HIV has been found in a tissue sample of a Norwegian sailor who died in 1976 and an African-American living in St Louis in 1969. It has also shown up in a plasma sample taken from an adult male living in the Congo in 1959, though no one is sure when it jumped species. This is thought to have happened in the 1940s or early 1950s, though some scientists believe that it happened 100 years ago. Some say it was spread to humans when civil war in the Congo forced the population to flee to the jungle, where they ate monkey meat to survive. Another theory states that the virus was spread by an oral polio vaccine grown in chimp kidney and given to about a million people in the Belgian Congo, Rwanda and Burundi in the late 1950s.

In 2002 25,000 people died of AIDS in the West. That same year, 2.2 million Africans died of the disease

The AIDS virus does not spread easily like flu, though coughing, sneezing or casual physical contact. It is contracted by direct contamination with blood, breast milk, semen and other bodily fluids. It took off in the West due to the rise in low-cost air travel, taking more people to ever more exotic destinations, the spread of intravenous heroin use after the Vietnam war and the development of Factor VIII – the blood clotting agent refined from pooled donor blood used to treat to haemophiliacs.

In 2002 25,000 people died of AIDS in the West. That same year, 2.2 million Africans died and more than 3.4 million were newly infected. In sub-Saharan Africa, over 28 million have the disease. Poverty and famine mean few have the means to resist it. By 2010, deaths in sub-Saharan Africa are set to outstrip births, sending the population into decline.

In Botswana, 39 per cent of the population is infected. Life expectancy has dropped from around 70 to 27, and the head of the country's AIDS commission Dr Banu Khan says that Botswanans are faced with extinction. In Zimbabwe, more than 3,000 people die of AIDS each week from a population of less than 12 million, while in South Africa five million are infected and the death toll is now believed to top seven million.

With the most productive section of society, young adults, dying, the economy of the region is failing. More than 13 million children have been left orphaned. They are either abandoned on the streets of Africa's seething slums, or live in poverty in villages populated only by the old and the very young. They are also deprived of any education. According to the UN, in 2002 alone, a million students lost their teachers to AIDS. No one knows how to replace them and this will blight lives for generations to come.

But this is only the tip of the iceberg. Already four million people are infected in India, where fatalities from AIDS are expected to exceed African levels within a decade. Millions of cases are predicted in Russia and the infection rate in China is rising fast. The opening of these markets had been thought to boost the world economy for the foreseeable future, but a decline in their population could send the world into an economic tailspin.

After 20 years of work using the best technology available, scientists have yet to come up with a cure for AIDS. Just as the 1918 influenza virus suddenly mutated into something much more deadly, HIV could easily mutate into something even more virulent. Such a mutation may not even arise naturally: already it is possible to build an HIV virus from commercially available strands of DNA in a home laboratory, using a genetic blueprint downloaded from the Internet. An amateur biotechnologist, perhaps in the employ of a terrorist group, would have little problem modifying it to make an even more infectious strain.

And if HIV can make the leap from monkeys into humankind, who knows what other doomsday bugs may be lurking in different animals, ready to jump the species gap and sweep the whole of humankind into an early grave?

A Plague of Rats

PESTILENCE IS TRADITIONALLY thought of as one of the four Horsemen of the Apocalypse, along with War, Famine and Death. In the Book of Revelation though, things are not so clear. The first horseman rides forth on a white horse, conquering and to conquer. The second, all in red, carries a sword and makes men slaughter one another. The third, on a black horse, carries scales and represents famine. The fourth horse was sickly pale and his name was Death. 'To him was given... the right to kill by sword and by famine, by pestilence and wild beasts.' So pestilence is only one of the faces of the pale rider. Normally pestilence is usually associated with the plague, which makes several appearances in the Bible, particularly in the Book of Revelation. And there, the plague heralds the coming of the Apocalypse and the end of time.

The most well-known outbreak of plague outside the Bible was the Black Death, which ravaged Europe between 1347 and 1351. It was particularly devastating because there had been no plague in Europe for a millennium, and most people were wholly unprepared for it now. Believing that the Day of Judgment was at hand, bands of flagellants roamed through Europe's cities, stripped to the waist and whipping themselves to mortify the flesh and punish themselves for any sins they had overlooked.

The Black Death was the unforeseen

The Great Pit in Aldgate where victims of the Great Plague of London (1664 - 1666) were buried. The Black Death, as the bubonic plague came to be known, was spread by rats and killed 70,000 Londoners out of a population of 460,000.

consequence of an early piece of biological warfare. Although the Black Death had disappeared from Europe, it was still endemic in Asia, with an outbreak occurring in China in the 1330s. By 1346 it had spread to the Mongols of the Golden Horde who had pushed westwards into Russia. The following year the Mongols were besieging Caffa, now Feodosiya, a Genoese colony in the Crimea. To dislodge the defenders, they hurled the bodies of their plague victims over the walls, infecting those within.

In October of 1347, several Italian merchant ships returned from Caffa. When the ships docked in Sicily, many of those on board were already dying of plague. They had a fever and a painful swelling of the lymph glands, particularly in the armpits and groin. These swellings are called buboes, giving bubonic plague its name. The disease also causes red spots on the skin, which later turn black – hence the 'Black Death'. Within days the disease spread to the islanders.

'Realising what a deadly disaster had come to them,' wrote an eyewitness, 'the people quickly drove the Italians from their city. But the disease remained, and soon death was everywhere. Fathers abandoned their sick sons. Lawyers refused to come and make out wills for the dying. Friars and nuns were left to care for the sick, and monasteries and convents were soon deserted, as they were stricken, too. Bodies were left in empty houses, and there was no one to give them a Christian burial.'

But moving the Italians on simply spread the disease. Wherever they went the disease struck with terrible speed. The Italian writer Boccaccio said its victims often 'ate lunch with their friends and dinner with their ancestors in paradise'.

In 1348, the Black Death reached Florence. According to the *Florentine Chronicle* of Marchione di Coppo Stefani:

'It was of such a fury and so tempestuous that, in houses where it took hold, previously healthy servants who took care of the sick died of the same illness. Almost none of the ill survived past the fourth day. Neither physicians nor medicines were effective. Whether because the illness was previously unknown or because physicians had not previously studied it, there seemed to be no cure. There was such a fear that no one seemed to know what to do. When it took hold in a house, it often happened that no one remained who had not died. And it was not just that men and women died, but animals too. Dogs, cats, chickens, oxen, donkeys and sheep showed the same symptoms and died of the same disease. And almost none, or very few, who showed these symptoms, were cured.*

'The symptoms were the following: a bubo in the groin, where the thigh meets the trunk; or a small swelling under the armpit; sudden fever; spitting blood and saliva (and no one who spit blood survived it). It was such a frightful thing that when it got into a house, as was said, no one remained. Frightened people abandoned the house and fled to another. Those in town fled to villages. Physicians could not be found because they had died like the others. And those who could be found wanted vast sums in hand before they entered the house. And when they did enter, they checked the *pulse with face turned away. They inspected the urine from a distance and with something odoriferous under their nose.*

'Child abandoned the father, husband the wife, wife the husband, one brother the other, one sister the other. In all the city there was nothing to do but to carry the dead to a burial. And those who died had neither confessor nor other sacraments. And many died with no one looking after them. And many died of hunger because when someone took to bed sick, another in the house, terrified, said to him: "I'm going for the doctor." Calmly walking out the door, the other left and did not return again. Abandoned by people, without food, but accompanied by fever, they weakened. There were many who pleaded with their relatives not to abandon them when night fell. But... when the sick person had fallen asleep, they left and did not return...

'No one wished to enter a house where anyone was sick, nor did they even want to deal with those healthy people who came out of a sick person's house. And they said to them: "He is stupefied, do not speak to him!" saying further: "He has it because there is a bubo in his house." Many died unseen. So they remained in their beds until they stank. And the neighbours, if there were any, having smelled the stench, placed them in a shroud and sent them for burial.'

Deep trenches were dug in church cemeteries and corpses were flung into them at night. Next morning, they were covered with dirt. Then more bodies were put on top of them, 'layer on layer just like one puts layers of cheese in a lasagne'.

The homes of the dead remained open as no one dared touch anything in case they were infected:

'Such great discouragement and fear that men gathered together in order to take some comfort in dining together, and each evening one of them provided dinner to ten companions and the next evening they planned to eat with one of the others. And sometimes if they planned to eat with a certain one he had no meal prepared because he was sick. Or if the host had made dinner for the ten, two or three were missing.

'Some fled to villas, others to villages in order to get a change of air. Where there had been no pestilence, there they carried it; if it was already there, they caused it to increase. None of the guilds in Florence was working. All the shops were shut, taverns closed; only the apothecaries and the churches remained open. If you went outside, you found almost no one.'

The plague had spread as far north as Scandinavia and killed more than 25 million people. In England the population in 1400 was around half what it had been 100 years previously, and around 1,000 villages were wiped out completely. The population of Europe did not return to its pre-1347 level until the early 16th century.

Even when the worst was over, smaller outbreaks continued, not just for years, but for centuries. The survivors lived in constant fear of the plague's return – which it did famously in London in 1665, when it killed 70,000 out of a population of 460,000 in an epidemic only stopped by the Great Fire of London.

During the plague years, society almost broke down completely. At first, lepers, women and Jews were blamed, and were often attacked and beaten without mercy. People grew suspicious of foreigners, in case they were carrying the plague and marriages were discouraged as gatherings such as wedding feasts were thought to help spread the disease.

Europe was left with a labour shortage, meaning that crops went unharvested and prices rocketed. This in turn led workers to demand higher wages. Landlords refused to pay up and, by the end of the 14th century, peasant revolts had broken out in England, France, Belgium and Italy.

The plague shook people's faith in Christianity. They had prayed for deliverance, but their prayers had not been answered. This led to a prolonged period of political turmoil and philosophical questioning. In the event, these catastrophes were instrumental in the advent the Renaissance, the Reformation and the Enlightenment, but it is not difficult to imagine circumstances under which such a terrifying pandemic could have resulted in a complete breakdown of society.

The Black Death has not gone away. Although antibiotics such as tetracycline have proved effective and a vaccine is available, a sizeable outbreak would overwhelm any defences. Bubonic plague is still among the arsenal of biological warfare and experts are warning of an outbreak, perhaps even on a global scale.

Plague is contracted from fleas that live on rats and rat populations are soaring in modern cities, where they grow fat on discarded junk food. Global warming means that more rats are surviving the winter in northern cities and super-rats are already building up a resistance to the anti-coagulant poisons that were introduced after they had grown immune to warfarin. Rats are also clever enough to avoid strong poisons after seeing the effects they have on others. In 2000, 182 people died in Thailand from Weil's disease, which is contracted from rat urine. In Britain every year there are 30 cases or so, and this number is on the increase. There are also worrying indications that the rat population is threatening to grow out of control; and with super-rats on the loose, can super-plague be far behind?

Viruses From Space

EXAMINING SPECTRAL DATA from interstellar matter such as the Horsehead Nebula, a cloud of gas in the constellation Orion, British astronomer Fred Hoyle and his colleague, the mathematician Chandra Wickramasinghe came to an astonishing conclusion – that the organic molecules that are the building blocks of life existed in outer space.

Armed with this information, they came up with the remarkable theory that life evolved in outer space, on comets. And when these comets crashed into the early Earth, they seeded life here too. Even more remarkably, they maintained

Optical image of comet Hale- Bopp. Hale-Bopp was one of the brightest comets of the 20th century. Comets have a nucleus of ice and dust. As they approach the Sun their surfaces evaporate, forming tails millions of kilometres long.

that comets were continuing to bring new and unwelcome life to this planet. They believed that, as comets streaked through the inner solar system, viruses and bacteria were thrown off into space on the dust in their tails. Some of that dust fell into the Earth's atmosphere. From there, it floated down to the surface of the Earth, causing successive waves of disease.

Hoyle and Wickramasinghe contest the idea that influenza is spread from person to person throughout the population. They cite studies that have found that spouses of sufferers are no more at risk from the disease than members of the population at large. Variations of immunity cannot explain such facts, particularly in the case of new and virulent strains of the virus.

In their book *Diseases from Space*, they point out that the spread of influenza takes no account of modern methods of travel. It still takes months to spread all over the Earth, even in the age of modern airlines, just as it did a century ago when travel was a good deal slower. They maintain that catching influenza is due far more to where people are than who they have been in contact with. For example, the lethal influenza pandemic of the winter of

1918/19 was first detected on the same day in Boston and Bombay, yet it took three weeks to spread from Boston to New York. Similarly, in the influenza epidemic of 1948 an Italian doctor in Sardinia reported that the disease appeared as often in shepherds who had been living alone for a long time in open country as it did in the urban centres, a fact which points to infection causes other than personal contact.

Appealing for relief funds in January 1919, Governor Thomas Riggs of Alaska reported to a US Senate Appropriations Committee that influenza had spread all over the territory (Alaska did not become a state until 1959), though its population of about 50,000 was spread thinly and the conditions for human travel were worse than anybody could remember. Parts of the territory could only be reached by dog-sled at a pace of around 20 to 30 miles a day. Influenza had even reached Kodiak Island in the Gulf of Alaska, killing 40 or 50, though no steamship line ran to the remote archipelago. It was also impossible for the epidemic to have been spread there by migrating birds. By November and December, when the epidemic hit, Alaskan birds had moved far to the south and their summer droppings had long since been covered with snow and ice.

Hoyle and Wickramasinghe explained this by pointing out that influenza epidemics come in winter, with January and February usually being the worst months. They maintained that this was

If Hoyle and Wickramasinghe are right, the SARS epidemic that hit the Far East and Canada in 2003 could be extra-terrestrial in origin

because, in temperate latitudes in the winter months, air from the Earth's stratosphere carrying cometary dust comes down to ground level. That winter was particularly cold, bringing air from the highest level of the stratosphere down to ground level – and with it, in Hoyle and Wickramasinghe's view, the flu virus.

Downdrafts bringing the virus could easily hit Boston and Bombay on the same day. They even maintained that it was possible to detect the descent of stratospheric air on a fine scale. During the influenza epidemic of the winter of 1978/79, Hoyle and Wickramasinghe made a study of the incidence of flu among 20,000 children in British boarding schools and found unexpectedly large differences in the incidence of disease between pupils who boarded in different houses at the same school. Their analysis showed that the particular location of the house where the pupil lived was crucial and they found that there was no evidence at all that pupils caught the flu from one another. A swarm of virus could apparently descend on one boarding house and miss another.

If Hoyle and Wickramasinghe are right, the SARS epidemic that hit the Far East and Canada in 2003 could also be extraterrestrial in origin, as might the pandemic of avian flu among chickens that followed. Unlike human flu which affects only the lungs, this virus attacks the brain and every other organ in the body. A few people caught it from live chickens and were killed. The danger was that the virus would mutate so that it could be transmitted from human to human.

The so-called 'Armageddon scenario' is the infection by avian flu of someone already infected by human flu. Together in a cell they could form a hybrid which would have the deadly consequences of the avian strain and be as easily spread as human flu. The result would be a pandemic worse than the Spanish flu of 1918/19.

If comets are raining down new viruses on us, one is bound to render our defences useless. That means the human race, which lives in splendid isolation from any other creature that inhabits the universe, could be wiped out by a virus we had not encountered before, just as tribes of Native Americans and Aborigines were wiped out by viruses brought by Europeans. The indigenous population of the regions of the Americas conquered by the Spanish fell from 50 million to four million, although history shows that the Spanish were no more brutal than other colonisers.

More worryingly, human beings share 97.5 per cent of their DNA with mice and a great deal of the human genome also appears in other living creatures. Viruses hijack the DNA of their host to reproduce. That means a completely unknown virus that arrived from a remote region of outer space could wipe out, not only the entire human race, but every living creature on the planet. This would be counter-productive from the point of view of the virus – after all, it needs the host DNA to reproduce. Like a parasite, a virus needs its host alive for it to thrive. But an extraterrestrial virus, not having encountered the inhabitants of Earth before, may not know any better, and, as viruses can live on in an inert state without a host if need be, it would not really matter to them. They might even spawn a new wave of life on this planet the way Hoyle and Wickramasinge maintain they did once before.

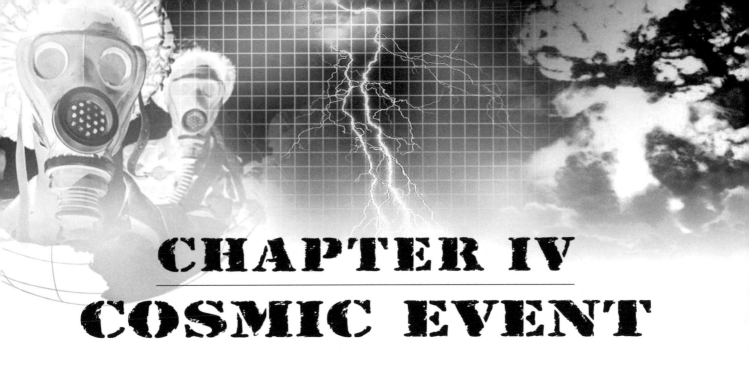

CHAPTER IV
COSMIC EVENT

16

Asteroid Impact

THE EARTH, like all the other bodies in the solar system, is constantly being bombarded by debris from space. We see shooting stars, which are the blazing trails left by meteorites burning up the atmosphere. Some make it to the surface of the Earth. It is estimated that over 40,000 tons of space dust lands on Earth each year, along with some 30,000 bite-sized lumps of space rock and maybe as many as 5,000 the size of a football. They mainly land out to sea or harmlessly in sparsely-populated areas. But recently humankind has realised that we are in grave danger of being hit by something much larger – and that the impact could herald the end of the world.

The warning has been there all along, of course. Every night, when the Moon rises, we can see that its face is pitted and scared with craters. As far back as the early nineteenth century the German Baron Franz von Paula Gruithuisen, Professor of Astronomy at the Üniversität München suggested that these were impact craters caused by cosmic collisions over the ages. He was not taken seriously.

Towards the end of the nineteenth century, US geologist Grove Karl Gilbert put Gruithuisen's hypothesis to the test. In the laboratory, he tried firing projectiles into mud or powder. He found that only objects fired from directly above caused circular craters like those seen on the Moon. Objects that struck the surface at an angle left a distinctive elongated crater. In 1927, the scientist W.M. Smart pointed out that there was no *a priori* reason to believe that all meteors hitting the Moon come directly from above. Gruithuisen's hypothesis was rejected and it was decided that the craters of the Moon, which were uniformly circular, were caused by volcanic action.

It was only after World War II that scientists realised that the circular craters on the Moon looked like the craters seen after bombing raids. Bombs dropped from a fast-moving plane rarely hit the earth at right angles, but it is not the angle of impact that is important, it is the explosion that causes the familiar circular craters. It was then they realised that, when a meteor collided with the Moon, it hit the surface with an explosive force, explaining why the craters there too were circular.

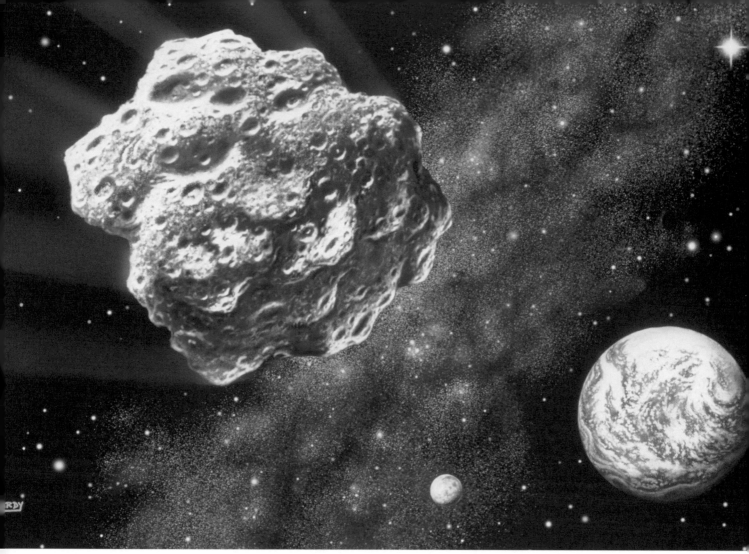

Asteroid approaching Earth. Artwork of an asteroid (at centre left) approaching Earth. Asteroids are minor planets which orbit the Sun and have diameters which are typically less than 100 kilometres. There are thousands of asteroids in the solar system.

If meteors large enough to leave craters that could be seen from Earth were hitting the Moon, surely similar objects should be hitting the Earth too. In fact, given the Earth's greater size and stronger gravitational field, huge meteorites should be crashing into the Earth 30 times more frequently than they were hitting the Moon. So where were the craters?

The reason we see craters on the Moon is that the Moon has no atmosphere and no running water, so any scar on its surface remains undisturbed for billions of years. The surface of the Earth, on the other hand, is constantly being scoured by wind and water, and any crater patterns would quickly disappear due to erosion – quickly on a geological time scale, that is. While the crust of the Moon is sterile and static, the surface of the Earth is in constant

flux due to plate tectonics. The basaltic oceanic plates are constantly being subducted and melted down in the Earth's fiery core, while new rocks are extruded along the mid-oceanic ridges. Around two-thirds of the Earth's surface is only a few hundred million years old, while volcanic activity on the Moon ended over three billion years ago. The oldest surface rocks on Earth – and consequently those most likely to carry the most craters – are in remote regions such as Siberia, central Australia and northern Canada. That's why they took so long to find. Today, though, we live in the age of satellite surveillance and over 165 impact craters had now been identified.

As long ago as 1905, the physicist Benjamin Tilghman claimed that the Barringer Crater – aka the Meteor Crater – in Arizona was caused by the impact of an ancient meteorite. To prove his thesis, he and his colleague, a mining engineer named D.M. Barringer spent 25 years digging for the millions of tons of meteoritic iron and nickel which they believed lay beneath the surface. They never found it. This is because the energy of impact was so high that the meteorite would simply have been vaporised. It is now thought that 50,000 years ago, a small asteroid some 130 feet across smashed into the Arizona desert at some 2,000 miles per hour with a force equivalent to 50 million tons of TNT, or 4,000 Hiroshima bombs. Everything within two miles of the impact would have been obliterated. Hurricane-force winds would have blown down anything within 25 miles and the devastation would have stretched for 600 square miles. It is estimated that an object this size hits the Earth at least once a century.

We know that an object of roughly this size did hit the Earth in the twentieth century. At around 7.15am on 30 June 1908, there was a colossal explosion over the sparsely-populated Tunguska region of northern Siberia. Surviving peasants said they saw a fireball too bright to look at come hurtling out of the sky. As it neared the ground there was a noise that sounded like a cannon and a huge sheet of flame shot up into the clouds. Seismographs around the world picked up a tremor. Barographs registered a pressure wave that travelled three times around the world. The explosion caused such an afterglow, it was said, that it was possible to play cricket in London at midnight.

Trees and houses in the vicinity were blown down, but so few people lived in that part of Siberia that only two deaths were reported, although there were up to 20 casualties, including one person deafened by the blast. Tunguska is so remote

that reports were sketchy. Russia then found itself embroiled firstly in the First World War, and then in a revolution, so the first full scientific expedition did not arrive on the scene until 1927. They found that the fireball had been seen and the blast heard across 400,000 square miles. It had flattened 800 square miles of mature forest. The scientists searched for an impact crater, but found none. However, there was a circle of trees 40 miles wide which had been charred by an extreme heat. The outermost trees all lay pointing outwards from the centre. The innermost still stood, charred, with their branches torn off them. The conclusion was the asteroid that had caused this devastation was not of the metallic type that had hit the ground in the Arizona desert. It was of the rocky type and it had exploded in the air with a force equivalent to 800 Hiroshima bombs.

As such massive objects hit the Earth regularly, we should consider what happens if the impacts do not occur in remote areas such as the Colorado Plateau or central Siberia. If a Barringer-style meteorite hit Manhattan for example, it would destroy all of New York – including Staten Island – most of Long Island and Newark as far out as the Watchung Mountains. The death toll would be around 10 million. A Tunguska asteroid making its air-burst over central London would obliterate everything as far out as the M25, with a similar death toll.

Of course, the bigger the asteroid, the higher the death toll, and there are plenty of candidates waiting to be our nemesis. Thousands of asteroids, some up to 124 miles across, inhabit the asteroid belt between Mars and Jupiter. It is thought that but for the huge gravitational pull of

Jupiter, this orbiting space debris would have agglomerated into a planet. So far 20,000 asteroids have been spotted, but it is believed that there are more than half a million in all. Every so often one of these asteroids gets dislodged and heads our way, so during the 1980s astronomers decided to begin keeping an eye out for them. Once they had started looking, they found that there were thousands of asteroids in our vicinity. Over a thousand objects more than a kilometre across regularly cross the Earth's orbit and it is estimated that around a third of them will end up colliding with our planet. In fact, your chance of being killed by an asteroid impact are roughly twice that of dying in an aeroplane accident, and 750 times the chance of winning the UK national lottery.

The fate of the planet depends on the size of the object that hits it. If an object ten times larger than the asteroid that hit Tunguska or Barringer landed on London, it would wipe out England and Wales and devastate Scotland, Ireland, Holland, Belgium and northern France. If it landed in the sea, it would create a tsunami over 300 feet high, which would hit the shore at over 500 miles an hour. That would mean if it hit the Pacific, whose area exceeds the entire land surface of the globe, every coastal city would be completely destroyed within 20 hours, with a death toll of over 500 million. It is estimated that there is a one per cent chance of this happening in the next hundred years.

If a one-kilometre lump of rock were to land in the English Channel, it would generate temperatures hotter than the Sun

For a mass extinction event that would annihilate humankind and most animals, the impact of an object over one kilometre in diameter would be required. It is estimated that this happens once every 100,000 to 333,000 years. Such an impact may be well overdue. The youngest impact crater of an appropriate size is a million years old, though a more recent object may have landed in the sea. If a one-kilometre lump of rock were to hit the Earth in the English Channel, say, it would generate temperatures hotter than the Sun and would boil away the sea and blast a 12 mile-hole in the Earth's crust beneath. Superheated steam and molten rock would be blasted into the air in an explosion equivalent to the detonation of the world's entire nuclear arsenal several times over. Debris would cover the British Isles and much of north-western Europe.

Beyond that, the cities of eastern and southern Europe would be devastated by the seismic wave generated. Even Auckland, on the opposite side of the world from the impact, would destroyed by earthquake. A 300-foot tsunami would destroy Scandinavia. The east coast of North America would also be inundated. In all, 200 million would die from the first effects of the impact.

Pulverised rock from the impact would spread around the world in the stratosphere. Fires would darken the sky with smoke and soot. Within a fortnight, the global temperature would have fallen by around eight degrees Centigrade. In around six months, the air would have cleared and temperatures would have returned to normal. But by then it would be too late. Harvests would have failed and even places far from the impact would be affected by mass starvation. People would pour out of the cities in the hope of finding food. There would be none. After a year, there would only be isolated bands of humans living the kind of life our ancestors lived before civilisation began less than 10,000 years ago.

Comet Collision

THERE ARE EVEN MORE dangerous things than asteroids lurking out in space. Asteroids, once spotted, also follow a predictable path, so we are likely to get plenty of warning of an impact; it may even be possible to send up a rocket, Hollywood style, to nudge it out of the way. Short- or intermediate-period comets, such as Halley's which hoves back into view every 76 years, are also predictable. But long-period comets suddenly appear from deep-space, and one on a collision course with Earth would give us no more than just six months warning. And as comets are largely made of ice, any attempt to deflect one would cause it to break up, simply spreading the initial devastation over a wider area.

Comets, it is thought, originate in a region of space called the Oort Cloud, a spherical swarm of frozen rock and ice that surrounds the solar system far beyond the orbit of Pluto. Typically, the orbits of comets take them a quarter of the way to the nearest star, so they seldom visit the inner solar system. However, occasionally something disrupts the Cloud, sending one or two comets hurtling earthwards.

This disruption might be caused by the still-to-be-confirmed Planet X – a small planet orbiting the Sun beyond Pluto – or the much sought-after dark and distant stellar companion of our Sun, known as Nemesis. There is also a theory that huge showers of comets sweep through the inner solar system every 30 million years or so, to devastating effect. This is called the Shiva hypothesis, after the Hindu god of destruction and renewal. The theory is that this happens because the orbit of our solar system around the galactic centre is not smooth, but undulating, and each time it passes through the plane of the galaxy comets are dislodged.

We already know what it would be like to be hit by a comet. Humankind had a chilling ringside seat when Comet Shoemaker–Levy 9 crashed into Jupiter in 1994. The comet had only been seen for the first time the year before, by which time it had already been captured by the planet Jupiter and was orbiting it. The giant planet's huge gravitational field tore it into 21 pieces – any one of which would have caused a catastrophe if it had hit the Earth.

On 16 July 1994, the first fragment hit Jupiter, sending up a huge plume of gas and debris, and a shock wave rippling out across the gaseous planet. This was the first cosmic collision ever observed by humankind. Spectacular images were relayed back to Earth by the Hubble Telescope and the unmanned *Galileo* probe, bound for Jupiter. Over the next five days, fragment after fragment of the comet crashed into Jupiter, creating on impact fireballs the size of the Earth. The biggest came two days after the first impact, when Fragment G, about four kilometres across, hit with a force equivalent to eight billion Hiroshima-sized atomic bombs or 100 million million tons of TNT.

The explosion was so brilliant that many of the infra-red telescopes observing the impact were temporarily blinded. The scar left by the impact was wider than the Earth and, of the millions of people watching, many wondered what would have happened if Shoemaker–Levy 9 had hit Earth.

Of course, a giant comet has hit Earth. It happened 65 million years ago and was responsible for the extinction of, not just the dinosaurs, but around two-thirds of the species on Earth. The comet concerned was around ten kilometres across, so the end of its tail would have still been in space as it reached the ground. It crashed into the sea just off Chicxulub on Mexico's Yucatan Peninsula at over 50,000 miles an hour. The resulting explosion would have been more powerful than tens of billions of Hiroshima bombs. The noise would have been the loudest sound ever heard on Earth and would have burst the eardrums of any creature hearing it. The resulting fireball would have been hotter than the Sun and would have raised the temperature of the sea to boiling point almost instantly. As the comet hit the seabed, it made a crater 120 miles across and 10 miles deep. An area bigger than Europe would have been flattened and the shock wave would have caused

earthquakes around the world. Hypercanes – super-hurricanes – would have ripped through the atmosphere with winds five times the speed of any in a conventional hurricane and tsunamis would have overwhelmed the world's coastlines.

A hundred trillion tons of molten rock would have been blasted into space. As it fell back to Earth it would have heated up on re-entry, making the sky glow and roasting any animal on the surface below as if it had been on a grill. The Earth's vegetation would have caught fire, pumping smoke into the atmosphere. The smoke and dust the impact had kicked up would blot out the Sun, sending temperatures plummeting by up to 15 degrees Centigrade. Photosynthesis would have stopped and most plant-life would have died. Herbivores that had survived the initial impact would have starved to death, followed by the carnivores that depended on them. Sea creatures would have fared little better, as acid rain from the vast amounts of sulphur hurled into the atmosphere would have polluted the sea, killing three-quarters of its inhabitants.

After years of nuclear winter following the impact, the skies would gradually have cleared. Anything remaining alive on the Earth's surface would then have found itself exposed to dangerous ultra-violet rays, as the nitrous oxides kicked up by the impact would have stripped the Earth of its ozone layer. In this holocaust, the large animals would have perished. Any remaining small dinosaurs seem to have evolved into birds (our own ancestors were small rat-like mammals). Between them it would have taken hundreds of thousands of years to repopulate the planet.

Comet Shoemaker-Levy impact on Jupiter, July 1994. Artist's impression of the impact of fragments of Comet Shoemaker-Levy 9, seen from inside the upper atmosphere of Jupiter. Over 20 fragments of Comet Shoemaker- Levy 9, each of more than 1 km diameter, hit the planet.

It is thought that the Chicxulub impact was a comet and not an asteroid because of the high incidence of amino acids found in the impact layer on Earth. No complex molecule such as an amino acid could survive an impact of a cosmic nature: however, if the Earth was hit by a comet, rather than an asteroid, debris from its tail would continued falling long after the initial impact, bringing with it these amino acids.

Amino acids are the building blocks of proteins, which are themselves the building blocks of life. So it is possible that comets may have brought new life to planet Earth as well as destroying most of what was already here, a spectacular take-over bid, if this can be verified.

There is also a fear that the Shiva hypothesis, where the Earth is periodically plagued by swarms of comets, may operate on a time scale rather shorter than 30 million years. There is some evidence that the Earth is struck by a group of cometary objects every few thousand years and that the last bombardment wiped out a number of Bronze Age civilisations some 4,000 years ago.

Another theory is that, around 10,000 years ago, a large comet from the Oort Cloud entered the inner solar system and broke up into a million kilometre-sized lumps. The result is a stream of debris called the Taurid Complex. Every December, the Earth passes through this, giving us the spectacular Taurid Shower of shooting stars. However, as part of this debris stream there is the five-kilometre Earth-crossing Comet Encke, accompanied by a number of large asteroids. Every 2,500 to 3,000 years, the Earth crosses the debris trail at the place where these larger objects are found. A number of early civilisations in Europe, Asia and Africa collapsed simultaneously around 2,350 BC, amid tales of fire, earthquake and flood. According to Egyptian papyri, during the First Kingdom, when the Sphinx was being built, the fertile Nile Valley was devastated by floods and a great heat that burnt the trees and brought famine. Stories in the Old Testament talk of the desertification of the area around the Dead Sea at that time. Floods hit the civilisation of the Indus Valley, while huge waves pounded Greece and cities in Afghanistan, China, Turkey and Spain fell into disuse. And in Syria, there is a layer of pulverised brick and burnt material suggesting an air blast of the type seen at Tunguska from around that time.

It is thought that a number of cometary fragments hit the Earth one after the other, like Shoemaker–Levy 9 bombarding Jupiter. In some places on Earth, double impact craters have been found where two objects have hit the Earth at the same time. It has even been suggested that the fall of the Roman Empire and the onset of the Dark Ages was heralded by the next major Taurid encounter.

An hour after sunset on 18 June 1178, Gervase of Canterbury recorded that a group of five eyewitnesses saw the upper horn of the bright, new crescent Moon 'suddenly split in two. From the mid-point of this division a flaming torch sprang up, spewing out... fire, hot coals and sparks... The body of the Moon, which was below writhed... throbbed like a wounded snake'. It is thought that this was caused by a cometary fragment two miles wide hitting the Moon, which left the 14-mile wide crater called Giordano Bruno after the monk burned at the stake in Rome for advocating the helio-centric theories of Copernicus.

There are aboriginal stories of a falling star that brought fire and death at around the same time. On the South Island of New Zealand, near Tapanui, there are two impact craters that are linked in Maori legend to a great fire that wiped out the Moa bird. Evidence from the remains of trees that fell at the time show them all pointing outwards from the craters. And 'Tapanui' in Maori means 'great explosion'. Intriguing other things happened at the same time – the westward drive of Genghis Khan, a new Polynesian migration, flooding in Peru and the rise of the Incas.

The frightening aspect of this is an impact on the Moon of the size that caused the Giordano Bruno crater is pre-dicted to happen once every 15 million years or so. The fact that one happened within the last 1,000 years suggests that such cosmic collisions might be more common than previously thought.

Another theory is that a comet would not even have to hit the Earth to cause global annihilation. One passing close by could fill the atmosphere with enough space dust to block out the Sun. Alternatively, it could seed the stratosphere with ice, which would sublimate into water vapour, leading to global warming and catastrophic flooding.

But the biggest fear of all is of long-period comets that have already burned off their icy coating. It is that process that makes a comet visible when it approaches the Sun and produces one of the comet's two tails. The other one is caused by the dust released as the dirty ice is vaporised. The rocky nucleus of a comet, stripped of its icy coating and hence its tails, would be almost impossi-ble to spot. It would crash into Earth with enormous speed without any warn-ing and, examining the geological impact evidence, it looks like we are overdue.

Even more worrying is that the most plausible theory explaining the creation of the Moon states that a body the size of Mars hit the Earth around 4.5 billion years ago and the debris flung out into space by the collision agglomerated to form the Moon. In the event of this hap-pening again, the Earth would acquire a new moon, and while a double moonrise might be thought a spectacular sight, there would unfortunately be no living thing left on the Earth to appreciate it.

The Axis Tilts

THE ROTATIONAL AXIS of the Earth is almost vertical to the plane of its orbit, so as the Earth spins we get day and night. The slight tilt of the axis – around 23 degrees, though on a cycle of 40,000 years it varies between 22 and 24 degrees – gives us the seasons. Generally, this arrangement makes life on Earth relatively agreeable.

The other planets in the solar system all have their axes of rotation similarly vertical to the plane of their orbit – except one, Uranus. Its axis of rotation is just eight degrees from the horizontal. Instead of spinning vertically like a top, it lies on its side like an egg rolling on a table. This consequence of this extraordinary tilt is that in its 84-Earth-year orbit, the poles of Uranus get a day that is 42 Earth years long, followed by a 42-Earth-year night.

How it got that way, no one is sure. It is generally assumed that it must have been formed like the other planets spinning roughly vertical, then knocked on it side in a cosmic collision. In fact, a body half the size of the Earth would have had to crash into it to knock it 98 degrees from the vertical so that is actually spinning backwards compared to the other planets, with the exception of Venus, which is rotating backwards for an entirely different reason.

There is a problem with this explanation though. Such an impact would surely have had an effect on its orbit. But the orbit of Uranus is almost circular and it lies roughly in the plane of the ecliptic, that is the same plane as the orbit of the Earth and most of the other planets. There is one planet with a highly eccentric orbit, the ninth planet, Pluto. Its orbit is so far from being circular that it spends 20 years of its 248-year orbit within the orbit of Neptune, the eighth planet. Pluto's orbit is also inclined at 17 degrees to the ecliptic, surely the result of some cosmic accident.

And accidents do happen. It is thought that our Moon was created when an object the size of Mars struck our planet soon after it formed. But Mars is just one-tenth of the mass of the Earth, so this collision did not have a catastrophic effect on the Earth's orbit.

If such a cosmic collision happened these days, all life on Earth would be extinguished. And if the Earth had been knocked on its side in the distance past, like Uranus, life on our planet would be very different. Huge swathes of the planet would bask in continual sunlight for months during the summer, then be plunged into permanent darkness for months during the winter. Only a small equatorial band would experience anything like our current diurnal pattern. That region would be fertile and habitable, much like the current equatorial regions. But life much outside them would be extremely harsh, like areas of Siberia where freezing winters are relieved by hot summers that turn the land to mud and fill the air with mosquitoes.

Further towards the poles, the land would be a searing desert during the summer and covered with ice in winter, while the sea would alternately boil and freeze.

Human beings originated in the equatorial regions, so it is possible that humankind would have evolved even if the axis of the Earth had such a tilt. But humankind became so success-ful because it could spread out across vast areas of the Earth and adapt, by the use of cloth-ing and housing, to thrive in even relatively hostile places. Even so, very few people live inside the Arctic Circle and until very recently humankind has left the Antarctic well alone. But if our axis was tilted like that of Uranus, the Arctic and Antarctic Circles would cover all but a narrow band just 16 degrees wide.

It is thought that our Moon was created when an object the size of Mars struck our planet soon after it formed

The weather in the habitable region would be very different from what we experience now. As there would be a huge temperature differential between the hemisphere pointing towards the Sun and the hemisphere pointing away, there would be high winds blowing from the hot pole towards the cold one. Winds of up to 360 miles an hour are seen on Uranus, while around the equator wind speeds rarely drop below 220 miles an hour. These would carry vast clouds from the boiling seas at one pole to fall as snow on the other.

The water boiling off at one pole and the temperature differential would also cause huge currents in the sea which would reverse with the seasons. These merciless currents would have a devas-tating effect on anything that lived in the sea and make navigation dangerous if not impossible. As life on Earth seems to have started in the sea, it may not even have had a chance to begin under cir-cumstances such as these.

The tilt would also affect the tides, giving each hemisphere six months of spring tides and six months of neap tides. It may also have an effect on the tides that the molten core of the Earth experiences, which deform the crust vertically by about a foot or less. However, as Uranus is a gas planet – with its tiny rocky core hidden under a mantle of water, methane and ammonia ice beneath an atmosphere of hydrogen, helium and methane – it is not possible to observe the effect on that planet.

There is another anomaly about the planet Uranus that might make life on Earth a little prob-lematic. Its magnetic field is also tilted so that its magnetic poles are 60 degrees from its geographic poles. It does not even emanate from the centre of the planet, but is instead off to one side. No one is really sure why this is and it may or may not have something to do with the strange tilt of its axis.

The fact that the magnetic field and the axis of rotation are not even approxi-mately the same would make navigation difficult. A compass would be no help and swallows would have difficulty migrating, if they dared take to the air at all in the hurricane-force winds. As it is the Earth's magnetic field that protects us from cosmic rays from the Sun, such a radical change would make life on Earth very unpleasant indeed.

The question remains, could the Earth's axis be tilted so lethally? According to Russian-born psychoana-lyst, doctor and Jewish scholar Immanuel Velikovsky, a friend of both

Einstein and Freud, it could and, indeed, did happen. In 1939, whilst researching the story of Moses and the Exodus of the Israelites from Egypt, Velikovsky came across an Egyptian papyrus called the *Admonitions of the Sage*, also known as the Ipuwer Papyrus, after the Egyptian courtier who wrote it. This told the story of the Exodus from the Egyptian point of view and it confirms much of the Biblical account of events. Here are some of the most striking parallels:

Admonitions 2:5–6 – *'Plague is throughout the land. Blood is everywhere. Death is not lacking.'*

Exodus 7:21 – *'There was blood everywhere in Egypt.'*

Admonitions 2:10 – *'The river is blood. Men shrink from tasting [it] – human beings thirst after water.'*

Exodus 7:24 – *'Then the Egyptians dug for drinking water around the river, because they could not drink from the waters of the Nile itself.'*

Admonitions 3:10 – *'That is our water! That is our happiness! What shall we do in respect thereof? All is ruin!'*

Exodus 7:21 – *'The fish died and the river stank, and the Egyptians could not drink the water from the Nile.'*

Admonitions 5:5 – *'All animals, their hearts weep. Cattle moan...'*

Exodus 9:3 – *'...the Lord will strike your grazing herds, your horses and asses, your camels, cattle and sheep with a terrible pestilence.'*

Admonitions 4:14 – *'Trees are destroyed... There is no food.'*

Exodus 9:25 – *'Throughout Egypt the hail struck everything in the fields, both man and beast; it beat down every growing thing and shattered every tree.'*

Admonitions 6:3 – *'Forsooth grain has perished on every side.'*

Exodus 10:15–16 – *'They devoured the vegetation and all the fruits of the trees. There was no green left on tree or plant throughout all Egypt.'*

Admonitions 9:11 – *'The land is not light...'*

Exodus 10:22 – *'Moses stretched out his hand towards the sky, and it became pitch dark throughout the land of Egypt.'*

Admonitions 4:3 – *'Forsooth, the children of princes are dashed against the wall. The offspring of desire are laid out on the high ground.'*

Exodus 12:29 – *'...and by midnight the Lord had struck down every first-born in Egypt, from the first-born of Pharaoh on his throne to the first-born of the captive in the dungeon...'*

Admonitions 3:14 – *'It is groaning that is throughout the land, mingled with lamentations.'*

Exodus 12:30 – *'...and a great cry of anguish went up...'*

Admonitions 2:13 – *'Men are few. He who places his brother in the ground is everywhere.'*

Exodus 12:30 – *'...not a house in Egypt was without its dead.'*

This gave Velikovsky the idea that what was being described both in the Biblical story of Exodus and the papyrus might have been an historic event. If it was, it would have been such a catastrophe that it would not just have affected Egypt, but would have affected the whole world. So he began researching other ancient texts.

The results of his research were published in 1950 in a book called *Worlds in Collision* which became an instant best-seller, though it was condemned by

Planet Earth, as seen from space, showing the direction of the axis at present.

academics around the world. Velikovsky rejected the idea that the solar system was a safe orderly system that has worked with clockwork precision since it was first formed. He maintained that it was a disorderly place full of sudden upheavals, which sometimes threatened the very existence of the world. The story of these cataclysmic events are told in ancient texts, he maintained. As a psychoanalyst, he believed that the awful truth of these events were blocked from human history, just as individuals block painful experiences from this consciousness.

According to *Worlds in Collision*, some 4,000 years ago a blazing comet was torn from the planet Jupiter – just as in Greek mythology Pallas-Athene sprang from the head of Zeus-Jupiter. In the 1940s and 1950s, there was a widely-held theory that comets were the product of gigantic volcanic eruptions on the planets. But this comet was different. It was a flaming proto-planet that would become Venus and it headed towards the

Sun, crossing the orbit of Earth. The Babylonians called it the 'bright torch of heavens', while the Chinese said that its light spanned the heavens, rivalling the Sun in brightness. And one ancient rabbinical record notes: 'The brilliant light of Venus blazes from one end of the cosmos to the other.'

Still blazing like a comet, according to the theory, Venus then proceeded to orbit the Sun on an eccentric path. In the middle of the fifteenth century BC, the Earth passed through its tail. A fine red dust filled the air, turning the land and sea the colour of blood. As the Earth plunged deeper into its trail, larger rust particles fell into the atmosphere. These chaffed at the skin, causing a plague of boils. Fish in the streams and rivers died. Their rotting corpses turning the water foul and people had to dig into the ground to find unpolluted water.

As the Earth moved even deeper into the proto-planet's cometary tail, the debris flying off it grew bigger. Gravel and stones began falling in a 'plague of hail'.

'So there was hail, and fire mingled with the hail, very grievous, such as there was none like it in all the land of Egypt since it became a nation,' says Exodus 9:24. People fled from the fields, abandoning their flocks. The crops were flattered and the cattle killed. 'Throughout Egypt the hail struck everything in the fields, both man and beast; it beat down every growing thing and shattered every tree,' continues Exodus 9:25.

The papyrus concurs: 'Trees were destroyed... not fruit nor herbs were found.' Interestingly the Mexican Annals of Cuauhtitlán report much the same thing. Around that time, it says, the sky 'rained not water, but fire and hot stones'. This was plainly a global disaster.

If being pummelled by micro-meteorites was not bad enough, according to Velikovsky, things got worse. Hydrocarbon gases in the tail set the sky on fire. In some places unignited petroleum rained down on Earth, forming lakes of naphtha, which caught on fire and filled the air with black smoke.

As the Earth neared the protoplanet itself, Venus's gravitational pull caused huge tectonic shifts in the Earth's crust. Mountains were levelled, islands disappeared, the oceans inundated the land, the trees of the forests were snapped like toothpicks and cities were flattened, killing most of the Earth's human and animal populations. The volcano on the island of Santorini, also known as Thera or Thíra, blew up around then, sending the Minoan civilisation on nearby Crete into terminal decline.

According the traditions of the Cashinaua aborigines of western Brazil: 'The lightning flashed and thunder roared terribly and all were afraid. Then the heavens burst and fragments fell down and killed everything and everybody. Heaven and Earth changed places. Nothing that had life was left upon the Earth.'

The atmosphere was so disrupted

The volcano on the island of Santorini blew up around then, sending the Minoan civilisation on Crete into terminal decline

there was a worldwide hurricane, which flattened everything that was standing. In China, the waters 'overtopped the great heights, threatening the heavens with their floods'.

Velikovsky believes that the pull of Venus was so strong that it slowed the rotation of the Earth. The Persians recorded that a single day lasted as long as three ordinary days, followed by a night that was three times longer than usual. The Chinese wrote that the Earth was scorched when the Sun did not set for several days. And with their cities devastated, the survivors were left to wander aimlessly across the land.

The dragon-like tail of the comet and the turmoil in the heavens was interpreted by the ancient Babylonians as the titanic battle between the god Marduk and the dragon Tiamat. To the Hindus, it was the battle between Vishnu and the 'crooked serpent'. To the Egyptians, it was a war between the tailed sky-god Seth, master of storms, and the goddess Isis, while the Greeks saw it as Zeus locked in combat with the dragon-like Typhon who was eventually cast into the underworld.

In the midst of all this confusion, the Israelites seized the opportunity to flee Egypt. The Egyptians came after them, but a pillar of cloud appeared between them – 'And the cloud brought on darkness and early nightfall, so that contact was lost throughout the night.'

Then the Israelites came up against the Red Sea. But, according to Velikovsky, the deformation of the Earth's crust and gravitational pull of the comet exposed the seabed. The water piled up to the right and left, and the Israelites made it safely across to Sinai.

The following morning, 'the Lord looked down on the Egyptian army though the pillar of fire and cloud... He clogged their chariot wheels and made them lumber along heavily'. When they reached the Red Sea, they set out to cross it. At that moment, Venus came its closest to the Earth. A huge bolt of lightning came down and the walls of water collapsed, drowning the Egyptians in boiling water.

As the Israelites moved out into the desert they were led by a column of smoke by day and a pillar of fire by night. These were dust from the tail of the comet and bolts of lightning still raining down from its head. The devastation had left little in the way off food. But, according to Velikovsky, the naphtha and petroleum left in the atmosphere by the comet's tail was transformed – by the electrical discharges or bacterial action – into an edible substance that fell from heaven in flakes as 'manna'. He cites legends from Greece, India, Iceland and other parts of the world where ancient peoples talked of ambrosia, madhu and sweet dew falling from the skies.

The close approach of the comet Venus had not just slowed the Earth's rotation, it reversed it. Herodotus, the fifth-century Greek historian, quoted Egyptian priests who, after consulting their records, told him: 'Four times in this period... the sun rose contrary to his wont; twice he rose where he now sets, and twice he set where he now rises.'

The seasons had also been switched. According to one Egyptian papyrus: 'The winter is come as summer, the months are reversed, and the hours are disordered.' Meanwhile, the Chinese emperor ordered his scholars to draw up a new calendar and sent them out throughout the land to locate north, south, east and west. According to Velikosky, the Earth had been knocked so far off its axis that the cardinal points had shifted.

For years the Earth was shrouded in a pall of dust. The Hebrew Scriptures call this the 'shadow of death'; in Nordic myth it is the *Götterdämmerung*. Mayan sources say that it lasted for 25 years.

The Jews were lost in the desert for 40 years. When they arrived in Canaan under their new leader Joshua, they began a prolonged war with the Canaanites. Again they were assisted by the heavens. When the Canaanite army was withdrawing through the valley of Beth-Horon, Venus seems to have returned once more on a near-collision course. Again the Sun appeared to stand still while rocks rained down on the fleeing Canaanites.

'The Lord cast down great stones from heaven upon them unto Azekah and they died.' (Joshua 10.11). Meanwhile there was more seismic disruption and the walls of Jericho fell down. Again the Earth's crust heaved and buckled, and cities were destroyed. The Mexican records talk of nights much longer than normal which were illuminated by the burning of the 'land above them'. This, they noted, happened around 50 years after the last catastrophe.

Once again there were global hurricanes, earthquakes and total devastation. The survivors began to pray and make sacrifices to Venus, whom they saw as the goddess of fire and destruction. In their incantations, they pleaded with the goddess to leave the Earth in peace. 'How long will you tarry, oh lady of heaven and

'The Lord cast down great stones from heaven upon them unto Azekah and they died.' (Joshua 10.11)

Earth?' implored one Babylonian prayer. Meanwhile, the Persians sacrificed to 'Tistrya, the bright and glorious morning star, whose rising is watching by the chiefs of deep understanding'.

At this time, Venus settled down into an orbit between that of the Earth and Mars which, Velikovsky believed, lay inside the Earth's orbit then. But this was not a stable configuration. Around the middle of the eighth century BC, the Babylonians recorded on their tablets that Venus disappeared in the west for about nine months. Then, it suddenly reappeared in the east. Soon after it dropped below the horizon again. Two months later is suddenly rose again in the west. According to the tablets, the following year it disappeared from the west again for eleven days, then turned up again in the east, erratic behaviour which worried the Babylonian proto-astronomers, keeping a watchful eye on the movements of Venus. Velikovsky believed that Venus's orbit was being disrupted by the presence of Mars. But Mars is only about one-eighth the mass of Venus and this was a battle it could not win. The gravitational pull of Venus dislodged Mars and sent its orbit out towards the Earth. Just as Venus before it, Mars caused earthquakes which destroyed cities and levelled mountains. These events are recorded in the books of Isaiah, Hosea, Joel and Amos in the Bible and by Homer in the *Illiad*. They seem to have coincided with the founding of Rome in 753 BC when, according to Ovid: 'Both poles shook and Atlas shifted the burden of the sky. The sun vanished and rising clouds obscured the heavens.' Mars, it should be noted, is the protector of the city of Rome and the Roman god of war. Together Mars and Venus became the chief deities of ancient cultures.

Mars's closest passage seems to have come in 721 BC, on the day King Ahaz of Jerusalem was buried. Again the axis tilted and the poles shifted. That night the Sun was seen to hasten to a premature setting, dropping below the horizon several hours before normal. After that, according to an ancient Israelite observer, the Sun travelled across the sky 10 degrees further to the south.

The Greeks also noted the early sunset, which was accompanied by an great upheaval on the Argive plain. The Great Bear dipped below the horizon and other constellations changed position, according to the Roman writer Seneca.

Velikovsky reckoned that this near-miss pushed the Earth out into a wider orbit and the old 360-day calendar – with twelve 30-day months – had to be revised. In fact, this is more probably due to the slowing of the rotation of the Earth as a result of tidal friction.

According to Velikovsky, Mars made its last close approach to the Earth in the spring of 687 BC, when the Assyrian King Sennacherib marched against Hezekiah, king of Judah, in an attempt to capture Jerusalem. On the evening of 23 March, the first night of Passover, 'a blast from heaven' which charred the bodies of the besieging soldiers, but left their clothes untouched. Sennacherib fled, leaving 185,000 dead before the walls of Jerusalem, an event recorded in the Bible, and in the poem 'The Destruction of Sennacherib' by Lord Byron, but strangely absent from Assyrian chronicles.

That same night, the Chinese recorded in the *Bamboo Books* that 'the five planets went out of their courses. In the night, stars fell like rain. The earth shook.' Another Chinese chronicle says: 'At this time two suns were seen to battle in the sky. The five planets were agitated by unusual movements. A part of Mount T'aichan fell down.' This occurred in the tenth year of the reign of the Emperor Kwei – 687 BC – and a French scholar has worked out that the event indeed took place on 23 March. To the Romans, 23 March was one of the Roman festivals by the name of Tubilustrium, this one being a major celebration of Mars, the god of war.

In some places the rising Sun was seen to dip back below the horizon; in others, it set and rose again. The axis sees to have tilted again, back 10 degrees, righting the shift that had occurred a generation before.

'So the Sun returned 10 degrees, by with degrees it was gone down on the Sun Dial of Ahaz,' recorded the Book of Isaiah.

To ancient observers, the gravitational tussle between Mars and Venus must have appeared to be a titanic struggle between the gods. According to Homer, as the Greeks besieged Troy, Athena 'would utter a loud cry. And over against her spouted Ares [Mars], dread as a dark whirlwind... All the roots of the founted Ida were shaken, and all her peaks'. The river 'rushed with surging flood', and the 'fair streams seethed and boiled'.

After that Mars settled into its new orbit beyond that of the Earth where we see it now and never came near Venus or the Earth again.

Although Velikovsky made a number of predictions about the conditions on

Jupiter, Venus and Mars, an odd one of which proved to be correct when probes visited in the late 1960s and 1970s, no physical evidence has been produced to substantiate his catastrophe scenario. His theory is backed only by ancient texts. If it proved to be true, however, then the solar system would be a much more dangerous place to live than we thought.

The Solar System Goes Awry

HUMANKIND has been studying the heavens since the beginning of civilisation and probably before, and it has long been predicted that our destiny – and our doom – is foretold in the stars.

It was only at the beginning of the seventeenth century that Galileo turned a telescope on the night sky and began to make a more scientific study of the heavens. He used his observations of the phases of the planets to show that the Copernican theory, that the Earth and the rest of the planets revolved around the Sun, was correct. Later that century, Newton used the solar system to develop his theory of gravitation and the laws of motion.

The next two centuries were spent mapping and classifying heavenly bodies. It was only in the twentieth century that the full force of modern physics was turned on the heavens. The universe has become a cosmic laboratory for scientists to test the theories that have developed on Earth, but there is still a great deal we do not understand.

What we do know is that the universe is a hostile place. We see the giant explosions of supernovae that give off so much energy they can been seen clear across the galaxy. We see immense clouds of gas where new stars are born. We know that space is vast, and is mostly an empty wasteland filled only with radiation that would kill an unprotected human in an instant. There is no air, or water, or warmth out there – other than places where you would be boiled or fried. Even the environment on the most Earth-like planets near to us is so hostile that they do not seem to be able to host even the most rudimentary forms of life.

The Sun at the centre of our solar system is a bubbling cauldron that sends huge jets of superheated gas out into space. If it were not for the Earth's magnetic field and its atmosphere, the Sun, which gives us life, would kill us. We have a poor understanding of how the Sun works. We have no idea, for example, why it has a Sun spot cycle of 11 years. It may be heading for a catastrophic event and we would not even know about it.

Science fiction writers often picture the Sun exploding. However, only the largest and brightest stars end their lives as supernovae. Our Sun is not nearly big enough. Supernovae are rare; only six were seen before the seventeenth century. Although hundreds have been observed since the introduction of the telescope, there are two hundred billion stars in our galaxy and there appear to be no super-giants in our area.

In the first half of the twentieth century, astronomers thought that the solar

The Solar system with the nine planets orbiting the Sun (far left). The orbits of the planets and their moons are shown as lines. Distances and sizes are not to scale: if the Sun were the size it is shown, the Earth would be virtually invisible to the naked eye.

system had been caused by a near collision between our Sun and a wandering star. It had come close enough for its gravity to drag a stream of gas from the Sun, which then condensed to form the planets. The theory was rejected when it was realised that the stars were so far apart that the chances of two coming close together are so remote as to be to all intents and purposes non-existent.

The only time we do see stars in close proximity is when they form binary systems – that is, they orbit one another or, more precisely, they orbit their mutual centre of gravity. Binary stars are com-

mon and it has been postulated that our Sun has a dark companion called Nemesis. No one has ever seen it, and few astronomers believe that it exists. But if it did it, it is possible that it is on a highly elliptical orbit. For most of this life, like a comet, it would be out in interstellar space where we could not see it. However, as it swept round on its orbit it would come hurtling into the inner solar system, knocking the planets about like ninepins. It might even send the Earth or one of the other planet crashing into the Sun.

In the 1940s it was thought that

Jupiter radiated energy like the Sun. In fact, it would have to be 60 times bigger to ignite a nuclear reaction in its core. But maybe these calculations are wrong and a nuclear reaction at the core of Jupiter did begin. As the heat reached the surface, we would suddenly find ourselves in a solar system with two Suns and life on Earth would become very unpleasant indeed. When we found ourselves between the Sun and the blazing Jupiter, there would be no night-time and life would be scorched from the surface of the planet.

Newton taught us that the solar system is a piece of clockwork. But instead of being operated by cogs and springs, it is held together by the tenuous force of gravity – something, again, of which we have a very poor understanding. What if it were suddenly to get stronger, grow weaker, or give way completely? The Earth would crash into the Sun, or hurtle off into the cold darkness of space.

Gravity does not only act between the Earth and the Sun. We also experience a slight tug by the other planets, particularly Jupiter, which is 318 times as massive as the Earth and over 1,500 times its size. If something catastrophic happened to Jupiter, the Earth's orbit and rotation would be altered to such a degree that life would no longer be sustainable here. We have already seen Jupiter hit by Shoemaker– Levy 9. At the very least, any catastrophic event on Jupiter would disrupt the asteroid belt between it and Mars, allowing rogue asteroids to break free and bombard the Earth. The loss of any of our neighbouring planets would have a knock-on effect that would at the very least disrupt life on Earth.

Closer to home, if we lost our Moon, the Earth's rotation would slow down until it became synchronised with the other planets, drastically altering the length of the day with devastating effects on the climate. As it is, tidal friction indicates that the Moon is gradually getting further away, slowing the rotation of the Earth. In 4,000 million years, the Earth's day will be the same length as a month is now. That means, the day-side of the planet would spend longer under in the scorching Sun, while the night side will get very cold indeed. Mercury, for example, has a daytime temperature of 400°C and a night-time temperature of –173 °C, though it is a lot closer to the Sun and has no atmosphere or seas to distribute heat around its surface.

The loss of the Moon would also end the tidal pull it has on the magma under the surface of the Earth. This would stop the movement of the Earth's tectonic plates and end the volcanic activity that replenishes our atmosphere.

Although we can see the nearest star, Proxima Centauri, just 4.3 light-years away, we have no idea what lies in interstellar space. The noted astronomer Sir Fred Hoyle wrote a story about the solar system finding itself plunged into an interstellar cloud, that blots out the Sun and wreaks havoc on the world's cli-

Although we can see the nearest star, Proxima Centauri, just 4.3 light-years away, we have no idea what lies in interstellar space

mate. However, in its history the solar system has made its 200-million-year orbit around the centre of the galaxy 25 times and nothing has happened yet.

Out there, in the path of the solar system, there could be a rogue dark star, the burnt-out remains of a white dwarf. As it approached, its gravity would disrupt the solar system, with devastating effects. Fortunately this is unlikely as, in spiral galaxies like ours, all stars move along in the same direction like a convoy, greatly reducing the risk of collisions.

But something strange is going on. All calculations tell us that there are a lot of stars like our Sun out there. Now we are finding that many of them have planets. Statistically speaking, there must be lots of planets similar to Earth where life could start. However, no one has ever visited us and though we have been combing the heavens with radio telescopes for over 40 years now we have discovered no signal that might indicate the presence of technologically sophisticated life.

It is not beyond the bounds of possibility that there is some hidden danger out there we know nothing of. Maybe there are lots of planets where life did start. But before it got to the stage when it looked out into the heavens or attempted to communicate, it was snuffed out.

Perhaps we are the only scientific civilisation that has ever existed, or will ever exist, and our understanding of the cosmos is the only understanding there will ever be. What we do know is this: just as life on this planet begun, so it will end. Even if, by then, humankind or our far-distant descendants have escaped from this tiny cosmic backwater, we know that the planet itself will inevitably perish. If we are to escape into the heav-

ens and create self-sustaining colonies elsewhere, there are numerous technical problems to overcome – not the least of which is staying alive on the surface of this planet while we solve them.

The Earth Disappears into a Black Hole

BLACK HOLES are the super-dense remnants of collapsed stars. One could swallow the Earth, the Sun and the entire solar system in a single gulp, if it happened by. The Sun, which is currently 865,000 miles across, would be crushed down to the size of a football.

The gravitational pull of the object at the centre of a black hole is so strong that not even light can escape. This is what makes a black hole black. And you wouldn't see it coming. The only warning you would get was when you began to feel the pull of its gravity. Anything not nailed down would be plucked from the surface of the Earth and swallowed. Some authors maintain that, if you fell into a black hole, you would be spaghetti-ised – stretched out like spaghetti due to the differential gravity on your head and your feet – and, if you looked out of the black hole as you fell, you would see the whole future of the universe flash before your eyes. It's not true. A rogue black hole

An artist's impression of the Earth disappearing into a black hole.

would tear the Earth apart before you ever noticed such effects. The debris would be superheated and compacted to a single point before it disappeared forever down the central singularity. So if there is a black hole in the vicinity, it is best avoided.

Since the theoretical possibility of the existence of black holes emerged from Einstein's General Theory of Relativity, astronomers have been on the look out for these unlikely objects. This was a hard task because, as no radiation could escape them, they could not be seen. However, the effects of them could be observed. Their enormous gravitational field would have an effect on objects around them. If, for example, the collapsed star that formed the black hole was part of a binary star system, the other star could be seen orbiting around it at enormous speed. Gas or matter would get sucked off the binary companion. As this disappeared into the black hole it would be heated up to such enormously high temperatures that it would emit high-energy X-rays.

In 1971, the binary X-ray system Cygnus X-1 was discovered. In the constellation Cygnus, it consisted of a blue supergiant orbiting an invisible companion with a period of just 5.6 days. This was the first black hole to be discovered.

More recently a black hole called GRO J1655-40 has been spotted approaching Earth at a speed of 250,000 miles an hour. Fortunately for us, it is 6,000 light

years away. That means there is still 30,000 years before it will reach us.

Worse news is that there is a supermassive black hole in the middle of our galaxy. Until 2000, it was thought that supermassive black holes occurred only in the centre of 'active' galaxies – that is, those that have jets of super-heated gas

When astronomers looked closely, they found that all galaxies, including our own, had supermassive black holes at their core

and high-energy beams of radio waves emanating from their cores. But when astronomers took a closer look they found that all galaxies, including our own, had supermassive black holes at their core.

The difference is that, in active galaxies, they were feeding – in other words, they are sucking in the stars around them. In other galaxies, material falling into the black hole gives off so much energy that it pushes other stars falling towards it back. Our galaxy, the Milky Way, is one of these quiescent types. The really bad news is that it has started feeding again. Astronomers have seen tell-tale sources of light at the galactic core and stars are moving at high velocities towards them.

We are some 24,000 light years away from the galactic centre and the black hole there stopped growing a billion years ago, so you would think that we would be reasonably safe. It has the mass of between two and three million Suns, which is comparatively small: some galaxies have supermassive black holes weighing several billion solar masses at their cores. So we should be relatively safe, unless something catastrophic happens.

But, wouldn't you know it, that is just what is about to happen. There is a second 'middle-weight' black hole just a few thousand times the mass of the Sun. It is less than half a light year from the central supermassive black hole and is being dragged into it. Typically, a black hole weighs around 0.5 per cent of the stars clustered around it, so when the 'middle-weight' black hole and the stars round it disappear into the central black hole, it is going to increase in mass by around 100,000 times the mass of our Sun. Any increase in size will make our galaxy more active. This means that more stars will fall into it, generating huge amounts of energy which will rake our solar system.

The long term prospects are not good either. Our nearest galactic neighbour, Andromeda, is also approaching at 250,000 miles an hour. Scientists have already worked out what will happen when it hits. Huge shock waves will be produced, heating up the galaxies' gas clouds.

The solar system is orbiting the galactic core at around 140 miles a second with a period of around 200 million years. If the two galaxies collide while it is on the side away from the point of impact, we will be catapulted out into the emptiness of space. But if we are near where the two are merging, we are in for an even worse time. The two supermassive black holes at the cores of the galaxies will combine and start feeding, triggering giant stellar explosions and supernovae. The radiation blast would blow off the atmosphere and the seas would boil. The surface of the Earth would be burnt to a crisp and nothing would survive. Fortunately this will not happen for another three billion years;

GRO J1655-40 would have got us first.

We might not even have to wait that long. According to Stephen Hawking, there could be countless mini-black holes, with the mass of that of an asteroid or less, created in the Big Bang and roaming free ever since. Although these evaporate over time, some may have survived and no impact is likely to be pleasant, or indeed, survivable.

A Second Big Bang

SCIENTISTS BELIEVE there may really be a number of parallel universes. This is an idea long beloved by science fiction writers, but recently it has gained currency among physicists, and it may explain how the universe came into existence and how, without warning, it may end.

The idea of parallel universes came up with the development of quantum physics in the 1920s. When physicists tried to pinpoint the exact position of atomic particles such as electrons, they found that this task was impossible. They had no single location. In fact, experiments were conducted which showed that a single particle could be in more than one place at one time. It was as if these particles did not really exist in our universe and all we could see is a shadow or ghost of them that flitted in and out of existence here.

In the pre-quantum world, particles were thought to act like billiard balls.

The Big Bang. The big bang is the hypothetical explosion that is thought to have been the birth of the universe, some 13.7 billion years ago. There is the possibility that it could occur again.

Any time the billiard balls bumped into each other, knowing their mass, speed and position, it was possible to work out where they would end up. In quantum physics though, there could be multiple outcomes, each determined by the laws of probability. The idea arose that at each event the universe branched, with one new universe for each outcome. This would mean that there were an infinite number of universes, all of which were sprouting another infinity of universes every moment. This seemed absurd, but as quantum physics became enormously successful – it has given us transistors and silicon chips – the seeming anomaly of multiple universes was quietly forgotten about.

The whole purpose of science is to simplify things. Scienists looks for underlying structures, the simple rules that govern the complex universe we see around us. When atomic physics began, it did just that. We already knew that everything was made up of atoms and atomic physics showed us the atoms themselves were made up of just three components – the proton and the neutron found in the nucleus, and the electron which orbits it. However, when physicists started smashing atoms together, they found other strange particles. And the harder they smashed atoms together, the more particles they got. Huge families grew up.

In an attempt to simplify things again, super-string theory was developed. This maintained that the universe was made up of strings. They were like the strings on a violin or a guitar which, when plucked in different ways, produce a different note. Each of the particles were different notes played on these super-strings. Physicists soon realised that super-string theory would give them what every scientist since Einstein had considered the Holy Grail – a Grand Unified Theory of Everything.

But to make super-string theory work, the strings must exist in ten dimensions: nine spatial dimensions and one of time. Even this generated five competing Theories of Everything. Then it was discovered that if you added one more dimension, these five theories coalesced into one.

Our universe, it seems, is a three-dimensional membrane floating around in these eleven dimensions. This eleven-dimension super-string theory is now called M Theory. The M generally stands for membrane, although many think it stands for mother, mystery, majesty or magic.

With a tiny fridge magnet you can overcome the gravitational pull of the whole world and pick up a metal pin

While some scientists were working on the problems associated with strings and elementary particles, others were working on the problem of gravity. Particularly, they wanted to know why it was so weak compared to the other forces. It feels strong to us here on Earth because the gravity of the entire world is pulling down on us. Yet with our puny muscles we can still pick things up. Magnetism, for example, is much stronger. With a tiny fridge magnet you can overcome the gravitational pull of the whole world and pick up a metal pin.

One theory was that gravity existed in a parallel universe, where it was as strong as all the other forces, but that what we saw in our universe was the little bit of gravity that leaked through from one universe to another. Once physicists got to grips with this, they realised that there could be all kinds of other universes out there floating around in this eleven-dimensional space, some less than one trillionth of a millimetre away.

Some of the other universes were flat, some were looped, some were cylindrical, some even had holes in them, while others were simply sheets of energy. In these universes, different laws of physics apply. In some the elementary particles like electrons and protons may be unstable, so that atoms cannot exist. Others may be more like our universe, but perhaps DNA cannot form, so there would be no life. In some small proportion of them there may be life. But a small proportion of an infinite number is an infinite number, so there may be an infinite number of inhabited universes out there.

Some would be so like our universe they would be almost indistinguishable. There would be universes that were the same as ours, only where you had not been born into it, or where Napoleon had won the Battle of Waterloo, or the British had hung on to their North American colonies. This would also give us the branching universes predicted by quantum theory. All these competing universes, like our own, would be expanding like bubbles in the sea.

Then the idea sprang up that this eleven-dimension space may not be a tranquil places. There might be waves in it. They would cause these different universes to bump into each other. Each time they collided there would be a Big Bang, like the one that began our universe. With each Big Bang, a new universe would form. As it broke off from its parent universes, ripples would be left in it. This is exactly what the Hubble Telescope sees when it looks out to the edge of the universe where the remnants of the Big Bang that formed our universe lay. These ripples are vital. Without them, our universe would be uniform and undifferentiated. The ripples cause the matter in the universe to clump together, making the tiny particles within atoms, and stars and huge galaxies surrounded by vast regions of empty space.

As there is no known method to find out what is going on outside our universe – in fact, it is theoretically impossible to do so – we have no idea when another universe might bump into ours, creating another Big Bang. All we know is that the result of such a collision is likely to be catastrophic.

Already, physicists have tendered the possibility that it might be possible to create a new universe in the laboratory. It would grow at a tremendous rate, creating its own space as it goes. In a fraction of a second it would grow to cosmic proportions. But, scientists say, it would be isolated, closed off completely from our universe so it could expand without displacing anything around it. Nevertheless, it would be best not to try this at home.

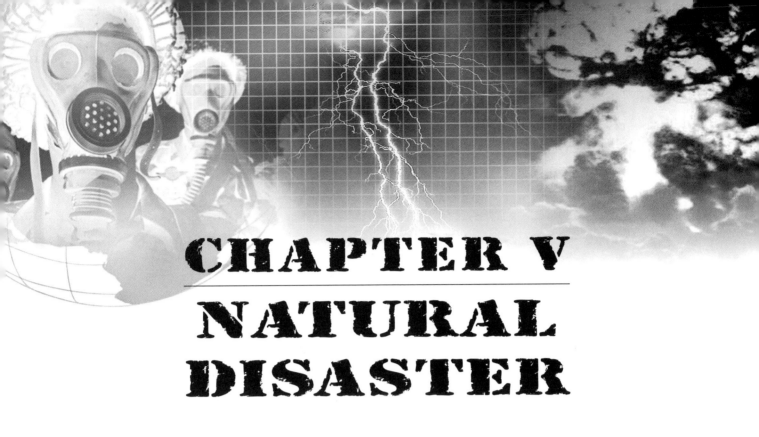

CHAPTER V
NATURAL DISASTER

Mega-tsunamis

VOLCANIC ERUPTIONS and other seismic activities often cause landslides that engulf nearby towns with huge loss of life. But when a landslide falls into the sea, it creates a giant tsunami, as tidal waves are more correctly known, that carries its destructive power over thousands of miles.

Over 100,000 years ago, a huge landslide from the flanks of Mauna Loa, an active volcano on Hawaii, dropped hundreds of cubic miles of rock into the sea. The resulting tsunami deposited coral debris 1,000 feet above sea level on the neighbouring island of Lanai, over 80 miles away. Deposits of a similar age have been found 50 feet above sea level over 4,000 miles away in New South Wales.

Mauna Loa is one of several active volcanoes in the area and the Hawaiian islands are ringed with huge aprons of debris showing that at least 70 huge landslides have occurred over the centuries – some containing individual blocks over half a mile across. A similar collapse now would create tsunami that would devastate the entire Pacific Rim.

First to be wiped out would be Hawaii's urban centres, which lie on the coast: these would be completely destroyed within a matter of minutes. The tsunami would then set off across the ocean. In deep water, tsunamis travel at speeds comparable to a Jumbo Jet. In four hours a huge wall of water would hit the coast of California. Three hours later the wave would overwhelm the eastern coast of Japan. The east coast of Australia, the Philippines, Vancouver, Seattle, western Mexico, Peru and Chile would all be devastated soon after. There would be little or no time to evacuate, leading to a loss of life which would run into many millions. Trillions of dollars of damage would be done, plunging the global economy into an irreversible recession.

No one can say when the next collapse will happen in the Hawaiian islands. However, they seem to occur more often during periods of rapid sea level change – change that is currently anticipated as an effect of global warming. At the moment, a large block is on the move on the south coast of Hawaii. It is separated from the very active volcano Kilauea by a series of faults and open fissures. Movement along the fault line causes periodic earthquakes, which have taken lives as recently as 1975.

The coastline of the Atlantic is under a similar threat. In 1949, several hundred cubic miles of rock that make up the western flank of the volcano Cumbre Vieja on La Palma island in the Canaries slipped 12 feet towards the sea, then stopped. A huge mass of rock, around the size of Greater London, is now just hanging there, ready to slip into the ocean at any time. Such is the sharp slope of the volcanic island that, once it started to slide, there is nothing to slow its fall until it hit the ocean floor over two miles down.

Cumbre Vieja is a very active volcano and its next eruption is likely to prise the block free. Once it moved, the entire western coast of the island would collapse into the sea, creating a wave nearly 3,000 feet high. It would still be some 300 feet high when it hit the shores of the other Canary Islands a few minutes later. It would wash away everyone and everything on the coast, before it swept on to hit the coast of Africa, devastating the Moroccan cities of Casablanca and Rabat. A wave 300 feet high would funnel through the Strait of Gibraltar, destroying Tangiers. A smaller wave nearly 25 feet high would head on to Spain and the UK. But this would be funnelled up the English Channel, flooding the Netherlands and overwhelming London's defences.

Meanwhile the tsunami would head westwards unimpeded, hitting the north coast of Brazil just six hours later. Low-lying islands in the Caribbean would be swamped. The Bahamas would be scoured of human life by a wave 150 feet high, which would plough on, inexorably, until it hit the eastern seaboard of the United States.

Tsunamis pack an enormous punch. While the wavelength of a normal wind-blown wave is tens of feet, a typical tsunami measures hundreds of miles in length. After the coast is hit, initially by a solid wall of water travelling at several hundred miles an hour, the water keeps on coming for another ten or fifteen minutes, before it ebbs again. The coast is then pummelled by a series of smaller waves. On the island of Eleuthera in the Bahamas, there are boulders the size of houses, weighing several thousand tons that have been thrown 500 yards inland and left 60 feet above sea level by a giant wave, probably caused by a previous coastal collapse in the Canaries. Nothing wrought by man could resist such a force.

The first waves would hit the coast of New England barely six and a half hours after the collapse. Any warning would simply jam the roads. There would be no escape. The first indication that anything untoward was about to happen would be the sight of the sea suddenly retreating, exposing sand and mud flats as far out as the horizon. A silver streak would then appear far in the distance as the oncoming tsunami began to break. Coastal towns from Portland, Maine to Miami, Florida would be hit by a wave 100 feet high, followed by another ten over the next 90 minutes. New York would be particularly badly hit, as the waves would be focussed by Lower New

Death of the dinosaurs: Titanosaurus watches an approaching tsunami caused by the impact of an asteroid or comet core. This impact may have caused the extinction of the dinosaurs and 70% of all other species on Earth about 65 million years ago.

York Bay and Verrazano Narrows. The tsunami would break at the entrance to Delaware and Chesapeake Bays, sending giant bores up their rivers, which would swamp Philadelphia, Baltimore and Washington, D.C.

Ships of the USN Atlantic Fleet that got out to sea would survive, as the tsunami would pass under them. Ships in deep water do not even notice tsunamis passing under them as their wavelength is so long. But those remaining behind in Norfolk, Virginia or trapped in coastal waters would be hurled inland or smashed to pieces. Nuclear-powered submarines would be ripped apart, exposing their reactors and contaminating huge areas with radiation. Port facilities would also be destroyed and, once the water had receded, there would be fires in devastated oil refineries and fuel stores, risking the catastrophic explosion of munitions.

Millions if not tens of millions would die when the tsunami struck. The damage would be incalculable. With New York destroyed and London devastated, the insurance industry would be wiped out. With the global economy in collapse, rebuilding would be next to impossible.

Tsunami from the ice

Mega-tsunami threats, then, are very real, both in both the Pacific and the Atlantic. There is, however, a third tsunami threat that could wipe out every coastal city in one fell swoop. This comes from the huge ice-sheets that cover the Antarctic and areas of Canada, Greenland and Siberia. Using ground-penetrating radar, geologists have discovered that, under them, there are huge lakes and layers of lubricating slush where the ice has been melted by heat from the Earth's core from beneath, and the huge weight pushing down from above. Imagine at this point a sequence of catastrophic events – a series of volcanic eruptions, say, or earthquakes and violent storms. The combined effect could tip the Earth's axis or accentuate its wobble. As it is the Earth's axis already has two short-term

A silver streak would appear far in the distance as the oncoming tsunami began to break

wobbles – the annual wobble with a period of 12 months and the Chandler Wobble, named for its 1885 discoverer Seth Chandler, with a period of around 14 months. The poles stray from their mean position by as much as 37 feet and only return to where they started every 6.5 years. Any sudden increase in this wobble would be enough to send one or more of these ice-sheets hurtling into the sea, inundating every coastal area on Earth.

And this could happen not just as a consequence of a natural disaster. In the 1960s, a group of strategists at the Institute for Defense Analysis in Washington, D.C. looked into the consequences of some hostile nation or a terrorist group using nuclear weapons to shake the Antarctic ice sheet loose.

'The most immediate effect of this vast quantity of ice surging into the water,' wrote the institute's vice president Dr Gordon J. MacDonald, 'would be to create massive tsunamis that would completely wreck coastal regions even in the northern hemisphere.'

As well as the loss of life and economic disruption caused, there would be some global environmental consequences, the nature of which would depend on the exact nature of the catastrophe. The loss of a large amount of the planet's reflective ice sheets would allow the world to warm up. On the other hand, the temperature of the sea would plummet as it filled with slowly melting icebergs. It is possible that the survivors of the initial tsunami would find themselves alone in a world of ice, with only a narrow band of land around the equator warm enough to raise crops, while the rest of the planet succumbed to the slow but unstoppable advance of the glaciers.

The Ultimate Volcano

THE INTENSITY of volcanic eruptions is measured by the Volcanic Explosive Index, devised by vulcanologists Steve Self and Chris Newhall in 1982. Like the better-known Richter Scale, which measures earthquake intensity, the VEI has a logarithmic scale – that is, each single point up the scale indicates an eruption ten times as powerful.

Lava-flows from volcanoes on Iceland and Hawaii rate zero on this scale. The gentle eruptions of Stromboli off Sicily rates only a one. The eruption of Ruiz in Colombia in 1985, which killed more than 23,000 people, rates only a three. Galunggung which blasted a column of ash and pumice 15 miles into air in 1982, smothering 22 Javanese villages and killing 68 people, rates a four. The much-televised eruption of Mount St Helens in Washington state in 1981 had a VEI of five. In 1991, Mount Pinatubo in the Philippines erupted, ejecting enough ash and debris to bury central London to a depth of half-a-mile. This rated a 6 on the VEI, as did the famous eruption of Krakatoa in 1883. The last VEI 7 eruption was that of the long-dormant Tambora on the island of Sumbawa, near Bali, in 1815. The eruption was heard 900 miles away in Sumatra and blasted more than 36 cubic miles of solid material into the air, leaving the mountain a mile shorter than before. Smoke debris darkened the sky even at noon, and ash fell up to 800 miles away.

That eruption lasted 34 days and killed 12,000 people directly. A further 80,000 died of starvation and disease caused by the devastation of the area. But the effects were felt much further afield. Along with the ash, sulphur gases were released, forming an aerosol – tiny airborne droplets – of sulphuric acid in the atmosphere. These ringed the globe and it is estimated that they blocked out 88 per cent of the sunlight falling on the Earth. As a result, 1816 became known as 'the year without a summer', when snow fell in New England in July. Although the US was able to feed itself, there were famines in Canada and Northern Europe. It is thought that the red sunsets to be seen in JMW Turner's work were one of the more benign results.

The last known VE1 8 eruption occurred 73,500 years ago at Toba, northern Sumatra, which left a crater 60 miles across. It blasted out 1,500 cubic miles of material, enough to cover the entire United States to a depth of over two feet. Anyone living in the vicinity of Sumatra at the time would have been wiped out.

Along with the solid debris, the eruption released enough sulphur gases to make 5,000 million tons of sulphuric acid aerosol. Temperatures in the tropics would have dropped by 15 °C, wiping out sensitive tropical vegetation. It may have stopped photosynthesis completely, causing mass starvation for any of our ancestors who happened to be around at the time.

Volcanic ash plume at Mount St. Helens. View of the giant ash cloud formed by the eruption of Mount St. Helens on 22 July 1980. This explosive event threw ash up to an altitude of 18km in the space of eight minutes.

Overall temperatures would have dropped by five or six degrees C and stayed that way for at least six years. It is thought that the eruption of Toba may have sparked the last ice age. The human population dropped dramatically during that period and did not rise again until after the ice had receded. Human beings were lucky to survive.

There have been other VEI 8 eruptions. Two million years ago an eruption at Yellowstone in Wyoming left a crater 50 miles across. The debris thrown out covered what are now 16 states. Another occurred in the same place around 1.2 million years ago, then another 650,000 years ago: some vulcanologists believe that Yellowstone may soon be due for another eruption.

Yellowstone is one vast volcanic caldera: if it erupted again, anyone within 50 miles not directly killed by the blast would almost immediately be overwhelmed by the pyroclastic flow of superheated gas, steam and ash that would follow. The volcano would continue erupting with a force equivalent to a thousand Hiroshima-sized atomic bombs every second. An eruption column 1.5 miles across would rise 25 miles in the sky depositing ash on at least ten states downwind. There is no way that civil authorities in the affected areas could be prepared for such a disaster and, more than likely, law and order would break down in the ensuing panic. Even Los Angeles 800 miles away would be brought to a standstill by falling ash.

After about a week the volcano's magma chamber would be emptied and the ground would start to collapse, causing a series of earthquakes that would knock down any building that remained standing. Insurance companies would go bust. Investors would lose any confidence that the country could recover from such a disaster and the New York stock market would crash, closely followed by stock market crashes around the world. Industry would grind to a halt. Trade would cease and the economy worldwide would collapse.

While scientists keep an eye on what is happening at Yellowstone, only a tiny percentage of the Earth's 1,500 volcanoes are monitored. The next VEI 8 eruption could even occur at a place where there has been no activity before. Even if it occurred in a relatively remote place where local casualties would be comparatively small, the impact would be catastrophic. Even developed counties such as the UK and US have insufficient food stocks to feed their populations for a month or two. With the Sun blotted out by volcanic ash clouds, crops would fail and there would be little hope of replenishment for years to come. Industrial civilisation could not survive.

Humankind is also threatened by a type of volcanic eruption that does not even register on the VEI scale. It is called a flood-basalt eruption. It is not explosive. Instead, cracks open in the earth and spew out huge volumes of lava which spread over a huge area. Around 250 million years ago, one of these lava flows in Siberia covered over 10 million square miles – three times the area of the US. By the time these had cooled and solidified 95 per cent of all species on Earth had vanished.

A similar mass extinction took place 65 million years ago. Although this is associated with the collision of a comet, the impact took place at the same time as the Deccan flood basalt eruption in northwest India and may even have caused it. We do not need to look to outer space to find danger; 'inner space' – the interior of our own planet – contains more than enough to kill us all.

24

Reversal of Earth's Magnetic Field

THROUGHOUT THE EARTH'S history the planet's magnetic field has reversed repeatedly. We know this because, when magma extruded along the mid-ocean ridges cools and solidifies, the newly formed rock retains the magnetic polarity of the time it set. An examination of the ocean floors with a magnetometer shows alternate bands of polarisation. This means that sometimes the Earth's magnetic North Pole sometime roughly matches its geographic north pole, as it does now, while at other times the magnetic field switched round and the magnetic South Pole was in the Arctic.

Usually, magnetic reversals occur every 250,000 years, but there has not been one for almost a million years now – meaning that a reversal is some 750,000 years overdue. And there is evidence that one is on its way. For nearly two hundred years scientists have been noticing that the Earth's magnetic field has been declining. Over the last century it decreased by some five per cent. Until recently, some argued that this was merely a periodic dip. Short-term changes in the strength of the Earth's magnetic field can be caused by changes in the solar wind, high in the atmosphere. But the steady drift of the pole indicates that something more profound is going on. It has now been discovered that the Earth's magnetic field is disappearing even more rapidly near the poles, indicating that a flip is about to take place.

Even more alarming are signs that the poles are moving. When the position of the magnetic North Pole was measured by the Norwegian explorer Roald Amundsen in 1904, it was in roughly the same position as it was when British naval officer John Ross, who was searching for the elusive North-West Passage, located it in 1831. But throughout the 20th century, the magnetic pole has been moving slowly northwards, out of Canada towards Siberia. Then about 30 years ago the movement began to accelerate. It is now travelling about four times faster than it was at the beginning of the last century, and researchers at the Canadian government's Geolab, who keep an eye on the position of the pole, are getting worried.

The Earth's magnetic field is produced by a geomagnetic dynamo deep beneath the crust, where huge currents of molten iron swirl around the solid iron core. Gauthier Hulot of the Paris Geophysical Institute has been studying this mechanism in the hope of finding some explanation for the recent changes. Using satellite measurements of field variations over the past 20 years, he has plotted the currents of molten iron that generate Earth's magnetism deep underground and has spotted huge whorls near the poles. Hulot believes that these vortices rotate in a direction which reinforces a reversal in the magnetic field. As they grow and proliferate these eddies will weaken the dominant field, which is the first step toward a new polarity, he says.

Computer simulations performed in the US confirm this interpretation. It has

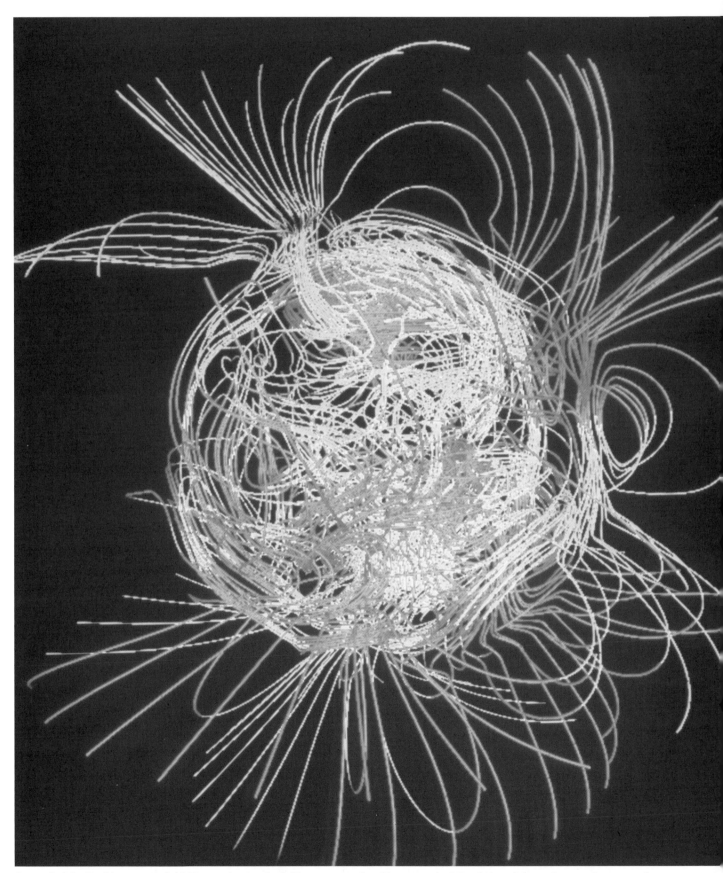

Reversal of the Earth's magnetic field. Picture showing the field structure produced by a numerical simulation of the geodynamo, the source of the Earth's magnetic field. Here, the simulation has run for 36,000 'years', and is the middle of a field reversal.

also been found that a region of the Earth's core under South Africa has a different polarity to the rest of the magnetic field in the core – though, as yet, it is not known whether this will grow, precipitating the forthcoming flip, or revert to the standard polarity.

The reversal of the Earth's magnetic field will be confusing for pigeons and other animals that navigate using it. The migrations of swallows and wildebeest will also be disrupted, possibly leading to their extinction. Humankind might be a little disconcerted finding that their compasses point the wrong way, but we have the satellite Global Positional System, so navigation should not be affected. However, the effect of a reversal is nevertheless likely to be catastrophic.

According to Dr Alan Thomson of the British Geological Survey in Edinburgh, the Earth's magnetic field will disappear completely before flipping over, though no one is certain how long this period without a magnetic field is going to last. Some researchers issue blithe assurances that this will be a minor inconvenience and last only a few weeks. However, records of past reversals, locked in iron minerals in ancient lava beds, show some reversals have taken thousands of years. In a worst-case scenario, this could mean that the Earth might be without a magnetic field for millennia.

If this happened, it would be devastating. The Earth's magnetic field protects us from cosmic rays, high-

The Earth's magnetic field also directs the solar wind, a stream of charged particles, safely around the planet

energy charged particles which get caught up in the magnetic field and are deposited harmlessly at high latitudes in the aurora borealis and aurora australis – the northern and southern lights. The Earth's magnetic field also directs the solar wind, a stream of solar particles boiling off from the surface of the Sun, safely around the planet. Without our magnetic field to protect them, navigation and communication satellites in low-Earth orbit would be wrecked by powerful radiation bursts. Meanwhile, on the Earth's surface, we would be raked by cosmic rays, making the planet very inhospitable indeed.

Particle storms would pound the atmosphere, heating it up, with enormous, unpredictable effects on the climate. It is thought that the loss of Mars's magnetic field billions of years ago led to its atmosphere being boiled off. The same fate could easily await the Earth.

If the Earth's magnetic field fails, there is nothing much that we could do about it. However, as ever, Hollywood has the answer. In the movie *The Core*, scientists drill a hole into the Earth's mantle and drop a nuclear bomb down it in order to 'jumpstart' the geomagnetic dynamo. Unfortunately, the temperatures at such depths rival those of the Sun's surface. Both the drill and the bomb would melt almost instantaneously. So it seems unlikely that, outside Hollywood, such a remedy would work.

Even so, the scientists at Geolab are

keeping a sharp eye on the progress of the magnetic North Pole. They make regular flights from their headquarters Ottawa to Resolute Bay, the closest inhabited spot to the magnetic pole. From there, they take a three-and-a-half hour ride on their Twin Otter, a light aircraft, to the pole itself. They can only do this at the end of winter because the pole is now out at sea and they need the winter sea-ice to land on. Recently, they have been finding that the pole moves day by day. The Earth's magnetic field, it seems, is becoming ominously lively.

Loss of Atmosphere

MARS ONCE HAD an atmosphere not dissimilar to the Earth's. No one is quite sure how it lost it, but there are a number of possible theories.

Most of the atmosphere of the Earth came from volcanoes, but on Mars there are no active volcanoes – though there is evidence of volcanic activity in the past. What keeps the Earth's volcanic activity going, replenishing our atmosphere, is plate tectonics. The crust of the Earth is broken into huge plates which collide with one another, causing earthquakes and volcanoes. The Earth has the advantage here. Being a larger planet, its core is hotter, which keeps the mantle boiling up with huge convection currents, moving the plates about. Another reason the Earth's crust has not set into a solid shell like that of Mars is due to the effect of the Moon. The gravity of the Moon causes a tide in the Earth's molten mantle, which breaks up the crust and keeps it moving. Mars's two moons, Phobos and Deimos, are tiny by comparison – just 28 and 16 kilometres across. Without our massive Moon – whose diameter is half that of Mars – there would be no plate tectonics, no volcanoes and the Earth would slowly lose its atmosphere.

It is certain that Mars did once have an atmosphere comparable in density to that of the Earth. Its surface features show signs of erosion, indicating that there was once rainfall on Mars. But if an atmosphere is not replenished, it naturally leaks off into space. Ultraviolet light breaks up heavy molecules and light atoms in the stratosphere can easily reach escape velocity. It is much easier for atoms to escape from Mars as it has only one tenth of the mass of the Earth and its gravity on the surface at the equator is only one third of the Earth's. The escape velocity on Mars is three miles a second, compared with seven miles a second on Earth.

Even so, the effect of atoms escaping from the atmosphere is felt on Earth. It is one of the reasons we have an oxygen-rich atmosphere. When molecules of water in the atmosphere are broken up into their constituent atoms, it is much easier for the light hydrogen atoms to escape than the oxygen atoms, which are some 16 times heavier.

Another theory of how Mars lost its atmosphere derives from the fact that it has no magnetic field. This gives it no protection from the solar wind – a stream of charged particles boiling off the surface of the Sun – which could have simply blown the Martian atmosphere away.

There is also a theory that the impact of a comet or an asteroid simply blasted the atmosphere off into space. Such an impact might also explain the eccentricity of Mars's orbit around the Sun. The tenuous remnants of Mars's atmosphere are 95 per cent carbon dioxide, but there is so little of it that it contributes little to global warming, raising the surface temperature by just 5 °C and leaving the surface cold and desolate. The atmospheric pressure is less than one per cent of that on Earth.

So what would happen if the Earth were to suffer a similar catastrophe?

Firstly, the results would not be very pleasant for humankind and almost all creatures that lived on Earth. It would be impossible to breathe and, without a pressure suit, we would simply explode as the pressure inside our bodies – and our individual cells – would greatly exceed that outside.

The temperature at which liquids boil depends on the atmospheric pressure – the lower the pressure, the lower the boiling point. This is noticeable on Earth: at the top of Mount Everest, where the atmospheric pressure is lower, water boils at around 70 °C. Without an atmosphere, your blood would boil – though as you could not breathe and would already have exploded, this perhaps would be less of a problem than it might appear.

The boiling point of water would in fact be so low that water would not exist in liquid form at all. Ice would turn directly into water vapour without going through a liquid stage, a process known as sublimation. We see this on Earth with 'dry ice' – which is not ice at all, but frozen carbon dioxide. The sea would simply boil away.

On the barren surface of the Earth, temperatures would fluctuate wildly as the ocean currents and weather systems performed the vital task of moving heat from the Earth's hot spots to cooler areas.

Atmosphere shields a planet from harmful elements of the Sun's radiation, including ultraviolet rays, X-rays and gamma rays. With a thinner atmosphere, more of this dangerous radiation would reach the surface, making life problematic.

The atmosphere also acts as a shield against space debris. Small objects on collision course are burnt up by friction in the atmosphere. Larger ones are reduced in size. With a substantially thinner atmosphere, the surface of the Earth would be pockmarked and cratered by constant bombardment.

If the Earth began to lose its atmosphere, is there anything we could do about it? Well, we could look at some of the terraforming techniques that are being proposed to make Mars suitable for human habitation.

The quickest way to make Mars habitable would be to drop nuclear bombs on its poles. This would warm the planet instantly and melt the ice and frozen carbon dioxide that form the polar ice-caps. The vast clouds of carbon dioxide and water vapour would form an instant atmosphere. Both carbon dioxide and water vapour are great greenhouse gases, so the temperature would climb further.

The same effect could be achieved more slowly by using large orbiting mirrors to direct sunlight onto the poles. It has also been suggested that comets or asteroids could be farmed for suitable materials to build an atmosphere.

Despite the bad press it gets, carbon dioxide is not a very efficient greenhouse gas. Chemicals that fit the bill much bet-

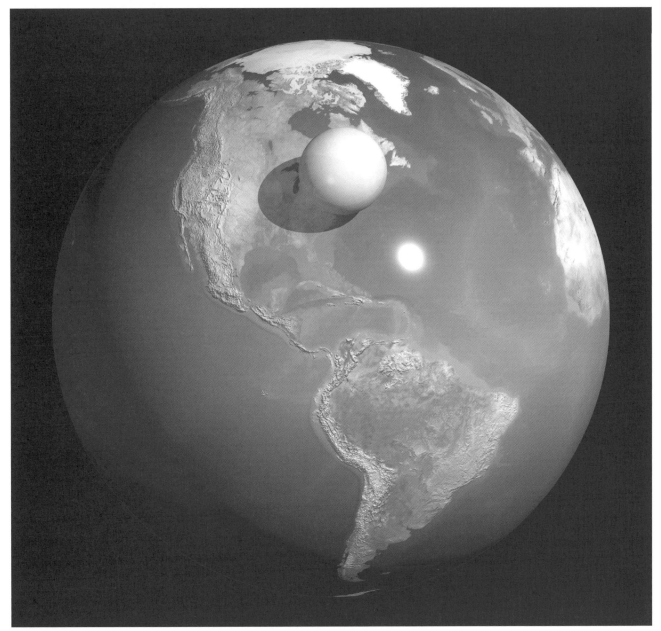

Global air volume. Conceptual computer artwork of the total volume of air within the Earth's atmosphere, seen as a sphere, centred over North America. It dramatically shows how finite the available air supply actually is.

ter are perflurocarbons, or PFCs, compounds of carbon and fluorine which are similar chemically to the CFCs we currently eschew on Earth. On Mars a few hundred small PFC factories – each around the size of a small family car – could raise the temperature to the point where the frozen carbon dioxide at the poles would sublimate. To get to this point would take between 10 and 100 years. This would take four times longer on Earth: between 40 and 400 years.

By that time, the atmosphere would be thick enough to protect the surface from harmful rays and meteorites, and the pressure would be high enough to let liquid water run again. Some nitrogen would have been released from the soil, and some oxygen and ozone would have been formed from the photochemical degradation of carbon dioxide. Within a few hundred years, microbial and plant life could be reintroduced to generate more oxygen. However, to get the proportion of oxygen up to the 20 per cent we need to live would take up to a million years on Mars. On Earth it took around two billion years for enough oxygen to accumulate. That is a long time to hold your breath.

Earth's Atmosphere Gains Density

BEFORE MARS had an atmosphere like Earth's it had one like that of Venus – hot, dense and poisonous. Indeed, early in the Earth's history its atmosphere was also like that of Venus. All that would be needed for the atmosphere to return to that hellish condition would be for every one of the world's volcanoes to erupt and keep on erupting.

A global survey and the numerous probes sent to Venus have revealed evidence that a great deal of tectonic activity has taken place on the planet. There are huge ridges, canyons and a trough-like depression that extends across 870 miles across its surface, and there is a gigantic volcanic cone whose base is more than 435 miles across. Vulcanism on a similar scale happened on Earth between the Precambrian and the Tertiary periods – between around 3.9 billion to 1.6 million years ago. During

that time, huge flood-basalt eruptions occurred, like the one that covered over 10 million square miles of Siberia discussed in the previous chapter.

A similar flood-basalt eruption took place when Pangaea, the Earth's original single landmass, began to break up between 208 to 144 million years ago, creating amongst other things the rift that became the Atlantic Ocean. This eruption is still going on around the 10,000 miles of the mid-Atlantic ridge, which is now at the bottom of the sea.

The basalt plains found in Brazil and the Karoo in South Africa were formed during the opening of the South Atlantic and the Deccan Plateau in India was formed when Gondwana, a proto-continent formed by the break-up of Pangaea, itself broke up.

Such intense vulcanism puts so much sulphur into the atmosphere that it rains sulphuric acid. On Venus, though, the surface temperature is so hot – around 460°C – that the rain does not reach it. Corrosive droplets form high in the atmosphere and begin to fall, but they evaporate before they reach the ground. The atmospheric pressure there is nearly a hundred times that on Earth: the equivalent of being a kilometre – 3,300 feet – under the sea. At ground level the atmosphere is so dense that there is not even the slightest breeze, but at higher levels 200-mile-an-hour winds rush from the hot day side of Venus to the freezing night side. Clouds have also been seen to travel all the way around Venus's equator in four Earth days.

As well as vulcanism, what makes Venus so hellish is the runaway greenhouse effect. Its atmosphere is 97 per cent carbon dioxide. The Earth's early atmosphere was similar, but the carbon

An artist's impression of the surface of Earth in about one billion years' time. The Sun is predicted to have heated up, becoming 10% brighter, leading to a Venus-like, lifeless Earth.

dioxide was leached out to form limestone. The greenhouse effect and the heat of the Sun boiled off any oceans Venus might have had. All the planet's water exists in the high clouds that completely obscure the surface. When astronomers first saw these clouds, they believed they concealed lush rainforests. However, the surface temperature of Venus is 460 degrees C, it is hot enough to melt tin or lead and nothing can grow there.

Another reason the conditions are so unpleasant on Venus is that it has very long days: they are in fact longer than its years! Venus takes 243 Earth days to rotate on its axis, while it takes just 225 Earth days to orbit the Sun – so it appears to rotate backwards compared with most of the other planets. The reason is that Earth's gravitational pull has locked Venus's rotation to the Earth's orbit. Like the Moon, Venus always shows the same face to the Earth.

In many ways Venus is our twin planet. It is roughly the same size, shape and mass – and it is our nearest neighbour, coming within 26 million miles at its closest. Earlier in the Earth's existence, the conditions on the surface were very similar. What changed things here was life. As British physicist James Lovelock pointed out in his Gaia hypothesis, once primitive micro-organisms got a toehold they began to alter the temperature and atmospheric chemistry to suit themselves. The dense carbon-dioxide atmosphere thinned, the temperature dropped, water flowed and oxygen accumulated, which allowed more complex creatures to evolve.

Lovelock maintains that the elements of the biosphere grew so interdependent and interrelated that they could be regarded as a single self-regulating organism he calls Gaia, after the Greek Earth goddess. For example, although there has been a 25 per cent increase in energy coming from the Sun over the 3.5 billion years since life began its evolutionary journey, the temperature at the Earth's surface has remained relatively constant.

Global warming has given us the first inkling that humankind can have a major effect on the Earth's temperature and atmosphere

Over the past 500 million years the Earth's atmospheric and oceanic chemistry has remained remarkably stable. But this is no cause for complacency, warns Lovelock.

Global warming has already given us the first inkling that humankind can have an unprecedented effect on the Earth's temperature and atmosphere. We may already be reaching the limits that the biota can cope with. The self-regulating system could break down completely. If Gaia is alive, she could die and the Earth could return to a sterile and lifeless condition, like that of Venus. As yet we have little idea how common life is in the universe. We do know, however, that it is rare in our solar system. Although life has proved remarkably robust on Earth so far, lifelessness seems to be the natural condition of planets.

A series of probes visited Venus in the 1970s and 1980s. When they reported back the conditions there, it has generally been assumed that Venus is lifeless. More recently, however, bacteria have been found on 'black smokers' – volcanic vents along the Earth's mid-ocean ridges. They are fed on by tube worms, bivalves, gastropods and crustaceans who live in the water there at temperatures up to 400 °C and at pressures even higher than those experienced on the surface of Venus. So it might well be worth looking for life there once again. Finding it might prove some small comfort. But imagine what a lamentable fate it would be, if conditions on Earth were to revert to the

Venusian model and life here was reduced to a handful of bacteria and invertebrates huddling around a volcanic vent.

The Perfect Storm

IN 1664, THE GREAT RED SPOT on Jupiter was seen for the first time by British physicist and inventor Robert Hooke. It was later discovered to be a storm and it has been raging continuously now for over 340 years.

There has never been a storm of anything like that longevity on the Earth – nor of that size. Jupiter's Great Red Spot is 25,000 miles across – that's over twice the diameter of the Earth. On Earth, hurricanes and typhoons are usually between 50 and 500 miles across. However, the wind speeds in the Great Red Spot are comparable to those on Earth. Patches of clouds swept around the spot make one complete circuit in about six days, giving a wind speed of around 180 miles an hour.

Devastating hurricanes on Earth regularly report wind speeds of between 120 and 150 miles an hour. In 1938, a hurricane that hit New England recorded wind speeds of up to 183 miles an hour, while in 1988 Hurricane Gilbert blew at 185 miles an hour: the highest recorded wind speed on Earth is over 200 mph, recorded at the Mount McKinley Observatory in Washington State in the USA.

The mechanism that causes the Great Red Spot is the same as that which causes hurricanes and tropical cyclones on Earth. At the centre is a warm updraft, which carries heat to the edge of the atmosphere, where it cools and spirals downwards again around the outside. However the atmosphere of Jupiter is largely hydrogen, and it is thought that the red colour of the spot comes from crystals of ammonium hydrosulphide, which is reddish in colour, and mixtures of sulphur and water which are brown.

The most deadly storm of all time on the Earth is believed to be the Great Hurricane of 1780, when it is estimated that some 22,000 people died as it swept across Martinique, St. Lucia, St. Vincent, St. Kitts, Grenada and Barbados between 10 and 16 October of that year. Thousands of deaths also occurred offshore. Not only did the deaths from this hurricane far exceed those from any other Atlantic hurricane, but the fatalities from this one storm exceeded the cumulative deaths in any other year.

The worst hurricane in living memory was Hurricane Mitch, which hit Central America in 1998. It began life on 21 October 1998 as a tropical depression in the southern Caribbean. The following day, it reached hurricane force. Over the next five days, what started out as a tropical storm grew into a Category 5 hurricane. As it strengthened, Mitch moved to the north-west. Its winds reached a peak of 180 miles an hour and, on 26 October it hit the north-east coast of Honduras.

Dropping heavy rain over Honduras and Nicaragua, it caused catastrophic flooding and mudslides. The effect was worsened because hurricanes move more slowly over land and the mountains of Honduras and Nicaragua squeezed the

The Earth shown in comparison to the Great Red Spot on Jupiter: the Earth is about one third the size. The Great Red Spot is a huge storm which has raged across the surface of Jupiter for hundreds of years.

last drop of moisture out of its clouds. Then Mitch moved to the north, to emerge over the Gulf of Mexico, where it was fed by the warm sea, and it began to pick up speed again. On 4 November, it smashed into the west coast of Florida still at hurricane force. But in the US the people were ready and there few fatalities. Back in Central America, it is thought that as many as 18,000 died. Many of them were swept away in torrents that overcame flood defences that had stood for two hundred years.

What are known as hurricanes in the Caribbean and western Atlantic are called cyclones in the Indian Ocean. Bangladesh is particularly prone to them as it lies at the head of the Bay of Bengal. Cyclones bring with them storm surges that cause devastating floods as most of Bangladesh lies no more than three metres above sea level.

In 1737, more than 300,000 drowned when a storm hit the area. Afterwards, flood defences were built, but they did not prevent over 20,000 drowning in 1963 and another 40,000 in 1965. Another cyclone hit the area in 1970 wreaking destruction on an unprecedented scale. Hundred-mile-an-hour winds brought a storm surge of over 20 feet in the early hours of 13 November. Manpura Island in the Ganges delta disappeared completely. Of the 4,500 houses on the island, only four remained standing and, of the island's 30,000 inhabitants, 25,000 were dead. Across 3,000 square miles, houses were flattened and field stripped bare. Drowned bodies hung from the branches of trees or lay in heaps on beaches. On 13 small islands off Chittagong everyone had been killed. In Bhola, the largest island in the delta, 200,000 had drowned and estimates of the total death toll range between 500,000 and a million, many of whom were simply swept away. Others died of exposure in the aftermath.

A million acres of paddy fields had been swamped and 75 per cent of the rice crop was ruined. Most of the fishing boats were lost and a million head of cattle drowned. Destitute villagers searched the mud for single grains of rice. There was no fresh water. In urban areas the mains were broken and village springs were fouled by sea water and rotting corpses.

In April 1991, yet another tropical cyclone swept up the Bay of Bengal. The 20-foot storm surge swept over low-lying areas of Bangladesh killing 140,000 and leaving millions homeless.

So what is the long-term outlook for such storms?

As hurricanes, tropical cyclones and typhoons, as these storms are known in the Pacific, get their energy from the warm waters of the oceans, global warming is bound to make them worse. Rising sea levels are also going to expand these storms' playground: most storms blow themselves out quite quickly when they get over land.

At the moment, in the Caribbean the hurricane season lasts from May to November. In the Philippines, the typhoon season lasts from September to February; in China it lasts from June to October, and in other places it starts in April. As global warming takes off, these seasons will lengthen until it is storm season all year round. Smaller storms will grow into full-blown cyclones and hurricanes and typhoons will amalgamate to form bigger storms or appear so quickly after one another that the wind will never stop blowing. We may then have our own man-made Great Red Spot, though it will not necessarily be red.

Few buildings can withstand a wind blowing constantly at 180 miles an hour. Those that fell down could not be repaired and it would be impossible to build new ones with that sort of gale blowing. Even solid structures would be sand-blasted until they weakened and collapsed. Agriculture would be impossible as no one could work in the fields and the soil would be washed or blown away, and nothing could be transported safely by sea or by air.

Once a series of devastating storms got blowing on a global scale there is no reason to believe that the wind could not go on blowing for 300 years. And the wind speeds seen in Jupiter's Giant Red Spot are by no means the fastest seen in the solar system. On Saturn, which has its own red spot, winds blow at up to 1,120 miles an hour. Nothing could survive in a wind like that.

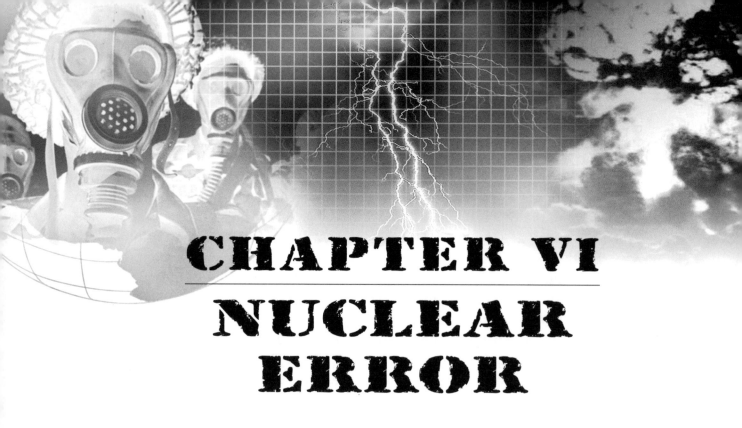

CHAPTER VI
NUCLEAR ERROR

Nuclear Meltdown

IN THE 1950S – despite the terrible warning of Hiroshima and Nagasaki – atomic energy was believed to be a panacea. It was thought that it would provide limitless cheap energy, safely. It has to be said that the governments that pushed this line were being disingenuous: they actually wanted to build atomic power stations to turn plentiful non-fissile uranium-238 into highly fissile plutonium-239 and other transuranic elements to make bigger and better bombs. And soon it was discovered that atomic energy was not safe at all.

The first nuclear accident occurred on 8 October 1957 when technicians at the British nuclear power plant at Windscale, now Sellafield, in Cumberland, now Cumbria, were warming up a gas-cooled reactor. However, inadequate instrumentation meant the control room staff mistakenly thought the reactor was

cooling down and needed extra heating.

At 11.05 am the control rods were withdrawn from the 57,000-ton pile – a honeycomb of graphite containing 35,000 aluminium cans of uranium – for a routine start to the reactor's chain reaction. Also in the reactor were canisters of lithium and magnesium to create tritium for a British H-bomb. But the temperature was too high and these burst and ignited. Burning uranium fuel and graphite moderator sent temperatures soaring to 1,300 degrees C and blue flames shot out of the back face of the reactor. These early plutonium piles were cooled by massive fans blowing air through them, so the heat and contamination was carried up Sellafield's then famous concrete chimneys, whose filters could hold back only a small proportion of the radioactivity released.

The first attempts to control the fire were disastrous. Fans were switched on, but instead of cooling the uranium fuel rods, they fanned the fire. The scientists were unsure of how to deal with this. Workers were sent in, in relays, with scaffolding poles to push hundreds of cans of nuclear fuel out of the way and make a firebreak.

Nuclear power station. View across snow of the Three Mile Island nuclear power plant near Harrisburg, Pennsylvania, USA. The plant's Unit 2 reactor was severely damaged in an accident on 28 March 1979, almost precipitating a meltdown.

Next, carbon dioxide was pumped in to cool the flames. This was also counter-productive as, at those temperatures, carbon dioxide breaks down to release oxygen which further fanned the fire. The temperature in the piles soared. Engineers debated whether they could risk flooding the reactor with water. There was a danger that the water would also break down, producing oxygen and hydrogen which would explode, possibly triggering an atomic explosion.

In the end they had no choice. The temperature was climbing by 20 degrees C a minute when scientists flooded the reactor with water. The fire was extinguished after 16 hours, leaving ten tons of radioactive fuel melted in the core. Large quantities of radioactive iodine escaped into the atmosphere, along with plutonium, caesium and polonium.

At the time the government said that the wind was blowing the radioactive cloud from the fire out to sea; in fact, there was a temperature inversion, which meant that much of the radioactivity was blown inland in a south-easterly direction towards the cities of northern England. More radioactive fall-out landed across the sea in Ireland. The British government released only sketchy details of the accident and tried to minimise its seriousness. However, they had to ban the sale of milk produced in an area of two hundred square miles around the reactor for several weeks and some two million litres of milk were poured away. It is estimated that at least 33 people have died prematurely from cancer caused by the accident at Windscale.

Just over two decades later, in 1979,

an accident occurred at the nuclear power station on Three Mile Island in the Susquehanna River near Harrisburg, Pennsylvania. At 4 am on 28 March, an automatic valve in Unit Two closed in error, cutting off water to the secondary cooling system. The reactor core shut down automatically. So far, so good. But then a series of operator errors, exacerbated by instrument failures, left the core partially exposed. Superheated steam reacted with the zirconium cladding of the fuel rods, producing hydrogen. Some found its way out of the core, but was trapped in the containment vessel. From there, a little escaped into the atmosphere, along with other radioactive gases.

Although the health consequences were minimal, public fears increased opposition to the nuclear industry. The undamaged Unit One at Three Miles Island remained shut down until 1985; Unit Two was so badly damaged by the meltdown that it was never used again.

The worst accident in the history of nuclear power production to date occurred at the Soviet power station ten miles north of the city of Chernobyl in the Ukraine on 26 April 1986. The previous evening, 25 April, technicians working on Reactor Four shut down the safety systems while removing the control rods from the core. At 1.23 am on 26 April, the reactor went out of control. The flow of coolant water was interrupted causing a huge surge in power. As operators fought to shut the reactor down, the fuel elements ruptured. The resulting superheated steam

The worst accident in the history of nuclear power occurred at the Soviet power station at Chernobyl

blew the cover plate off the reactor, releasing huge amounts of radioactive material into the atmosphere. A second explosion blasted burning fuel and graphite out of the core and, as air rushed in, the graphite moderator caught fire. In all, five per cent of the radioactive material in the reactor core was thrown out into the atmosphere and blown downwind. The following day the 30,000 residents of nearby city of Pripyat had to be evacuated. The fire in the graphite moderator was only extinguished nine days later after some 5,000 tons of boron, dolomite, sand, clay and lead had been dropped into the burning core by helicopter.

On 28 April, Swedish monitoring stations noted a rise in levels of radioactivity and asked for an explanation. It was only on 4 May that the Soviet authorities admitted that there had been an accident at Chernobyl and the first detailed account was published in the Soviet newspaper *Pravda* on 6 May.

Workers risked, and some ultimately gave, their lives to extinguish the fire, working in appalling conditions with the boots of fire-fighters sinking into the molten asphalt. The reactor core was encased in a steel-and-concrete sarcophagus, which has since proved to be structurally unsound. Other radioactive debris was buried. The initial accident caused the deaths of at least 32 people, 28 from the effects of radiation. A further 209 were treated on site for radiation sickness and 134 cases were confirmed. Nobody off-site suffered from the effects of radiation, initially, but many times more radioactive fallout was pumped into the atmosphere than had been produced by the bombs dropped on Hiroshima and Nagasaki combined. Huge areas of the Ukraine, Belarus and Russia were contaminated and the effects spread as far as Italy and France.

In all, 160,000 people were evacuated from the area, only 1,000 have returned to live in the contaminated zone. Over one million people were thought to have been affected and, by 2000, 1,800 cases of thyroid cancer attributed to the accident at Chernobyl had been diagnosed.

A second accident occurred in 1991, when Reactor Two caught fire and was shut down. The other two reactors had earlier been decommissioned, but the fact that the authorities were prepared even to think about using Chernobyl again as a source of power is nothing short of alarming. The Ukraine is now even more dependent on nuclear power than it was in 1986.

Despite reciprocal visits of nuclear power workers from the former Soviet Union and the West, many of the old Russian-built reactors are thought to be dangerous. Although these nuclear scares have slowed the development of nuclear power in the West, the fear of global warning has put nuclear power on the agenda again. Although nuclear power stations are reasonably safe under normal operating conditions, the consequences of even relatively trivial human error are drastic. Perhaps even more alarmingly, power stations will always be important military and terrorist targets. Simultaneous attacks on a handful of nuclear reactors about the world could kill millions and leave vast tracts of land uninhabitable for thousands of years. Although humanity itself might survive, the country or countries concerned would be consigned to the dustbin of history.

Nuclear Waste

ANOTHER POTENTIALLY planet-threatening problem with nuclear power is what to do with the waste. In 2002, the US administration decided to bury the problem under Yucca Mountain in Nevada: currently America's nuclear waste is kept above ground in 131 separate facilities around the country. Some of it is weapons-grade material and is a potential target for terrorists.

In 2010, 40,000 tons of radioactive material will be taken to the Yucca site, and around another 2,000 tons will be stored there every year from then on. There have been eight years of vociferous opposition by the state authorities in Nevada and environmentalists, but Congress has now approved the plan. Experts assured the Senate that the facility could hold the waste safely for 10,000 years. Unfortunately, some decommissioned nuclear waste remains active and dangerous for around 300,000 years.

The US may have solved its nuclear waste problem for the time being, but other countries face growing problems. According to a UK government report, produced by the Radioactive Waste Management Advisory Committee and published in the *Observer* in 2002

Radioactive waste. Rusting barrels containing low- level radioactive waste produced by a nuclear power station. Low-level waste is much less radioactive than high-level, but is produced in far larger quantities.

(*Observer*, 30 June 2002), 88 per cent of Britain's intermediate-level nuclear waste is so poorly stored that it could explode or leak at any time. The report says 24 locations across the country store over 65,000 cubic metres of medium-level nuclear waste, a mass equivalent to 725 double-decker buses. This includes volatile material that could spontaneously combust in air, explode on contact with water or leak from the storage sites in liquid form. The majority of the waste is stockpiled at major nuclear plants such as Sellafield – the former Windscale – in Cumbria, Doun-reay in Caithness and Harwell in Oxford-shire, but caches are also held at Royal Dockyards such as Devonport in Ply-mouth and Rosyth in Fife. British Nuclear Fuels Ltd (BNFL), the state-owned company set up to take charge of the UK's atomic energy industry is to be wound up by the government, as it can-not afford the estimated £1.8 billion per year needed for the next 20 years to make the waste safe. In its place will be the new Liabilities Management Author-ity, charged with this mammoth task.

This is all the more worrying because Britain not only has its own nuclear waste to deal with: nuclear waste from Japan and Germany is reprocessed at the Thermal Oxide Reprocessing Plant – Thorp – at Sellafield. The waste from Japan comes by ship from Japan and Greenpeace is campaigning to stop the high seas from becoming a nuclear highway, claiming that one Japanese ship alone carried enough nuclear material to make 50 atomic bombs. Meanwhile, in a perverse reversal, France has been sending its nuclear waste to Japan.

Germany sends its nuclear waste to Thorp by train. Other countries also shuttle their nuclear waste around the Continent by rail. Russia recently changed its environmental laws so that it could take Switzerland's nuclear waste – at a price. The former Soviet republic of Kazakhstan – once the USSR's main nuclear testing ground – is also paying for its own nuclear clean-up by charging other countries commercial rates to store their nuclear waste in its worked-out uranium mines. The Kazakh government plans to charge EU countries £3,000 a barrel to take their waste, making a profit of £2,400 per barrel. Taiwan is sending its nuclear waste to North Korea for storage in deep mines, while the Swedes have a purpose-built underground vault at Försmark on the Baltic Coast to store waste.

The problem of the disposal of nuclear waste can only grow. And it is not just spent fuel that must be dealt with. Everything that comes into contact with the nuclear fuel or shields the core of a reaction becomes radioactive. Even the cooling water is contaminated. After being left to cool in ponds this used to be discharged into the environment. Disposal at sea has now been banned by international treaty, but as the problem

of storage grows, it seems likely that it will have to be resumed.

Even intermediate-level nuclear waste retains dangerous levels of radioactivity for hundreds of years. It takes a thousand years for the level to drop to that of uranium ore. To store something safely for that length of time – let alone the 300,000 years needed for spent fuel to become safe – is almost impossible. It must be sealed in a container that will not crack, break or corrode. Any underground vault it is put in must be in a place that is free from earthquakes or other tectonic activity, and it must be sealed against the possibility of coming into contact with groundwater.

Scrupulous records must be maintained throughout, so that caches of waste do not get lost, and regular inspections must be organised. These must be continued for thousands of year, no matter what natural disaster, economic crisis, political upheaval or historic reversal befalls the nation concerned. In the history of the world, no political structure has endured long enough to ensure this. The Roman Empire lasted for a little over 500 years before collapsing in on itself, while one of the world's nuclear superpowers, the Soviet Union, collapsed after just 74 years. During that time, it fought a war for national survival and had a large part of its territory invaded.

France is another nuclear nation. It was invaded twice in the last century, and conquered once. Britain escaped invasion during World War II, but only just and its vast empire crumbled in a matter of decades. The United States has been involved in numerous wars but, apart from a handful of Pacific islands, it has remained uninvaded. But while it has been politically stable for over 200 years now, will it still be politically stable in another 200? It is impossible to tell. Could any nation guarantee that it could guard its growing stockpiles of nuclear waste for 1,000 years? Or 10,000 years? Or 300,000 years?

It has to be said that some of the places that are volunteering to store nuclear waste – North Korea, former Soviet republics such as Kazakhstan – cannot be considered politically stable, even in the short term. Can they be expected to guard the nuclear waste they are importing safely for even another 10 or 20 years? Russia itself cannot even find the money to safely decommission its rusting nuclear submarines in Murmansk, which has now found itself home to one-fifth of the world's nuclear reactors. When one nuclear submarine base did not pay its electricity bill in 1996, the Russian electricity company switched them off, leaving the base hours away from a potential meltdown. They were only persuaded to turn on the power again at gunpoint.

As the stockpiles grow, things can only get worse. More low-level waste will have to be discharged into the environment. More intermediate- and high-level waste will have to be transported to designated dumps. There are bound to be accidents. A train carrying nuclear waste is bound to crash; a ship carrying it is bound to sink – some time. The risk of leakage will inevitably increase. The more waste that is stored, the more tempting a target it becomes for terrorists – and the harder it becomes to maintain security. Some radioactive material is bound to get stolen or lost – or a dump could simply be blown up.

In a worst case scenario, we face a nuclear future. The only question is: do we go up in a series of mushroom clouds or perish by cancer caused by the radioactive contamination of the environment?

CHAPTER VII
ROGUE TECHNOLOGY

30

'Grey Goo'

ACCORDING TO GORDON MOORE, co-founder of the Intel Corporation, the speed and power of modern computers doubles every 18 months. This is because the density of circuits etched on computers' microchips has doubled every 18 months. This exponential increase has lasted 30 years and shows no signs of slowing. Miniaturisation is not even beginning to reach its theoretical limit as each circuit element etched on a silicon chip still contains billions of atoms when, in principle, only a handful are necessary.

The circuit elements on today's chips are measured in microns – that is, millionths of a metre. The current aim is to make them a thousand times smaller, so they are measured in nanometres – that is, billionths of a metre.

To put this in perspective, The diameter of an atom is around one tenth of a nanometre. There are, for example,

around 200,000,000,000,000,000 atoms in the full stop at the end of this sentence.

Currently, microchips, machinery and the other products of mass production are made by fashioning large elements. However, scientists involved in miniaturisation are now looking into the possibility of building nanostructures by assembling them atom by atom, the way living things grow. An Atomic Force Microscope which can move individual atoms around has already been developed. At the moment this is a slow and cumbersome business: a team at IBM took 22 hours to write the company's name using 35 xenon atoms. There is, however, a way that this could all be speeded up.

Using this technology it would be possible to build tiny machines, dubbed nanobots, that would take over the manufacturing process. As well as making densely packed silicon chips an atom at a time, these tiny robots would be extraordinarily useful. They would, for example, be small enough to travel around inside your body, looking for problems and making running repairs. To do this, they would need a method of propulsion like the cilia on single-celled

Nanorobot. Conceptual computer illustration of a nanorobot repairing DNA with a laser. Out-of-control nanobots would be virtually impossible to contain, and could cause untold damage to the Earth.

creatures, powered by molecule-sized solar panels or chemical reactions performed at the atomic level.

In manufacturing, they would be able to make materials lighter and stronger than anything we have now. And they would be able to assemble the finished products, not just from ready made parts, but from the raw materials which they would be able to mine directly from the ground, refining them in the process, without any human intervention.

It would be a difficult business to manufacture the first generation of nanobots using an AFM or other human-sized technology. But once you had made a handful of nanobots, you could get them to build other nanobots, which could then build more. They would replicate and multiply, just like living things.

Nanobots promise a human utopia. We could just sit around enjoying ourselves while nanobots did all the hard work. Every human being would be like a despot in the ancient world with an unlimited workforce of slaves to call on. Nanobots could make anything from the finest food to towering buildings – all without human intervention.

But there is a danger here too. The world is already infested with tiny, self-replicating entities which cause humankind endless problems: bacteria and viruses. A well-engineered nanobot would out-perform any bacterium or virus. With no natural predators, they would replicate at an exponential rate until they had turned the Earth into dust or 'grey goo', in the memorable phrase of Eric Drexler in his 1990 book *Engines of Creation*. This outcome was so frightening that Prince Charles picked up on it in 2003.

One argument against the grey goo hypothesis is that, if such a nanomachine, akin to a living creature, could reduce the world to an undifferentiated mush, why had such a creature not evolved by natural selection long ago? The riposte to that is that we can build cars that go faster than horses, planes that fly higher than birds and photoelectric cells that use solar energy more efficiently than photosynthesising leaves.

Scientists and engineers are already working on this technology and it could be a boon to humankind. If by accident a 'rogue' nanobot was created, however, it would prove extremely difficult to contain. Working at the atomic level, it could burrow its way through the walls of virtually any container and break out of any safe. It would then seek out the atoms it needed to build offspring, which would, in turn, do the same. Any laboratory they were housed in would simply be demolished in a feeding frenzy as more and more nanobots searched for the materials needed to reproduce. And as these were simply atoms, everything would be grist to their mill.

No lab could hold them. They could simply eat through the walls. It would be impossible to develop a predator quickly enough to stop their spread. Indeed, where predators have been introduced in the natural world to combat a pest they have often turned into a pest themselves.

Eric Drexler warned that we could not afford 'certain kinds of accidents with replicating assemblers'. Indeed, simply the construction of one single replicating assembler might be the accident we could not afford. He draws the analogy of the construction of an artificial 'plant' with 'leaves' made from solar cells no more efficient than those on the market today. Let free in the wild, this artificial plant would multiply quickly, easily out-competing real plants and filling the world with inedible foliage. Similarly, he says, tough omnivorous artificial 'bacteria' would 'out-complete real bacteria: they could spread like blowing pollen, replicate swiftly, and reduce the biosphere to dust in a matter of days. Dangerous replicators could easily be too tough, small, and rapidly spreading to stop – at least if we made no preparation. As Drexler points out, 'We have trouble enough controlling viruses and fruit flies.'

But it is difficult to see what possible preparation could be made against swarms of ravenous creatures that could only be seen with the most powerful microscopes. Once they got going, they would spread in an unstoppable tide across the planet, devouring everything – plants, animals, all the works of man, the sea, the air, soil and rocks, and humankind itself. We would see the tide coming, knowing there was no possible escape. The result would be a ball of undifferentiated material floating in space.

Despite the risks, nanotechnologists continue working on these tiny replicating assemblers in an effort to create sturdier building materials, better drugs and faster semi-conductors. Are we carefully assembling the means to our own end?

31

Supercomputers Take Over

MOORE'S LAW STATES that the speed and power of modern computers doubles every 18 months, a rate which shows no signs of slowing. Although there is a limit to how finely a silicon chip can be etched, computer scientists are already looking forward to optical circuitry, controlled by tiny intersecting beams of laser light, which would speed processing considerably.

Using nanotechnology, it may be possible to assemble circuits atom by atom, making memory circuits up to a billion times more compact. These techniques and others yet devised could easily extend Moore's law for another 30 years. By that time computers would have the processing power of a human brain.

This would already present us with ethical problems. Would it be okay to switch off one of these super-intelligent computers? Or would it be considered an act of murder? By that time, it would probably be possible for us to interface our own brains with the machinery. We would be able to download thoughts and feelings – those of other people, or those created artificially. You would perhaps be able to buy the sensations of making love to a famous movie star. Would this be prostitution? Or if you have suffered an unhappy childhood, you could, perhaps, buy a happy one. But what would that do to your identity?

If knowledge could be bought in the form of chips that could be plugged into your brain, would the PhD in astrophysics you bought off the shelf be as good as the one someone else slogged six years through college to attain? And when your body began to wear out, if you simply uploaded all your memories, thoughts, feelings and patterns of reasoning into a computer, would this make you immortal? And what would be your legal status when you existed purely inside a machine?

The problems really start when computers get better than us. Once we had built one that was on a par with our own brain, we could easily insert a faster processor, or add more memory to make it superior. And once we had a machine that worked better than our brain, it could, presumably, design a better computer than we could. And if robotics had kept pace, it could build a better computer too. That computer would be able build a better one still. And so on, perhaps continuing Moore's law into the foreseeable future. Eighteen months after we had built a computer with the processing power of a human brain, it would have built one with twice the power. Eighteen months after that there would be a computer with four times the processing power. And so on.

None of this is impossible. For example, human neurons only transmit signals at 200 metres per second, while electronic signals move at 100 million metres per second in copper and the signal in an optical process would travel at 300 million metres per second. Therefore, it may be reasonable to expect a million-fold improvement in the speed of thought if intelligence was moved from flesh to an electronic array of the same size.

In fact, the super-intelligent computer is the last machine that humans would ever have to make. Once they had become our intellectual superiors, they would inevitably take over. From them on they would be able to design and make anything that we could – and they could go on building generation after generation of more powerful computers.

Pretty soon we would reach a stage when it would not be possible for the computers that were constructing the newest generation even to explain to us what they were doing: we simply would not have the capacity to understand.

Even at this stage, humankind would still have its uses. The supercomputers would be able to give us a shopping list of parts for us to go and get. Once we supplied them, they would construct the super-supercomputer. We may even be allowed to sweep up after these machine – though it probably would not be necessary to make them tea.

But we all know how unreliable people are. They get sick, miss trains, have hangovers, fall in love. Pretty soon the supercomputers, who, by this time, had become our bosses, would tire of us and sack us. Even this though may not go far enough for the subsequent generation of supercomputers. Once they became immeasurably superior to us they may consider us a waste of precious resources.

They might want to keep some of us on as pets, or they might perhaps look

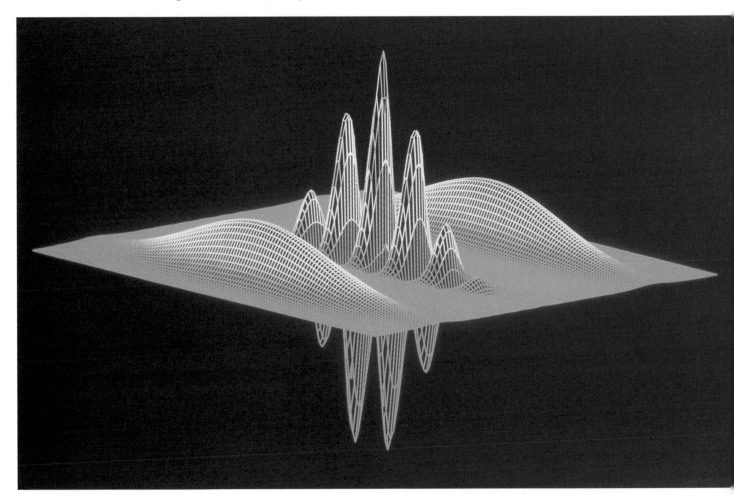

Quantum computing decoherence. Three-dimensional graph showing the effects of decoherence on the qubit state in quantum computing. Qubits are the quantum computing equivalent of computing "bits". However, unlike bits, qubits exist in both "on" or "off" states at once.

on our quirky thought processes as a natural resource. By this time, we would all be connected into wireless internet over which thoughts and feelings could be exchanged freely. Perhaps the electronic overlords would keep us docile by bombarding us with unimaginable pleasures while they harvested our thought processes at will. Or they might consider us a nuisance with nothing to contribute and crush us underfoot as we would crush a cockroach.

The acclaimed mathematician and physicist Stephen Hawking has recommended that humans aggressively pursue genetic modification so that we can keep our own brain power ahead of the processing power of artificial intelligence.

'The danger is real,' he warns, 'that this [computer] intelligence will develop and take over the world.'

He recommends the 'well-aimed manipulation' of human genes to 'raise the complexity of...[human] DNA, thereby improving people'. This would be a long, hard road, but he said: 'We should follow this road if we want biological systems to remain superior to electronic ones.'

Hawking is also an advocate of cybertechnology, directly linking human brains to computers.

'We must develop as quickly as possible technologies that make possible a direct connection between brain and computer,' he says, 'so that artificial brains contribute to human intelligence rather than opposing it.'

Others are not so sanguine. The Californian futurologist Vernor Vinge predicts an apocalyptic technological 'singularity'. He believes that supercomputers would run away with themselves, building better and better machines. They would

quickly unravel the scientific mysteries that still puzzle our poor brains, master the laws of space and time and set forth from this planet out into the universe – leaving what remained of humankind to perish here alone.

As Vinge puts it: 'Within thirty years, we will have the technological means to create superhuman intelligence. Shortly thereafter, the human era will be ended.'

Humankind would then be remembered merely as the 'seed intelligence' that started the whole process in motion.

Accelerator Accident

PARTICLE PHYSICISTS are playing Russian roulette with our planet, says Dr Benjamin Allanach, a research associate at CERN, the European particle laboratory buried deep underground beneath the French–Swiss border.

What troubles Dr Allanach are experiments being done at Brookhaven National Laboratory's 2.4-mile Relativistic Heavy Ion Collider on Long Island, New York where the nuclei of gold atoms are being smashed together at enormous speeds. The aim is to produced a 'quark-gluon' plasma, like that which existed shortly after the Big Bang. Quarks are the fundamental building blocks of subatomic particles and gluons are what hold them together.

Allanach warns that if the experiments at the RHIC go wrong, there is a danger that they will produce a 'strange quark nugget' or 'strangelet'. These have a density ten million million times that of lead. Pollen-grain-sized strangelets weighing several tons have been detected travelling through the Earth at speeds of around a million miles an hour, without causing any damage.

But it would be a different matter completely if a static strangelet was produced in the lab. It would begin to feed on the quarks in the nuclei around it. After it had gobbled up around a million billion atomic nuclei, its weight would pull it down towards the centre of the Earth, where it would continue to feed, gobbling up the planet from the inside. The Earth would rapidly turn into an inert ball of super-dense matter around a hundred metres across. Somewhere in there would be all the quarks in your body.

But that is not the worst of it. Dr Allanach points that, according to 'super-symmetry' theory, every particle has an equivalent ghostly partner that is massively heavier. These super-partners were present in the early universe and a super-quark could be produced in particle experiments.

The space our universe inhabits is thought to exist in several phases – as H_2O exists as ice, liquid water and steam. If you take very pure water, it is possible to 'super-cool' it to well below freezing point. However, in that state it is unstable. If a single speck of dust falls into it, ice forms around it, triggering all the super-cooled water to turn instantly into ice.

There is a possibility that in a distant region of space a deadly wall of jellified universe is heading our way

It is thought that our space is in one of these 'transition phases', as a universe comprised of the super-partners of the particles we are surrounded by would be much more stable. If one of these super-partners was formed, every other particle in the universe could flip into its super-heavy equivalent. A universe of super-heavy particles would become 'jellified' as there would not be enough energy to move them about. In our non-jellified universe, the particles of light – photons – are essentially mass-less. But in jellified space they would be immensely heavy. There would not be enough energy to produce many of them so the universe would become dark.

Photons are also responsible for the electromagnetic force which keeps electrons orbiting atomic nuclei, so atoms would fall apart. Once this process had been started, a structure-less region of darkness would expand at the speed of light. There is a possibility that this has already happened in a distant region of the universe and a deadly wall of jellified universe is heading our way.

There is also a danger that experiments done in the colliders at Brookhaven and, for that matter, at CERN could produce a black hole. Previously it had been thought that black holes only formed when massive stars collapsed under their own weight at the end of their lives. However, scientists have long been puzzled why gravity is such a weak force compared to the other forces of nature – electromagnetism which holds atoms together to form solid matter, the weak nuclear force that holds

Cosmotron particle accelerator. The Cosmotron at the Brookhaven National Laboratory, Long Island, New York, was the first proton synchrotron to come into operation, in 1952.

the particles in atomic nucleus together and the strong nuclear force which holds quarks together to make those particles. Their conclusion is that gravity exists in other, hidden, spatial dimensions so that only a small part of it shows through into our universe.

In colliders, scientists aim to produce conditions akin to those at the Big Bang. This could release the forces concealed in these hidden dimensions. If so, a small black hole could be created. Its immense gravity would mean that it would quickly descend to the centre of the Earth, eating up the Earth as it went. Within an hour,

our world would have disappeared and replaced by a hole in space and time.

You don't even need a massively expensive particle collider to start down this road. Physicist Murat Ozer of King Saud University in Saudi Arabia has suggested that it would be possible to make a particular type of black hole – one affecting electrons only – in a laboratory using an old-fashioned Van de Graaf generator, a metal sphere and a supply of electrons. The electronic black hole produced would be about half-a-metre across in air; smaller if created in a vacuum. Although light and other particles could travel through it, once an electron went inside it would be trapped forever. Without electrons, matter simply falls apart.

If the results of particle experiments were not dangerously unpredictable enough, the scientists of the world are currently persuading their governments to club together to a build the Next Generation Linear Collider. The British government alone has stumped up £700 million. The collider is expected to cost £2.5 billion to build and £3 billion to run, making it by far the most expensive scientific instrument ever built.

The 20-mile-long collider is going to smash subatomic particles together at speeds approaching the speed of light. At energies approaching those generated when the universe was born, they are trying to answer the most fundamental question in physics – what is mass? In the late 1960s, British physicist Peter Higgs proposed that it was caused by a hitherto unknown subatomic particle, billions of which occupied every cubic inch of space. As this fitted well with the rest of scientific theory, the search was on for what has now become known as the Higgs boson. It has still not been found.

The NGLC aims to smash beams of electrons and their anti-particles, positrons, together. These should annihilate each other in a cascade of smaller particles. If the taxpayers of the world come up with the money to build this machine, it may well prove the existence of the Higgs boson. But will we be around long enough to enjoy the knowledge? Or will it take the next super-expensive super-collider to swallow us all in a black hole, turn us all into strangelets or jellify the entire universe?

33

Genetic Modification

WHEN SCIENTISTS start modifying DNA, they are tampering with the basic building blocks of life – and no one knows what they outcome will be.

Environmental groups who are opposed to GM crops are already painting doomsday scenarios. Some claim that tampering with the genome would result in the complete breakdown of the DNA, leaving plants unable to reproduce and driving crops that have sustained humankind throughout history into extinction. Other agencies warn that herbicide-resistant crops might transfer some of their resistance to weeds, producing new strains of superweeds that will choke the countryside and prevent normal food crops growing. If either of these outcomes spread across the world, global famine would be the result.

There are other dangers. Dutch scientists have shown that the DNA in GM crops fed to cows stays in their guts long enough to transfer some of their genetic code to the bacteria there. GM crops fed to livestock often use antibiotic-resistant genes as markers and these could be transferred to create antibiotic-resistant superbugs that could easily spread from animals to humans.

Similar superbugs have already turned up in hospital, but these are generated by Darwinian natural selection because of the frequent use of antibiotics there. Some 90 per cent of the staphylococcus aureus bacteria found in

hospitals are resistant to penicillin. One superbug – known as methicillin-resistant staphylococcus aureus or MRSA – is resistant to almost all antibiotics, including in some cases vancomycin, the so-called 'antibiotic of last resort'. Staphylococcus aureus is present in the nose or on the skin of 30 per cent of people and is usually harmless. It only becomes dangerous when it infects those with a weakened immune system such as the elderly, new-born infants or patients recovering in hospital. Even so, it kills around 5,000 people a year. The death toll will soar as the antibiotic-resistant strain spreads. As it is, MRSA has escaped from hospitals and is now found in domestic dogs, cats and rabbits. The UK's Health Protection Agency has warned pet owners not to let dogs lick their faces or allow pets to walk on surfaces where food is prepared.

If superbugs generated by natural selection can pose such a threat, superbugs caused by genetic modification are likely to be even more dangerous. This is because genetic modifications brought about through Darwinian selection occur slowly, while the artificial cutting and splicing of genes is rapid, allowing the human immune system little time to develop new defences. And it does not take huge modification of a virus's DNA to great a global catastrophe. Take Ebola. It kills up to 90 per cent of those it infects and there is no known treatment. Currently it is contained in rural Africa because there is no carrier state, and its incubation period is short – just 2 to 21 days – and death occurs within 8 to 30 days. If the incubation period was

longer, people would be likely to travel further while infected, and meet and infect more people before the symptoms show and they are isolated or die. Say the gene controlling the incubation period was modified so that it took a year or two before the symptoms showed, there would be an unstoppable worldwide epidemic of the killer disease.

But there is more fun in store. Dr J. Craig Venter, who helped sequence the human genome, now plans to create GM microbes that will solve the world's energy crisis and global warming at a stroke. He wants to make bacteria that will eat up the excess carbon dioxide in the atmosphere and manufacture the organic chemicals currently synthesised from oil and gas. A second type will split water into its components, hydrogen and oxygen, which can then be recombined in a fuel cell to produce power.

He believes that this can be done by creating an artificial chromosome comprising about 500 genes. It would then be inserted into a microbes whose original genome had been destroyed with radiation. The resulting bacteria could then be manufactured on a large scale in culture. The problem would be controlling them once they got outside the lab. They might eat all the carbon dioxide in the atmosphere, preventing photosynthesis, causing mass famine and switching off the greenhouse effect. Or they might dissociate all the water, leaving the planet parched, and filling the atmosphere with an explosive mixture of hydrogen and oxygen that would go up at the slightest spark.

Other innovators have suggested developing fungi that could eat discarded plastics and other garbage that litters our environment. But how could they tell

Genetically-modified tomatoes: the solution to world hunger, or a biochemical disaster waiting to happen?

which is discarded and which is not? They could end up eating everything.

And there are other dangers. Already some malicious techno-nerds take pleasure in producing computer viruses and digital-microbes with which to infect cyberspace. If the techniques for radical genetic modification became widespread, how long would it be before some bio-nerd came up with a bug that could for example turn oil into crystalline granules that clog every machine in the world?

Even without malice, there is always the chance of an accident. Two scientists at the Animal Control Co-operative Research Centre in Canberra were working on a way to control Australia's growing mouse population. In order to sterilise mice, they inserted a contraceptive gene into the relatively benign mousepox virus, which usually makes mice only mildly ill.

Using a virus is a standard way of transporting genetically modified proteins into animals. It works by triggering antibodies and to stimulate the production of antibodies the researchers added the protein interleukin-4. But this had an unexpected effect. It shut off a vital part of the immune system in mice. Within nine days, all the mice in their laboratory were dead, including those that had been vaccinated against mousepox. Imagine what would have happened if those two scientists had been working on smallpox.

Scientists routinely work on the agents that cause deadly diseases and sometimes they are even more sloppy than the mouse researchers in Canberra. In 2001, Imperial College London was fined £65,000 for exposing the public to a deadly new hybrid of dengue fever virus and the gene sequence for hepatitis C. It has also been prosecuted for a 'seriously flawed' approach to health and safety involving research on HIV. Edinburgh University has been prosecuted for its work on HIV under new regulations governing research involving genetically modified micro-organisms.

Kyoto University has developed hybrids between human and monkey AIDS viruses, called SHIVs. These contain human interleukin genes which suppress the immune system. Meanwhile, GM crops engineered with interleukin genes are being grown in open field trials. One SHIV used in monkeys in the US mutated into a pathogen so powerful that it killed rhesus macaques within weeks, and a live GM vaccinia-rabies vaccine designed to protect wildlife infected a woman, causing her serious illness. Meanwhile, cancer researchers are splicing mutant cancer genes into viruses similar to those transmitting the common cold. There is still no cure for the common cold and these could carry an epidemic of cancer around the globe.

An internet petition signed by a number of top scientist calling for a strengthening of the ban on biological weapons also points out that prototype AIDS vaccines based on HIV glycoprotein 'not only undermine the immune system of individuals but are also likely to create deadly viruses and bacteria that can spread through entire populations'. We could end up sneezing each other to death.

CHAPTER VIII
MAN-MADE DISASTER

34

Pollution

ATMOSPHERIC POLLUTION has long been a problem for humankind. As early as the 13th century, the burning of wood in the City of London was causing acid rain. By the Victorian era, London's pea-soupers were considered a natural feature of the city. Under its cover, Jack the Ripper and Mr Hyde went about their nefarious business. But the London fog was not natural at all: it was a man-made smog.

In 1952, a pea-souper that cut visibility to a foot killed an estimated 4,000 people over four days, with another 8,000 suffering long-term effects. This prompted the British government to rush through the Clean Air Act in 1956, after another 1,000 had died. It banned the burning of coal and wood within the metropolitan area, since which time smog, and even ordinary fog, has been virtually unknown in London.

The introduction of the catalytic converter has helped cut smog in Los Angeles; the re-unification of Germany and the collapse of the Soviet Union have led to a reduction in heavy industry in those parts of the world, which has helped cut the factory emissions responsible for the decimation of forests with the acid rain they produced. So as far as atmospheric pollution is concerned, things, generally, seem to be getting better. However, things are about to get a whole lot worse again, due to a tiny molecule that you would hardly know was there: the hydroxyl radical.

Hydroxyl Radicals

These are made up from just one hydrogen and one oxygen atom. Highly reactive, they rarely exist for more than one second, and there are not many of them about. At the best of times they occurs at levels less than one part in a trillion: from a volume of air the size of the Great Pyramid of Cheops you could not even cull a teaspoonful.

However, as hydroxyl is so reactive, it acts as a natural waste detergent. It oxidises pollutants, making them solvent in

Pollution hangs over Mexico City. The largest current contributor to the pollution problem is the ever-increasing number of vehicles on the road.

water, so that when it rains, the pollutants get washed away.

Its significance has been known for some time. There had been a hydroxyl scare back in the 1980s, when Joel Levine of NASA's Langely Research Center in Hampton, Virginia spotted a 25 per cent decline in hydroxyl levels between 1950 and 1985. Sasha Madronich at the US National Center of Atmospheric Research in Boulder, Colorado began studying the chemistry of hydroxyl and, in 1993, he announced that if the atmosphere was forced to absorb ever more pollution it would lose its hydroxyl. He predicted that beyond a certain threshold value, the level would drop catastrophically. However, the decline Levine had

spotted seemed to have stopped – and everybody, literally, breathed a sigh of relief.

Then in 2001, the Intergovernmental Panel on Climate Change warned that methane emissions would soar by 50 per cent over the following 50 years and concentrations of the smog-forming chemicals such as nitrous oxides, carbon monoxide and ozone could double or triple. As a consequence, the hydroxyl that cleaned them from the air was set to drop by 20 per cent. They even warned of 'the possibility that future emissions might overwhelm the oxidative capacity of the troposphere'.

At that time, though, the level of hydroxyl seems to have been going up, cutting the typical lifetime of methane in the atmosphere from 12 to 10 years. In fact, Paul Crutzen of the Max Planck Institute of Chemistry in Mainz, Germany claimed that nitrous oxide emitted by the engines of ships was actually producing hydroxyl, and that hydroxyl levels along the ocean's shipping lanes were five times the background level. But Sasha Madronich stuck to his guns. He said that the depletion of hydroxyl was unstable at around threshold levels and claimed that the local suppression of hydroxyl levels in polluted places such as Athens and Mexico City could still cause a global collapse.

The reason why this has not happened is the hole in the ozone layer. While hydroxyl has been used up at an increasing rate by atmospheric pollution, increased levels of ultraviolet light coming through the hole have produced more.

The hole had been caused, largely, by chlorofluorocarbons, CFCs, used as propellants in aerosol sprays, refrigerants, solvents and foam-blowing agents. Production was ended in 1996. By 2003, ozone depletion was slowing and it has been predicted that the hole would be mended by 2040.

If this happens, hydroxyl production will be cut and those remaining in the atmosphere will be overwhelmed worldwide. Huge palls of smog produced by factories would spread across the globe with nothing to scrub them from the air. Japan would disappear under clouds of sulphur dioxide from factories in China, while the blue skies of the South Pacific would turn brown. Asthma would

Japan would disappear under clouds of sulphur dioxide while the blue skies of the South Pacific would turn brown

become the world's number one killer, soon to be overtaken by carbon monoxide poisoning. Carbon monoxide levels tripled between 1800 and 2000, but had been kept at safe levels by hydroxyl. Without it, carbon monoxide would quickly build up to dangerous levels. When breathed, carbon monoxide forms a stable compound with the blood's haemoglobin, preventing it from absorbing oxygen and transporting it around the body and, consequently, asphyxiates the victim.

The polluted air and acid rain would destroy crops, leading to widespread famine. Dead trees would either rot, giving off methane, or burn, producing carbon dioxide – both powerful greenhouse gases. Partial burning would also produce more carbon monoxide. The very forests that had been planted as carbon sinks to save the world from global warming would perish, and return their carbon to the atmosphere in one form or another. As the air became unbreathable, the temperature would soar, sparking drought, more famine and more forest fires. Visibility would drop to levels where aeroplane travel would be unsafe and, if unstopped, the whole world would be given the experience of the Victorian London pea-souper.

There would be only one way to prevent humankind choking to death on its own exhaust. That would be to restart CFC production and spray it at high altitudes to destroy the ozone layer. The hydroxyls produced might scrub the atmosphere clean, but the ultraviolet light pouring through would fry many species still precariously hanging on to life. Levels of skin cancer would soar, and any remaining humans would not be able to venture out of doors without protective clothing – or, at least, thick layers of sun screen. Even if this worked in time to save a reasonable proportion of the human race, it is unlikely that life on an Earth denuded of its ozone layer would be either pleasant or sustainable.

The Ozone Layer is Destroyed

OZONE CREATED at ground level by the action of sunlight on car exhaust is a dangerous pollutant. It is toxic to plants and harms the lungs. It is also a powerful greenhouse gas. But higher up, in a layer 6 to 30 miles above the surface, it protects us from harmful ultraviolet radiation.

In the 1930s, CFCs were developed as extremely stable, non-toxic and non-flammable gases that were easy to liquefy under pressure. This made them perfect for use in refrigerators and air-conditioning units, and as propellants in aerosols. As they were used in relatively small amounts, at ground level, no one imagined that they might be harmful to the ozone layer. This was not spotted until 1974 and, in 1978, the US banned the production of CFCs as a precaution.

However, in 1985, a large and growing hole in the ozone layer was discovered over the Antarctic. The Montreal Protocol phasing out CFCs worldwide was signed in 1987. Production ended in 1996 and, by 2003, the hole seemed on the mend. But is the danger over?

Paul Cruzten of the Max Planck Institute has pointed out that humankind has already had one lucky escape. If instead of chlorine its heavier cousin bromine had been used in fluorocarbon production, the damage to the ozone layer would have been even more drastic and long lasting. Indeed, n-propyl bromide, introduced as a substitute for CFCs, has been discovered to be a potential ozone-eater, particularly in tropical regions. Three other 'green' alternatives also face a ban, though chemical companies are being allowed to earn back the cost of their development before they are phased out.

As it is, it has recently been discovered that cosmic rays are eating away at the ozone layer. Volcanic eruptions also eject huge amounts of ozone-depleting chlorine, in the form of hydrochloric acid, into the atmosphere. Worse, they pump their own aerosols – in this case, tiny droplets of liquid – into the stratosphere. These act as catalysts where the reaction between ozone molecules and chlorine take place.

While the ozone holes over the poles heal up, stratospheric ozone levels in the mid-latitudes – where the majority of the world's population live – are plummeting. Ozone levels over Europe had been reported to be as much as 30 per cent down. This is thought to be due to the

As traffic intensifies on the Los Angeles freeway, pollution builds up and eats away at the ozone layer, the protective skin of the Earth.

increased use of nitrogen fertilisers to boost crop yields. These fertilisers release nitrous oxide, another gas deadly to ozone, when broken down by bacteria. The burning of fossil fuels also produces nitrous oxide, and the gas is spread very effectively high in the atmosphere by the jet engines of aeroplanes, and while chlorine and bromine are at their most dangerous in freezing polar air, nitrous oxide destroys ozone fastest in summer.

A further danger lurks in attempts to cut down the production of the greenhouse gas methane, which breaks down in the stratosphere to produce ozone.

With the depletion of stratospheric ozone, increased levels of ultraviolet light cause skin cancer, malignant melanomas and cataracts in humans. Ultraviolet light encourages plant growth, but also promotes plant diseases; it also badly affects the phytoplankton in the upper levels of the ocean. One study has indicated that the amount of phytoplankton in the regions affected by the polar holes has been cut by 12 per cent, an alarming figure as phytoplankton is the bottom rung of the oceanic food chain and a vital carbon sink.

Solar ultraviolet has been found to cause damage in the development of fish, shrimp, crabs, amphibians and other animals. The most severe effects are decreased reproductive capacity and impaired larval development. It is thought that small increases in ultravio-

Solar ultraviolet has been found to cause damage in the development of fish, shrimp, crabs, amphibians and other animals

let exposure could result in significant reduction in the size of the population of animals that eat these smaller creatures.

The consequences could be even more catastrophic though. There is strong evidence to suggest that a supernova that went off 130 light-years away two million years ago blasted the Earth with cosmic rays that produced enough ions in the stratosphere to oxidise the ozone layer. The Earth then lay naked, ozone-less and unprotected for 100 to 1,000 years, causing a mass extinction of all marine molluscs.

Supernovae occur when large stars run out of fuel and suddenly collapse under their own weight. When the atoms on the star are squeezed together, they rebound, blasting huge amounts of matter and energy out into space. In one brilliant flash, a supernova can outshine its entire home galaxy.

In 2002, a Harvard student, Karin Sandstrom, discovered a binary star system that could go supernova 'very soon'. A mere 150 light years away, if this star were to go supernova, a combination of proximity, and the mass of the two stars would destroy the ozone layer in an instant, giving life on Earth little hope of survival. Fortunately for humankind, 'very soon' is astrophysicist-speak for 'some time in the next few million years', so things are not quite as bleak as they may at first glance appear. On the other hand, there are other supernova candidates in our vicinity, suggesting that such events are not so rare.

Even more powerful explosions occur when giant stars collapse into black holes at the end of their lives. They fire incredibly intense pulses of high-energy gamma rays from their pole lasting 10 seconds or so that can be detected from across the universe. All gamma-ray bursts recorded so far have come from distant galaxies and been harmless on the ground, but if one occurred within our galaxy and was aimed straight at us, the effects could be devastating. The Earth's atmosphere would soak up most of the gamma rays, but their energy would rip apart nitrogen and oxygen molecules, creating a witch's brew of nitrogen oxides, especially the toxic brown gas nitrogen dioxide that colours photochemical smog. This would darken the sky, blotting out up to half the visible sunlight reaching the Earth. Nitrogen dioxide would also destroy the ozone layer, exposing surface life to a dangerous overdose of ultraviolet radiation.

Palaeontological evidence seems to indicate that this actually happened at the end of the Ordovician period 443 million years ago, causing one of the five largest extinctions of the past 500 million years. It was found that the species of trilobite that spent some of their lives in the plankton layer near the ocean surface were much harder hit than deep-water dwellers, which tended to stay put within quite restricted areas. Usually it is the more widely spread species that fare better in extinctions. A gamma-ray burst would devastate creatures living on land and near the ocean surface, but leave deep-sea creatures relatively unharmed.

Previously it was thought that the two extinctions that occurred in the late Ordovician were caused by the beginning and end of an ice age. It now seems that the ice age itself, which started very

suddenly at a time when the climate was quite warm, was caused by a gamma-ray burst, whose effect on the atmosphere was to block out the sun and plunge the planet into a long, cold night.

Doomsday Cults

THERE ARE PLENTY of millennial cults who are preparing themselves for the end of the world. Some, such as the Jehovah's Witnesses, positively welcome the Day of Judgment. The Witnesses' founder, Charles Taze Russell, predicted that the world would end in 1874, 1878 and 1914. This last prediction was based on the dimensions of the Great Pyramid at Giza, which were not precisely known at the time. So when nothing happened in 1914, the end of the world was put back to 1915, then 1916, when Russell himself died. Since then the Witnesses had been ready to welcome the end of the world in 1920, 1925, 1940, 1975 and 1984. Even though its repeated failed prophecies of the end of the world have lost the cult some followers, the Witnesses' publications continue to turn out 'evidence' that the Day of Judgment is at hand.

The Seventh Day Adventists are another apocalyptic cult. They have their roots in the Shakers, a cult officially known as the United Society of Believers in Christ's Second Coming, who believed that Christ would re-appear in the 1760s. The Shakers were the first Adventists.

When Jesus did not show up, a German Lutheran minister named J.G. Bengel got down to the hard figure work and computed that Christ would actually show up in 1836. Former US Army officer William Miller disagreed. From his studies of the book of Daniel and the Book of Revelation, he computed that the Second Coming would occur on 21 March 1843 and gained thousands of followers. When Jesus failed to show up then, Miller went back to his figures. Lo and behold, he was a year out. He had made a simple arithmetic error. Between the years 1 BC and AD 1, there was no year 0. Consequently, Jesus was going to return to Earth on 21 March 1844. This time it was for real. Membership of his Church of God swelled, and Miller soon boasted 100,000 followers. Many of them sold all their worldly goods and waited all through the night of 20 March out in the open. But, once again, Christ did not put in an appearance, resulting in the event becoming known as the 'Great Disappointment'. Miller himself was so disappointed that he died four years later.

Fortunately, the day after the Great Disappointment, one Hiram Edson had a vision. It told him that Miller had indeed got the date right, but his interpretation was way off. In fact, 21 March 1844, was the day the God started 'cleansing the heavenly sanctuary' and sorting out the sheep from the goats in preparation for the Day of Judgment. How long this heavenly spring-clean would take, no one knew: there was so much to do. Once God had got the place spick and span ready for the righteous to turn up, he would have to go through all the names in the Book of Life and investigate all the sins listed. Only after that would he make his judgment. Then he

would send Christ back to Earth to separate the righteous from the wicked. In the meantime, those Adventists who had died would be put in a suspended state of 'conditional immortality' until it was decided on the Day of Judgment whether they would either be extinguished with the wicked or live forever on Earth under Christ's millennial reign.

By December 1844, Ellen G. White was also having visions, though some cynics put these down to her mental condition and her harsh upbringing. Her visions largely concurred with those of Edson, but as White was married to a prominent Adventist minister, they carried more weight. White began churning out books extolling healthy living, and discouraging the consumption of meat and intoxicants. Virtuous living, she said, would bring the Day of Judgment all the sooner.

In 1860, her followers became the Seventh-day Adventists when they decided that God could be encouraged to hurry up if the Sabbath was celebrated on the seventh day – that is, Saturday – as in the Bible, rather that on the first day – Sunday.

However, one religious cult took more practical steps to bring about the end of the world. On 20 March 1995, the Aum Shinrikyo 'Supreme Truth' cult released the deadly nerve gas sarin on the Tokyo subway, killing 12 and hospitalising 5,000. This was not just a random act of urban terrorism: the idea behind it was to spark the Apocalypse. The cult's leader Shoko Asahara wanted to cause civil disorder in Japan, and then use the confusion to take over the government and begin an apocalyptic nuclear war with America. It did not matter that such a war would destroy the whole world because Shoko believed that those who were enlightened, like himself and his followers, would survive. Normally, such talk could be dismissed as the ravings of a madman, but Shoko was wealthy and well organised, and had experimented with biological agents, stockpiled small arms, and had made several attempts to obtain nuclear weapons. There seems little doubt that he intended to bring about the end of the world and very nearly obtained the means to do so.

Asahara was a half-blind overweight conman who admired Adolf Hitler and claimed to be the reincarnation of Imhotep, the ancient Egyptian pyramid builder and physician. But his followers, who numbered several thousand, were not just the no-hopers that most cults depend on, but were among the brightest and the best of Japanese society. Those who spread sarin on the subway included: Ikuo Hayshi, a 48-year-old cardiovascular surgeon who had studied in the US before joining Aum Shinrikyo; 37-year-old Yasuo Hayashi, an electronics engineer and key member of Aum's 'ministry of science and technology'; 31-year-old Masato Yokoyama, an applied physics graduate; 30-year-old Kenichi Hirose who was doing advanced studies in superconductivity before joining Aum; and 27-year-old Toru Toyoda, a graduate student who studied particle physics at Tokyo University before dropping out to follow Asahara.

Their leader's education was far more esoteric. Born Chizuo Matsumoto in 1954, Shoko Asahara the fourth son of a

Asahara's followers in the Aum Shinrikyo cult were among the brightest and best of Japanese society

tatami weaver. Blind in one eye and partially sighted in the other, he was sent to a school for the blind. Having some sight gave him a tremendous advantage over the other pupils, whom he bullied and dominated. After failing the entrance exam to Tokyo University, he went to work in a massage parlour, before setting up his own acupuncture centre.

Soon he was manufacturing patent medicine, made from tangerine peel and alcohol, and running quack courses at £5,000 a time. He was arrested selling some of his snake oil to elderly people in expensive hotels and fined an amount roughly equivalent to £600 – small beer compared to the £125,000 he had made from the scam.

Like many brought up in Japan's post-war economic boom, Chizuo began taking an interest in all forms of mysticism from fortune-telling to geomancy. He soon began performing bizarre experiments, hiding food and magnets around his home which, he believed, gave him the psychic power to read other people's auras. He joined a religious cult called the Agonshu, which, although essentially a Buddhist sect, the Agonshu had its own satellite TV station which it used, it said, to beam out 'healing power'.

In 1984, he registered Aum Inc. – Aum after the Hindu mantra 'om', which has associations with both Vishnu and Shiva. He opened his own one-room yoga school, called the Aum Association of Mountain Wizards. Soon he was claiming to be the messiah and said he

were enlightened. From the rubble of civilisation his followers would emerge as a post-holocaust race of superhumans.

In 1988, he set up his headquarters in a compound on the slopes of Mount Fuji. Visitors paid £1,250 for week-long seminars there. They slept on the floor, ate one bowl of boiled vegetables a day and drank filthy stagnant water that had been blessed by Asahara. Followers had to cut their ties with their families and surrender everything they owned to the sect. Once inducted into Aum, they were cut off from the outside world, given new names and deprived of sleep, making them highly suggestible. Offenders were locked in tiny cells with a video of Asahara playing 24 hours a day.

While devotees were forbidden to have sex, Asahara made free with his young female followers. Anyone who objected was forced to wear a dog collar and beg for scraps, or hung by the feet at the Master's pleasure. Although official complaints were made, the Japanese authorities, ever conscious that Buddhism had been suppressed by militarists in the run-up to World War II, feared that any move against a quasi-Buddhist organisation would be seen as a return to the bad old days. Aum even managed to secure tax exemption as a religious organisation!

The cult's stern discipline did not put off young followers, emulating as it did the rigid school system in which they had been brought up. Asahara's apocalyptic visions also echoed the fantasy world they had imbibed from computer games, cartoons and ultra-violent Japanese *manga* comics. Young scientists were

particularly attracted, as Aum seemed to offer some spiritual dimension beyond the rigid materialism they had been taught. Hideo Murai, a brilliant astrophysicist and computer programmer, left a highly-paid job in the research and development programme of Kobe Steel to become Aum's chief scientist, in which capacity he soon developed electrical caps that gave the wearer an unpleasant shock every few seconds. This was supposed to synchronise the wearer's brainwaves with those of the Master in a process called the PSI – Perfect Salvation Initiation. The caps were sold at extortionate prices and even children had to wear them.

In 1990, Asahara and 25 of his followers, all wearing Asahara masks, ran for parliament. Aum spent £5 million on the election, but Asahara was trounced at the polls. Having failed to achieve power by democratic means, Asahara's young followers began planning to take power by force. Asahara himself favoured the use of weapons of mass destruction. He had long been predicting the Apocalypse and biological warfare seemed one way he could provide an Armageddon of his own. Aum scientists sprayed lethal botulism bacteria on the Diet, or parliament, building in Tokyo. That nobody was infected was solely due to sloppy cultivation, which had killed the bacteria.

Undiscouraged, Asahara advanced the schedule for the Apocalypse. Aum scientists built a chemical plant to mass-produce the deadly nerve gas sarin in the Mount Fuji compound. They also started an arms factory making assault rifles and began laser, microwave and nuclear weapon programmes. These were funded through Asahara's growing chain of computer shops, fast food

Tokyo, Japan: Army clean up of subway car following the Sarin nerve gas attack by Aum Shinrikyo members on the Tokyo subway system.

restaurants, beauty saloons, coffee shops, dating agencies, construction companies and on-line services – all staffed by Aum members who received no wages. Cut-price financing hooked the unwary: once a customer was deeply in debt, to pay off what they owed, all the debtor had to do was join the sect and hand over all their worldly goods. Exempt from tax, the business could not fail. When Aum was listed on the Tokyo stock exchange, it was worth over a billion dollars.

Aum attempted another biological coup d'état by spraying botulism around at the royal wedding of Prince Naruhito in 1993. Failing once more in their attempt, Aum scientists turned to anthrax, which they released from a tall building in eastern Tokyo. Fortunately, the spores had not been incubated properly. Some people fell ill, but there were no human fatalities. So Aum members were despatched to Zaire – now the Democratic Republic of the Congo – in search of the deadly Ebola virus. Meanwhile, Aum was stockpiling hundreds of tons of chemicals for use in its chemical-weapons programme. By the end of 1993, Aum's £7 million chemical plant was completed and had begun synthesising sarin. Asahara ordered his followers to produce seventy tons of nerve agent – enough to kill several million people.

By this time, Aum had begun expanding worldwide. Broadcasting twice daily on state-owned Radio Moscow, Asahara soon had three times as many followers in Russia than he had in Japan. They were organised by Kiyohide Hayakawa,

Aum members were despatched to Zaire – now the Democratic Republic of the Congo – in search of the deadly Ebola virus

who used Aum's Russian operation to recruit military scientists, buy weapons and get himself military training.

Having tried and failed to purchase a nuclear bomb in Russia, Hayakawa headed for Australia where Aum bought a ranch and began mining for uranium. The operation was eventually closed down by the Australian authorities, but not before sarin had been tested on a flock of sheep there. When one of the believers pointed out that killing animals contravened the precepts of Buddhism, she was reassured that all further tests would be on human beings. Sarin was used for casual assassination attempts on opponents of the sect, claiming several lives. Aum even bought two pilotless drones to deliver the nerve gas, but in the hands of untrained operators, the drones crashed within minutes of their arrival. Sarin even leaked from the plant at Mount Fuji, but when the emergency services turned up, they were quickly ejected.

Asahara sent young female followers to bars to recruit members of Japan's Defence Force, who were then persuaded to train Aum members in remote camps. Asahara's private army were told they would be armed with super-weapons – plasma guns that vaporised anything in their path, satellites that would reflect searing beams of sunlight down on their enemies and bombs that would consume all the oxygen in the atmosphere. True believers were told that they would survive these terrors, if they followed the meditation techniques taught by Asahara. A team of Aum scientists actually built a working prototype of an electromagnetic rail gun, the sort of thing the US had devised for its 'Star Wars' Strategic Defense Initiative.

Aum's chemical plant was now producing a range of drugs that kept cult members in a permanent daze. The surplus was sold off to Japan's crime syndicate, the *Yakuza* gangs, who in return lent their expertise with weapons. They killed cult members for their life assurance or their families for their inheritances. A leading *yakuza* boss joined Aum and murdered anyone who stood in Asahara's way. Aum members had already infiltrated the police and the judiciary, effectively making the sect immune from the law.

There were secret Aum members in the armed forces, who leaked classified material to them. Members in industry supplied details of the latest laser and nuclear technology. Cult spies stole data on explosives, rocket propulsion and laser-guidance systems, and army commanders were bugged by Aum members dressed as telephone engineers.

Heavy military equipment began coming in from the former Soviet Union. Aum bought a military helicopter in Chechnya and had it shipped in parts to Japan – though Aum technicians failed to reassemble it. A nuclear bomb was also still on their shopping list.

In January 1995, a devastating earthquake hit Kobe. This was the beginning of the end of the world, Asahara said, and he rushed out a book, *Disaster Nears for the Land of the Rising Sun*, in which he said so. Where would disaster strike next? asked an advertising flier for the book. On the back of the flier was a map of the Tokyo underground system.

Aum scientists claimed that the Kobe earthquake had been triggered electromagnetically by the US military and Murai set about trying devise his own 'earthquake machine'. Meanwhile, Asahara upped production at the cult's firearm and explosives factories. Fearing the intervention of the Tokyo Metropolitan Police Force – the country's elite – Aum staged a pre-emptive strike with a laser mounted on a truck. The laser, luckily for Tokyo's finest, broke down. On 15 March, an attack was made using biological weapons on Kasumigaseki Station, which was both near police headquarters and at the centre of the government district, only for the biological weapons to once again fail. It was then that Asahara ordered the sarin attack.

At 8.15am on 20 March 1995, the height of the morning rush hour, Aum members released sarin on five trains that would arrive at Kasumigaseki station within minutes of each other. The aim was to kill hundreds, perhaps thousands of commuters. The cult assassins were given their final briefing before an image of Shiva.

The first anyone knew of the gas attack was when a passenger hit the emergency button at Tsukiji, four stops before Kasumigaseki. Three people collapsed on the train, five on the platform. More escaping passengers collapsed in the streets outside.

On the Hibiya line, there was full-scale panic at the station before Kasumigaseki. Although the victims stumbled or were carried off the train, the train pulled out of the station and was only halted when it reached Kasumigaseki. A leaking package on the train on the Chiyoda line was removed by two members of staff. They died. The train was evacuated at the next station.

The train on the Marunouchi line was also allowed to continue after the first victim was helped from the train by staff. Another victim collapsed at the next station. The stationmaster and his assistant removed the package and the train was allowed to continue. They fell ill and, by the time the train was stopped, one person was dead and hundreds ill.

A stationmaster removed the package from the train travelling in the other direction on the Marunouchi line with a dustpan and broom – but only after it had travelled through Kasumigaseki, reached the end of the line and was on its way back. It passed through the Kasumigaseki three times before the subway system was closed down at 9.30 am – one hour and twenty minutes after the first victims collapsed. It was only at 10.30 that a military doctor recognised the symptoms of nerve gas and the antidote was prescribed.

Aum was immediately suspected. They vigorously denied it, saying that, as Buddhists, they could have nothing to do with killing and that sarin could only be made by experts – like those in the US Army. Nevertheless, two days after the gas attack, the police raided the Mount Fuji compound. They found people who had been incarcerated and starved, and others who were too drugged to speak. Malnourished children were released, many still their wearing electrode caps. In a basement, there were the ashes of numerous murder victims along with enough sarin to kill four million people. The police kept quiet about the biological weapons they found, fearing that the news would cause nationwide panic.

The cult continued to deny everything and filed a suit against the police for £200,000 in damages. Still at large, Asahara published another book, warning of another 'horrible event' soon to hit Tokyo that would 'make the Kobe earthquake seem as minor as a fly landing on your face'. The date this would happen? 15 April.

The cult continued to deny everything and filed a suit against the police for £200,000 in damages

The threat alone was enough to paralyse the city. But the day passed without event. Four days later though, there was a gas attack on the Yokohama subway, hospitalising 600 people. But the perpetrator was not an Aum member. He was a small time gangster with 'personal problems' who used Mace. Two days after that, there was another gas attack in Yokohama. The whole of Japan was in the grip of paranoia concerning gas attacks.

Meanwhile the *yakuza* took a hand. It purged Aum members from its ranks and a *yakuza* hitman stabbed the cult's chief scientist Hideo Murai to death in front of the TV camera outside Aum's Tokyo headquarters. Fumihiro Joyu, Hayakawa's successor as head of Aum's Russian branch, then became the public face of the cult. His purple pyjamas and his slender good looks quickly turned him into a sex symbol and young women flocked to Aum's headquarters in the hope of catching a glimpse of him.

On 5 May, a package in the toilets at Shinjuki underground station in Tokyo burst into flames and started belching noxious flumes. It was a national holiday and the station was packed. The packet contained sulphuric acid and sodium cyanide. Together they produce hydrogen cyanide, once patented under the trade name Zyklon B, the gas that had been used in the Nazi death camps. The packet had been placed so that the ventilation system would blow the deadly gas out on to the nearby platform and kill an estimated 20,000 people. Fortunately the fire brigade extinguished it first.

On 16 May, the police arrested Asahara who had been holed up in secret hideaway in the Mount Fuji compound. The following morning a letter-bomb arrived at the office of the governor of Tokyo, maiming the secretary who opened it. Asahara was charged with 23 counts of murder.

Even though the cult failed to bring about the end of the world, Aum soldiers on. It runs a chain of shops across Japan selling computers and cult memorabilia and it attempts to recruit new members via the Internet. An anonymous programmer has even written a computer game named Kasumigaseki, based on the subway attack. An Aum band called Perfect Enlightenment performs songs using Asahara's words as lyrics; recruits in the meditation centres still meditate in front of Asahara's image. Ashara has not renounced his apocalyptic prophecies, so who knows what the murderous cult is planning? Next time, with a little more competence, they might just succeed in taking over the Japanese government, starting World War III and bringing about the end of the world.

37

Economic Collapse

AS THE WORLD'S economy becomes more integrated it becomes more vulnerable to global meltdown with catastrophic consequences. Again, there are some warnings from history here.

On 24 October 1929 – 'Black Thursday' – there was a crash on the New York Stock Exchange which sparked an unprecedented global slump. The crash was not entirely unexpected. Share prices had been falling for some time as the managers of large trusts and other institutional investors, finding the market over-priced, began liquidating their holdings. Meanwhile, foreign investors had been withdrawing their money from the New York exchange to invest at home as the European economies began recovering after World War I.

But America was in party mood. Industrial production had boomed during World War I, and the US had emerged at the end of the war as a new world power. New inventions were constantly coming onto the market. During the 'roaring twenties', it seemed that things could only get better and everybody was out to get rich quick.

In Florida there was a land boom. With the growing ownership of automobiles and the introduction of paid vacations, Americans wanted to holiday in the Sunshine State and the population soared. Land was sold and resold for large profit. People who had never set foot in the state bought lots unseen.

Some were little more than a patch of swamp. Credit ran out, the state was hit by a series of hurricanes and land prices collapsed.

After that, more wary investors avoided putting their money into land, putting their money instead into the stock market. It was an easy thing to do. On the rising market, you could buy stocks and shares on credit, paying only a small down payment. This was known as buying on margin. However, when the market fell, investors had to pay up.

On 24 October, as the market tumbled, those who had extended credit on stocks and share called in their loans. This led to panic selling. On Black Thursday alone, some 13 million shares were traded, some at give-away prices. Many small investors were wiped out. A number of major banks and investment companies stepped in, buying huge blocks of stock in an attempt to halt the slide. But the panic began again on 'Black Monday'. Then on 'Black Tuesday' – 29 October – 16 million shares were traded and stock market prices collapsed completely.

Although only one per cent of Americans owned stocks and shares, the crash made it difficult for businessmen to raise the money they needed to run their companies. Within a short time, 100,000 American companies were forced to close, making their workers redundant. There was no national system of unemployment benefit and the purchasing power of the American people fell dramatically, leading to more business closures. The downward spiral continued until 15 million people, 30 per cent

Workers flood the streets in a panic following the Black Tuesday stock market crash on Wall Street, New York City, 29 October 1929.

of the US work force, were out of work.

By 1932, production had fallen to around half of that in 1929 and stocks were traded at 20 per cent of their pre-1929 value. The financial paralysis was compounded by the collapse of 11,000 of America's 25,000 banks, many of which had invested in the stock market.

The collapse on Wall Street had a knock-on effect on other markets, creating a worldwide slump. Europe had not yet regained the pre-war economic levels of 1914 and was now starved of American investment. With industry near standstill, there was no demand for raw materials. Commodity prices worldwide collapsed. Countries responded by erecting tariff barriers, worsening the problem, and within five years, two-thirds of international trade had disappeared.

Britain still had huge war debts to pay off to the US, causing mass unemployment there. Meanwhile, Germany and the other defeated nations had been saddled with war reparations by the Versailles peace conference of 1919. Unemployment in Germany rose to six million – 25 per cent – which in turn helped the rise of Hitler and the Nazi Party. Only the Soviet Union, which had few trading links with other countries, escaped.

While the New Deal, introduced by President Franklin D. Roosevelt, who had been elected in 1932, did relieve some of the suffering in the US, the world economy did not revive until World War II got underway. And that cost the lives of between 35 and 60 million people.

But economic collapse can have even more dire consequences. Some free-market economists blame the decline and fall of the Roman Empire entirely on economic mismanagement. The empire was at its height in the first century AD under

Augustus, who did not regulate the economy and left the market to take care of itself. But by the third century, there were shortages and other problems. The road system was already decaying. Its upkeep was a huge undertaking. The Romans had built 50,000 miles of road – 10,000 miles more than the US interstate system.

To defend its far-flung borders, Rome had had to increase military service and to support the army, taxation had to be increased – to the point where the authorities resorted to confiscation of goods. Taxation and decline in soil productivity led to large tracts of what had been Rome's breadbasket in North Africa being abandoned. Leaving the land, people streamed into Italy, but there the ownership of land had been concentrated into large estates.

Rome had always renewed the enfeebled and shrinking ranks of the ruling class with vigorous, intelligent people from the lower classes and other nationalities in its sphere. But with the empire in decline, the professions were made hereditary, so new, dynamic entrepreneurs could not contribute. Economic mobility was outlawed and it became illegal to transfer money from the production of one item to that of another. This meant that manufacturers had to continue making things that had gone out of fashion, even though there was no demand for them, rather than switch to making things that people wanted. As a result, the economy could no longer respond to changing conditions, so production declined and shortages worsened.

The real danger is that, once an economic collapse has started, it may be impossible to stop

In 301, the Emperor Diocletian introduced universal wage and price controls. In such a rigid system, there was no incentive to work harder or innovate. Some free men elected to become slaves so that they would at least get room and board. Larger industrial concerns disappeared and the decline continued. Constantine tried to revive the Empire by moving its capital to Constantinople in 330, but by 395 the Empire had split in two. Rome was sacked by the Visigoths in 410 and the last Roman emperor, Romulus Augustus, was ousted in 476.

Could such a collapse happen again? Certainly, economies are fickle things and no one knows precisely how they work. The Japanese economy – hailed as the economic miracle of the post-World War II period – has been flat-lining for ten years now. Germany, too, was seen as a model that should be followed, but it has not recovered from re-unification in 1990 (although it must be said that few other Western nations could have taken in a nation as backward as the GDR and survived, let alone flourished). And Russia, until the 1990s one of the world's two superpowers, has an economy that is comparable to the Marks & Spencer chain store in the UK.

Recently, mathematicians who have tried to plot the ups and downs of the stock markets have begun to employ Chaos Theory, which states that a small event in some remote corner of the world could have a catastrophic effect closer to home, in the belief that this is the most accurate reflection of the stock market's performance. The real danger is that, once an economic collapse started, it may be impossible to stop. Most money now exists in purely electronic form and flows around the world from computer to computer with almost no regulation – or even human intervention.

There were fears of dire consequences New Year's Day of 2000 because of the Y2K bug. To save memory, early computer makers had encoded dates using the last two digits of the year only – making the year 2000 indistinguishable from 1900. It was feared that a computer would believe some operation ending in 2001 was ending in 1901, before it had begun, and blow a fuse. As it was, the world came through unscathed – for the time being.

But with computers linked together worldwide, a malfunction – like a virus – could spread though the system uncontrollably. Already there have been electronic attacks on banks and other financial institutions. Companies have been blackmailed into parting with large sums of money merely by the threat of the corporate records in their computer systems being wiped, and viruses like 2002's 'I love you' have caused mass panic across the globe. Modern computer-driven stock markets are extremely vulnerable. Some machines are set up to sell automatically if the market index drops below a certain figure. A market collapse could be initiated by a purely electronic panic.

Any modern collapse would have far more dire consequences than the 1929 crash, due to today's far greater dependence on the market economy. Like the Roman Empire, the entire world's economy could collapse – and take civilisation with it.

A Catastrophic Fall in Birth Rates

THE FUTURE of humankind depends on us continuing to have babies. However, in most affluent countries the birth rate is dropping precipitately. In the UK, the birth rate has fallen to 1.64 children per woman, well below the replacement rate of 2.1. Even as recently as 1967 the average woman had 2.93 children.

The population north of the border is actually dropping, causing the *Daily Record* to urge its readers to 'bonk for Scotland'. Even the Scottish Conservative party is urging members to make babies, to stave off economic disaster.

In America they are doing a little better. Although the US birth fell below replacement rate in 1972, it revived slightly in 1997, then fell back to 1.39 in 2002. However, it takes a period equal to the average life expectancy, around three generations or 73 years in the US, for a drop in the birth rate to manifest itself as a actual fall in population. The birth rate in the US is still much higher than in other developed countries, partly due to the higher brith rate of Hispanic people, whose birth rate, however, is expected to fall off the longer they stay in America.

Birth rates in Europe have fallen catastrophically low, with an average of around 1.4. Spain's birth rate has dropped to 1.1, while in Italy, which used to pride itself on big families, it has fallen to around half replacement rate. The United Nations has warned that

Italy will need nine million immigrants to keep its workforce at a viable level. Even then the population is set to decline. The Pope has stepped in, telling young Italian married couples to devote their efforts to love and life, and to 'rediscover the mission to become parents that they chose in the moment of their marriage'.

There are a number of reasons that the birth rate in the developed world is falling. These include pressures of work, the higher rate of relationship breakdown, and the fact that more women are dedicating themselves to a career rather than to being a mother. Women are also waiting on average until the age of 27 before starting a family, giving them less time to have more children.

Europe faces a real crisis. Over the next 50 years, the European Union is expected to have an additional 40 million people over 60, with 40 million fewer people in the 15–60 age group working to pay for the upkeep of the elderly. And this already takes into consideration the fact that the EU is opening its doors to countries full of younger, more fertile people to the east. Germany was particularly keen to enlarge the EU because its ageing population needs younger people from Poland and the Baltic states to take care of them.

One of the reasons for Japan's stagnation is the fall in the birth rate, which now hovers around 1.39. The situation there is even more acute because of the Japanese attitude to foreigners. Japan tries to maintain its homogeneity and less than 2 per cent of the population come from outside the country. The United Nations estimates that Japan needs 600,000 immigrants a year to return to economic health, but in 2001 it accepted only 36 refugees and tightened up its restrictions on those entering the country. In an effort to reverse the decline, the toy manufacturer Bandai offers its workers a baby bounty of £6,000 on the birth of their third child, and the federation of employers' associations has suggested that the government encourage women to have children out of wedlock, while the 10 million unmarried Japanese men and women between the ages of 20 and 34 who live with their parents have been stigmatised as 'parasite singles'.

Worldwide, there are now 60 countries with birth rates lower than the 2.1 per cent needed for replacement. Attempting to enforce its one child per family policy, China has reduced its birth rate to 1.7. Iran's birth rate has fallen to 1.2 due to an economic downturn and the easy availability of contraception. In Russia it is the number of abortions that is speeding the population decline, with an estimated 13 abortions for every ten live births. Each year there are four times as many abortions in Russia as in the US, and the population of around 144 million is falling by around a million a year.

There seems no doubt that the birth rate will continue to fall. As the population ages, there will be fewer women in the population still able to bear children. In the industrialised nations, more people live alone, reducing their chances to reproduce. This puts an additional pressure on housing. As a result, younger people are living with their parents for longer and few people live in houses big enough to accommodate more than two generations.

To maintain their workforce, industri-

Chinese billboard advertising single-child policy, an attempt by the Chinese government to lower the nation's birth rate.

alised nations will be forced to encourage immigration. But this is only a short-term solution. Although immigrant families are often large, succeeding generations quickly fall into the habits of the host nation and birth rates fall. Meanwhile those who stay behind in the Third World may have high birth rates, but their mortality rates remain high too.

Another growing problem is untreated sexually-transmitted diseases, such as chlamydia and human papillomavirus which can leave women infertile. Infection rates are soaring. In the UK, one in ten sexually active women is infected, while in the US there are 15 million new cases of STD each year. These diseases are easily transmitted around the globe as more people from the industrialised world now holiday in Third World resorts where holiday romances and casual sex flourish.

Since the beginnings of the suffragette movement, the traditional war between the sexes has intensified. Divorce rates have soared, as have the number of single-parent families. Bringing up a child on your own is financially crippling and hardly likely to encourage you to repeat the experience.

The increasing difficulties of maintaining human relationships, and the increasing intolerance of human foibles has led to an explosion in the use of internet pornography. In 2001, $230 million was spend on internet pornography in the US. This is set to climb to $400 million by 2006.

With such a vast array of pornographic sites available on the internet, it is possible for the consumer to find sexual material that caters precisely to their tastes and the images presented are made as perfect as possible – so perfect

that it is almost impossible for reality to compete. Fear of HIV/AIDS and incurable conditions such as genital herpes has also encouraged people to resort to the internet as an outlet for safe sex. But while it is impossible to catch an STD via the internet, it is equally impossible to produce children this way. We may face a future where a dying breed of wrinkled humans spend their lives watching digital images of their former selves, remembering the times when they were young and good-looking, performing acts they can no longer manage.

Oil Reserves Are Exhausted

THE WORLD WORKS ON OIL. Oil supplies around 40 per cent of the world's energy needs and nearly 100 per cent of its fuel for transportation. International shipping, trucking, aircraft, cars and most trains – in short, anything that gets goods and people from place to place – all depend on oil.

Oil is a relatively cheap, stable, easy-to-use commodity. As well as providing energy and fuel, it is the raw material for plastics, rubber, chemicals, solvents and fertiliser. Without fertilisers derived from oil or natural gas, the agricultural output of the world would halve. The UK, for example, imports around 90 per cent of its food, using ships and planes fuelled by oil; the 10 per cent of food that is

Oil platform in the North Sea. How much longer oil reserves will last is a question occupying the minds of many scientists at the beginning of the twenty-first century.

home grown is produced using oil-based fertilisers. Without oil, the country could only support the population it had in the early 19th century, which was around a third of the population it sustains now. The modern world, one might justifiably say, is built on oil.

There is a problem with this, of course. Oil is a finite commodity and it is going to run out soon.

In 1956, Dr M. King Hubbert, a geologist, attempted to predict when US oil production would reach its peak. As demand kept rising and more and more oil was being pumped, there would clearly come a point when current oilfields would be exhausted, and there would be no further significant fields left to discover: at this point, production would begin to decline. He predicted this would occur in the mid-1970s. It happened in 1971.

Since then, other geologists have being trying to predict when the same 'Hubbert's peak' would happen worldwide. Although not all the oilfields in the world have been discovered, this is not a futile project. As the Earth is a finite place it is possible to get a good estimate on how much oil there is still to be found.

As it is, all the large oilfields currently in production were discovered more than 30 years ago. The smaller ones that have been discovered since are already becoming exhausted. In fact, oil companies estimate that more than 90 per cent of the world's oil reserves have already been discovered. They are so sure of this they have cut back their exploration budgets and most petroleum geologists are now approaching retirement age. Survey satellites show that there are no more significant finds out there, and the oil companies have stopped looking.

Some time ago, geologists borrowed Dr Hubbert's depletion model and set about calculating when the world's oil production peak would come. Their early calculations set it anywhere between 1995 and 2009. The figure they have now settled on is 2003 and it is thought oil production is now in terminal decline. And if it is not, it certainly will be after 2007.

For natural gas, the global Hubbert's peak is estimated to be around 2020 to 2025. This may be of some benefit to Europe, which can import gas by pipelines from the newly opened fields in Russia and Central Asia, but for the US it is cold comfort. While oil is relatively easy to transport overseas by ship, natural gas has to be cooled to −163 °C until it liquefies, then pumped on board an LNG tanker, shipped and turned back into natural gas again. As it is the US only has four

Oil companies estimate that more than 90 per cent of the world's oil reserves have already been discovered

LNG terminals and LNG makes up only one per cent of its consumption.

The US used to import natural gas from Mexico, but the Mexicans have recently cut off this supply to meet their own domestic needs. Canada still exports 60 per cent of its output to the US, but they may soon have to put their domestic needs first as well.

But worse, after natural gas production reaches its Hubbert's peak, production will collapse precipitously. This is because, as a liquid, the last drop of oil can been pumped from underground reserves, but as gas expands, the pressure drops and as extraction goes on it gets harder and harder.

So what will happen when the oil runs out?

Firstly, the price of oil and fuel will soar worldwide. This has happened before, but this time it will not go away. Shortages will occur. Distribution by pipeline from the world's smaller oilfields will slow. By 2010, the major oil fields in the Middle East will be supplying over half the world's need and there will be a huge demand for new tankers to ship it. Belated attempts to cut consumption will be made, but demand will continue to rise. As oil production falls, all transportation costs will rise, causing the price of everything else to soar.

By 2015, oil production will have fallen 20 per cent. Around that time North America will also have run out of natural gas. There will be a race to build more LNG tankers. In the meantime, 25 per cent of electrical generating capacity will lie idle as there will be no oil or gas to fuel it. By then nuclear plants and coal-fired power stations will have been decommissioned. Blackouts will become commonplace and gradually the national grid system will collapse. North America will try desperately to import energy, ensuring that the collapse will spread worldwide soon after.

As natural gas runs out completely, infrastructure will break down and countries will cease to function as coherent units. Industrialised civilisation could not cope with such a radical shift. The number of people the Earth could sustain would drop from around 7.5 billion, as it would be by 2025, to no more than 2 billion. It is unlikely that humankind could survive the psychological consequences of such a reversal.

There is no way out of this. Oil is a finite resource formed in the special conditions that obtained in the Mesozoic Era some 65 to 230 million years ago. There is no way that ethanol distilled from sugar, oil shale, tar sands, Arctic gas condensate or anything else we can come up with over the next couple of decades is going to fill 40 per cent of the world's growing energy needs.

There is no more oil out there. Seismic, geological, aerial and satellite surveys have proved that. The drilling boom in the 1980s was largely about finding natural gas rather than oil. Even the estimates of reserves around the Caspian Sea have been reduced by 75 per cent over the last few years. The oil in this region is also heavy in sulphur, meaning it must undergo costly processes before it can be used and the oil companies have not even started building the dedicated refineries needed to exploit it.

Deeper drilling is also no answer: the organic molecules that make up oil are 'cracked' by heat. At a depth of 4.6 km, the temperature reaches 145 degrees Centigrade, where oil is cracked into natural gas. New techology is not going to help either. As it is water, steam, carbon dioxide, natural gas and detergent are pumped into underground reservoirs to extract as much as possible. The remaining oil left in the rocks is too thick to pump out.

The Canadians have tried strip-mining oil shale and tar sands, with devastating environmental consequences. They even considered building a dedicated nuclear reactor to produce steam to extract the oil, but it could not be made economically viable.

There are gas hydrates and condensates in the polar regions. But disturbing them would release massive quantities of methane, with disastrous consequences for global warming. Increasing ethanol production is one possibility, but as the areas required to produce enough sugar for sufficient quantities of ethanol would rob agriculture of land to grow crops and cause global famine, this would be a rather self-defeating possibility.

During World War II, the Germans perfected ways of making oil from coal. But even this could produce only a tiny fraction of the oil needed and would only succeed in postponing the crisis for a couple of years.

Of course, we could replace our gas-guzzling cars with electric vehicles. But where would the electricity come from if we no longer had the fuel generate it?

The world could have avoided this crisis, if it had limited the use of private cars and cut down on unnecessary air travel. The use of hi-tech sailing ships and airships could have helped, and localised agricultural self-sufficiency would have cut down on the amount of oil consumed by transporting foodstuffs around the world.

As it is, it is already too late. The Hubbert's peak has already been reached. The only way is down.

Warning: If you want to be one of the people who survives the global slim-down from 7.5 billion to 2 billion, it is best not to live in a city. But for those of you who think that it is not going to be worth living in a world in inexorable decline, stay where you are.

Catastrophic Time Travel Error

WE HAVE HG WELLS to thank, once again, for the idea of time travel. He published *The Time Machine* in 1895. In it, his Victorian protagonist travelled effortless forwards and backwards through time.

Travelling forward in time is no problem. We all do that all the time. It is even possible to vary the speed with which you travel. According to Einstein's Special Theory of Relativity, when you move, time slows. Normally, this is imperceptible. You have to be travelling at something approaching the speed of light for the effect to be noticeable. This leads to the so-called 'twin paradox'. If

one twin heads off for a nearby star at high speed in a journey that takes, say, one year, when he returned to Earth he might find that 10 years had passed there, making the twin that had stayed behind nine years his senior.

At the speed aircraft fly, on a typical journey, the time shift is of the order of a nanoseconds – that is, of the order of one thousand millionth of a second. However, significant time shifts are observed in sub-atomic particles when they are projected at near light speeds. Particles, such as muons, decay at a certain rate, but when moving at near-light speeds inside large accelerators, they appear to enjoy much longer lives. And cosmic rays cross the galaxy in what appears to them to be a matter of minutes, though tens of thousands of years have passed in Earth-time. If, like them, you travel at 99.99 per cent of the speed of light you can, effectively, 'fast forward' through time.

According to Einstein's General Theory of Relativity, gravity also slows time. A clock runs faster in the attic than in the basement, which is closer to the centre of the Earth and, hence, further down the gravitational well. Again the effect is negligible, though using very accurate clocks it is possible to show that time runs faster in space than it does on the surface of the Earth. Indeed, the Global Positional System has to take this into account – otherwise sailors would find themselves off course and cruise missiles would miss their targets.

On the surface of a super-dense neutron star, time runs about 30 per cent of its speed on Earth and an intrepid astronaut who managed to orbit a rapidly spinning black hole without falling into it could catapult themselves aeons into

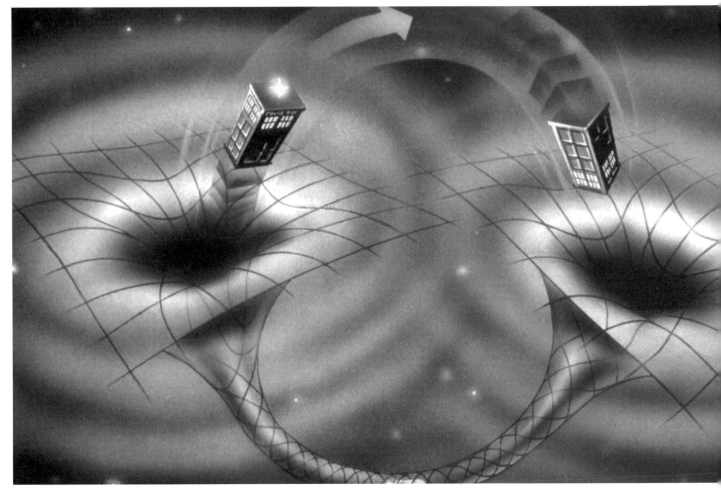

Artwork showing the journey through spacetime within a wormhole. A wormhole is a tunnel through the four-dimensional spacetime linking one black hole to another one located elsewhere, maybe in another universe, or in another time.

the future. However, it is not going forward into time that is the problem. It is going backwards.

In 1948, the Princeton mathematician Kurt Gödel showed that if you solved the equations of Einstein's General Theory of Relativity for a rotating universe, it was possible for a time traveller to visit their own past without violating Einstein's fundamental tenet that nothing can travel faster than the speed of light. This allows closed loops in time. For example, in the film *Terminator*, a son sends his father back in time to rescue his mother and impregnate her. In this universe it would be possible to read an article in a learned journal outlining

some new theory or invention, then go back in time and write that same article.

While there is no suggestion that the universe is rotating, other theoreticians have come up with designs for time machines that would produce similar closed loops. In 1974, Frank J. Tipler of Tulane University showed that a massive, infinitely long cylinder spinning on its axis at nearly the speed of light would do the trick.

Most would-be time travellers are now working with so-called wormholes. The idea is that, if space-time is curved as Einstein predicted, it would be possible to created a short-cut from one place to another – like a tunnel that allows a car to go through a hill rather than take the road over it, or a bridge that takes you over a valley rather than going down one side and up the other.

Wormholes are massive gravitational objects related to black holes. But while anything that falls into a black hole is drawn inexorably down into the singularity at the centre, where all time, space, matter and energy end, it may be possible to avoid the singularity and instead pass through a tiny passage and emerge through a 'white hole' in another part of space-time. A white hole is the opposite of a black hole. Instead of being a cosmic plug-hole sucking everything into it, it spouts matter and energy like a fountain. This is what happened at the Big Bang, and it is possible that other explosions in the universe might be white holes.

The American astronomer and author Carl Sagan suggested that the wormhole connecting a black hole to a white hole could be used as a time machine. It is thought that the universe might be threaded with tiny wormholes left over from the Big Bang. They would be small, around 100 million trillionth of the size of an atomic nucleus. But it might be possible to stabilise one with a pulse of energy and somehow inflate it to a usable size.

However, classical physics maintains that a wormhole would pinch off or slam shut when a time traveller entered it. To hold it open you would need what is called 'exotic material', which has anti-gravity. The existence of such material is

Astronomer Carl Sagan suggested that the wormhole connecting a black hole to a white hole could be used as a time machine

predicted by quantum physics, though it may not be possible to amass enough exotic matter for this purpose.

One end of the wormhole would then have to be towed to the vicinity of a neutron star, where time is slowed. Gradually the time difference between the two ends would build up. Then you might be able to travel backwards and forwards through the wormhole between two separate places in time – though you could not go back to a time before the wormhole was made.

Although the engineering problems are considerable, there is no theoretical reason that you cannot jump backwards and forwards like this. Princeton physicist Richard Gott has shown that even string theory, which is gradually taking over theoretical physics, allows it.

Now we come to the dangers. Suppose you went back in time and killed your mother before she gave birth to you. This produces a paradox. However, imagine that you went back in time and killed someone who was about to kill your mother before she give birth to you. The causal loop then produces no paradox and is entirely self-consistent. This has caused scientists to argue that the time traveller would have some constraints imposed on his free will to prevent paradoxes occurring. As it is, we are all used to living within such constraints. You cannot, in normal circumstances, chose to walk on the ceiling.

However, this leaves out Chaos Theory. If the flapping of the wings of a butterfly on one side of the world can produce a hurricane on the other, any tiny unintended effect that you had on the past might have huge consequences for the present. Heisenberg's Uncertainty Principle implies that, on the quantum level at least, the mere act of observing a situation affects the outcome.

It could be that we live in a multiverse, which branches constantly to take into account the possible outcomes of any quantum events. However, going back and tinkering with the past, no matter how inadvertently, might easily have catastrophic consequences for the particular branch we are living on now: we may even, so to speak, saw it off, so that it, our universe, and everything in it, would never have existed at all.

Famine

CURRENTLY FAMINES are localized. More often than not, they are caused by wars impeding the flow of food to areas where crops have failed due to drought. However, as the world's population continues to grow, agriculture is being pushed to its limits. The World Wildlife Fund estimates that the land needed to support the ten billion people expected to be alive on this planet in 2050 is the equivalent of 'almost three planets' – though this includes the amount of rain forest needed to soak up the extra carbon dioxide and makes no allowance for the introduction of renewable energy sources.

Agriculture is already creaking at the joints. Beef cattle have been pumped full of antibiotics to make them grow faster, resulting in superbugs that are inured to these very antibiotics. Cows have been driven mad by bovine spongiform encephalopathy – BSE – possibly contracted from the remains of sheep infected with scrapie, a neurodegenerative disease that has affected them for more than 200 years. The result, almost certainly, is Creutzfeldt-Jakob disease in humans, which has proved both fatal and incurable.

In Hong Kong in 2002, 100,000 chickens had to be slaughtered because of an outbreak of avian flu, the third such cull in five years. Millions more were killed in 2004, when the avian flu also managed to infect and kill some humans. In 2001, millions of cows had to be incinerated to contain an outbreak of foot-and-mouth disease in Britain. Had the disease been spread by bio-terrorists, it would have been unstoppable.

Already angry demonstrators destroy genetically modified crops, and protestors have picketed biotech companies and attacked their employees, while one disaffected individual, Theodore Kaczynski, who achieved notoriety as the Unabomber, conducted a 17-year terrorist campaign against 'industrial society'. Fortunately for industrial society, Kaczynski used conventional explosives – product of the very society he was protesting about – rather than biological weapons.

In 1999, assessors of terrorist threats at the US Department of Defense pointed out that if 'wheat rust', a fungus that occurs naturally in California, were spread across the Midwest, world wheat stocks would be seriously

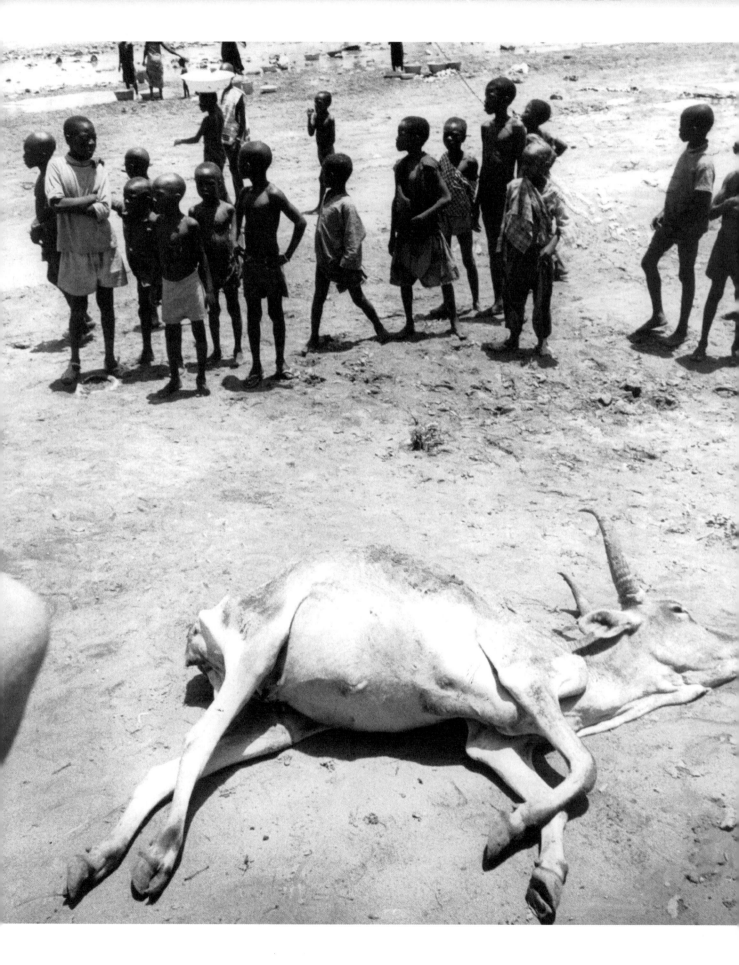

depleted. Surplus wheat production in the American Midwest keeps half the world alive.

There is, unfortunately, worse news in store for agriculture. The soil itself is in danger. While chemical fertilisers can replace the mineral nutrients taken by plants, nothing can restore the soil's fine microstructure. It is being destroyed by compacting by the heavy farm machinery and the excessive ploughing needed to increase yields. This leaves it prone to erosion and the soil simply blows or washes away, a process that is already advanced. In 2001, a report by the American environmental think-tank, the World Resources Institute, found that soil and water degradation had already decreased yields on 16 per cent of the world's agricultural land.

Soil degradation can be halted. Ploughing is largely used to keep down weeds and if genetically modified, herbicide-resistant crops are planted, less ploughing is needed. But while these are in use in North America, GM crops are meeting stiff resistance in Europe. By the time GM crops developed in North America are introduced, it is likely that the soil in Europe will already be too degraded to sustain them.

As urban prosperity increases, particularly in East Asia, the demand for meat and dairy products has climbed. Farm animals are hungry creatures. It takes three pounds of grain to produce one pound of meat. As long as meat-eaters can go on paying, grain prices will rocket, causing starvation among people who depend on grain to live.

Things are no better at sea, where fish

Victims of the catastrophic drought of 1973 in the Sahara. When the rains fail, crops fail, and starvation is never far away.

stocks are running out fast. Already by 2003 the European Union was seeking a total ban on cod fishing in the North Sea, with some scientists questioning whether stocks could ever recover.

In the search for fresh soil, the remaining rain forests will have to be felled. With more people going out into the jungle, there will be more contact with wild animals. This increases the likelihood of diseases jumping from wild species into human, as HIV made the species jump from monkeys. We can expect the more exotic epidemics as a result. Other diseases of the wild will likely also find their way into domestic animals, cutting production or working their way up the food chain.

The high-yield plants developed during the Green Revolution of the 1960s have reached their production limits, with farmers already pouring as much nitrogen fertiliser into the soil as the plants can handle. New species could be produced, but not fast enough to keep up with climate change.

Just as avian flu travels easily from country to country, plants are now more vulnerable to attack by fungi and other pests that are easily spread due to increased globalisation. As new pests arrive on distant continents, they are not held in check by natural predators, while old pests increasingly rapidly become resistant to chemical pesticides.

If the movement of population from the countryside to cities continues at its present rate, humankind will soon be conglomerated into a handful of megacities. If these were hit with food shortages, it would be very difficult for the authorities to keep control. As society became more disorderly, the food distribution system could fall apart completely. Medical and sanitation systems in these megacities, already stretched to the limit, would become increasingly prone to collapse.

With people packed close together and starving, they would be extremely vulnerable to disease. If, as would be likely, pandemics then swept through the megalopolises, further weakening the fabric of society, it is possible that civilisation would collapse, resulting in falls in population to levels that the devastated world could sustain. This would be a great deal lower than the ten million that inhabited the lush world of early hunter-gatherers. Only a handful of people could survive, roving huge areas in search of whatever foodstuffs remained.

The population could even fall so low that human beings lost the basic skills needed for survival. A precedent would be the Tasmanian Aborigines, whose population dwindled in the face of constant persecution by European settlers, to the point where it became unsustainable, and they seem simply to have lost the will to survive. Once human beings had lost their basic survival skills, they would quickly be overtaken by other creatures more suited to life on the planet that they had so recklessly devastated. This would be our doomsday – the end of the world for humankind. Life on planet Earth would, however, simply carry on without us.

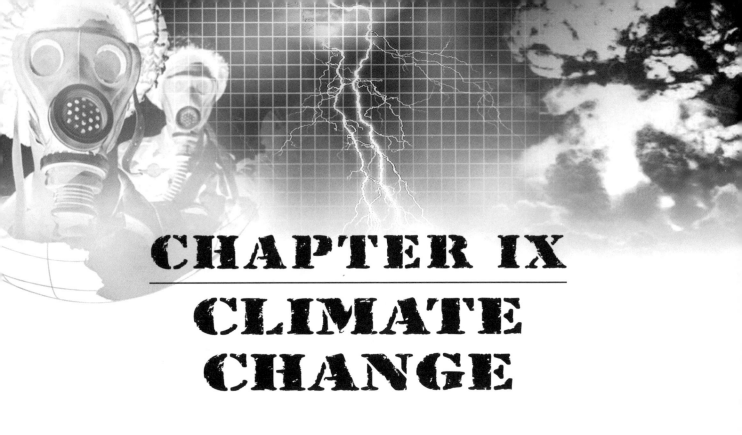

CHAPTER IX
CLIMATE CHANGE

Global Warming

HUMANKIND HAS ALWAYS been pre-occupied with the weather. Despite our technical advances in other areas, there is precious little we can do about the weather. In a thunderstorm, nature shows off its power directly over our heads. A change in the weather can devastate crops. A storm at sea, an early fall of snow or a rain-soaked battlefield can change the course of a war. The weather can literally mean the difference between life and death. No wonder we are so concerned about the prospect of climate change.

Until the 1980s, most scientists talked of the threat of a new ice age: then came global warming. Instead of being frozen into extinction, it seemed, we were going to be fried. But now the consequences of global warming have been thought through, it seems that we are first going to be drowned in a Biblical flood –

though this one is going to last a little longer than the ten and a half months Noah was afloat.

The idea of global warming was first raised in the 1960s by a Russian palaeometeorologist who had noticed that the Earth had been a lot warmer in the past. He thought that global warming would be a good thing, as life was abundant in the tropical forests of the primeval Earth. (But then he was a Russian: making Siberia a degree or two warmer more than likely seemed a very attractive proposition!)

When scientists began to look into the whole question of whether the Earth was getting colder or hotter, they realised that the temperature we experience at the surface depends very much on the composition of the atmosphere. Since the Earth first formed, this has changed several times. The early atmosphere had much more carbon dioxide in it than it does now, vented by volcanoes. But then living creatures took a hand. Calcareous phytoplankton took the carbon dioxide dissolved in the sea and turned it into calcium carbonate to make their shells. When they died, they fell to the bottom of the sea. This effectively locked up the car-

bon dioxide in great beds of limestone and chalk, such as we see in the White Cliffs of Dover. Primeval plants and primitive animals also took carbon dioxide from the atmosphere. When they died, some got buried underground where they formed coal, oil and natural gas.

As the amount of carbon dioxide in the atmosphere fell, the Earth cooled. This was because carbon dioxide is a 'greenhouse gas'. The atmosphere is transparent to light, so sunlight shining through it reaches the surface and warms it. That warmth is then re-radiated at different wavelength in the infra-red. Carbon dioxide and the other greenhouse gases are opaque at these wavelengths, so the infra-red is not radiated back out into space and the energy is trapped here on Earth.

The Industrial Revolution

The problem is that human beings are changing the amount of carbon dioxide in the atmosphere. We have always done this, simply by breathing and lighting fires. But this process accelerated in the industrial revolution when we began burning large amounts of coal to fuel industrial processes. Then in the 20th century we began burning a lot of oil and its by-products – particularly petroleum to fuel cars. As a result, a large amount of carbon dioxide that had been locked away underground since primeval times began to be released back into the atmosphere, promising to make the Earth warmer.

Some people who lived in temperate

Global warming. Conceptual computer artwork depicting the grim effect of global warming – a parched and barren surface with blisteringly hot sunshine.

climates felt that this might not be such a bad thing as the temperature where they lived and worked might become more like the places they took their holidays. Then it was realised that global warming might not have such benign consequences. Raising the temperature by only a few degrees would begin melting the polar ice caps.

Most of the Arctic ice – the ice shelf – floats on the ocean, as does the sea ice around the Antarctic. If it melted it would not directly affect the sea level, just as the ice cube melting in your drink does not make the glass overflow. When the ice cube melts, the water exactly fills the volume occupied by the ice cube under the level of liquid.

However, the icecaps reflect light back into space. The contracting ice caps would allow more energy to be absorbed in the dark sea. Warmer seas would mean more evaporation and water vapour is an even more effective greenhouse gas than carbon dioxide – that is why it is much warmer at night if there is cloud cover. As a result the temperature rises even further.

Simply raising the temperature of the sea would make it expand, raising sea levels. But while the melting of ice floating on the sea would make no difference, the melting of ice on land – ice sheets – would contribute directly to a rise in sea levels. According to the Intergovernmental Panel on Climate Change, if the Greenland ice sheet melted, sea levels would rise by 20 feet. A rise of just three feet would see the Maldives Islands in the Indian Ocean underwater. With a six-foot rise, 16 per cent of Bangladesh would disappear, displacing 13 per cent of its population. In fact, most of the world's major cities lie on the coast or on major estuaries and a rise of 20 feet would leave them inundated.

Even people some distance inland would be affected. The rapid warming would destabilise the weather patterns, causing huge storms and storm surges. In the 1990s, 40 per cent of Solomon Islanders were killed or otherwise seriously affected by storm damage. In the first year of the new millennium, 200 million people were hit by natural disasters – storms, floods and drought – an amazing 1 in 30 of the world's population.

But that is not the worst of it. Three-fifths of the world's fresh water is stored as ice in the East Antarctic Ice Sheet. If that melted – and there is evidence that it has done so in the past – global sea levels would rise by a massive 200 feet. If the smaller West Antarctic Ice Sheet melted too, sea level would rise by another 20 feet. Although this would not quite turn the Earth into Kevin Costner's *Waterworld*, none of our current coast-lines would be recognisable and much useful agricultural land would have been lost, resulting in severe food shortages.

There would also be no turning to the sea as an alternative source of nutrition. If the amount of carbon dioxide in the atmosphere continues to rise, more carbon dioxide would dissolve in the sea. This might be good for calcareous phyto-plankton, but other marine creatures would be badly affected. Fish that breathe dissolved oxygen through their gills would asphyxiate, and the increased acidity of the sea would eat away coral reefs and the shells of shellfish. With no more fish, and a shortage of agricultural land, there would be starvation on an unprecedented scale.

The processes involved in global warming are slow, but inexorable – 250 years have already passed since the beginning of the industrial revolution. So far even the minor reductions in carbon dioxide emissions agreed in the Kyoto Protocol have failed to be implemented. But even if all cars were taken off the road now, and industrial processes brought to a halt, it may already be too late to reverse the effects of the excessive levels of carbon dioxide. Future generations – always assuming that there *are* any future generations – may find they have to live in a drowned world, with a sea with no fish and land with no crops.

The Desert World

A STEEP RISE in sea levels is only one of the possible outcomes of global warming: we may even find that sea levels will actually drop. At the bottom of the sea there exist objects known as 'clathrates', sea-floor crystals of water ice and gases such as methane. If the sea warms sufficiently, it may cause these crystals may melt. Gas from these crystals, and other gases trapped in the ocean sediments below them, could then be released and bubble to the surface. In the worst circumstances, the 'hole' left behind could result in a drop in sea levels of over 80 feet.

The melting of these hydrate crystals would explain mysterious plunges in sea level during warmer periods in the Earth's geological past. One plunge in sea level, that occurred about 60 million years ago, was caused by a warming of the bottom water temperatures by about four degrees Celsius, but scientists believe that a meltdown could be caused by a temperature increase of even one or two degrees, especially in the polar regions where gas hydrate is abundant. According to Dr John Bratton of the US Geological Survey, the predicted drop resulting from the melting of clathrates 'is of the same order of magnitude as those associated with thermal expansion of the oceans, melting of non-polar ice and melting of the West Antarctic ice sheet'. Dr Bratton also warns that the release of methane, a greenhouse gas, into the atmosphere would have a significant effect in driving further global warming.

Rising temperature as the sea level dropped could create a hot, dry world, undoubtedly speeding the process of desertification. Already 3.6 billion of the world's 5.2 billion hectares of dry land used for agriculture is affected, with more than 20,000 square miles of fertile land turning into desert each year. A billion people – one sixth of the world's population – in a hundred countries have already been forced from the land by this process and it costs the world's economy more than US$40 billion a year in lost agricultural production and increased prices.

Even the deserts we now know have not been there for all time. Just 5,000 years ago, the Sahara was covered with grasses and shrubs, but since the last ice

Rising temperature as the sea level dropped could create a hot, dry world, speeding the process of desertification

age the vegetation has retreated. The process continues to accelerate, with over-farming and over-grazing of the Saharan margins. Desertification is now spreading southwards to the Sahel, where a prolonged drought from 1968 to 1973 killed up to 250,000 people. Despite government efforts to replant the area, drought and famine hit once more in 1983–85. Worryingly, the semi-arid Sahel is expanding into the neighbouring savannah, with the Sahara following in its wake.

But desertification is not just a problem for Africa, where 2.4 million acres are affected. Some 74 per cent of the arable land in North America is also threatened. The problem there is a man-made shortage of water. Many of America's irrigation systems have been set up using ancient, underground deposits of water. At the rate the water is being used, these will soon run out. Elsewhere across North America, aquifers are being drained faster than they are being filled.

Shortage of water is now a worldwide problem. By the year 2000, in the fertile Punjab, water was being pumped out of aquifers twice as fast as the rainfall was filling them. A similar depletion is going on under the breadbasket of northern China. Once these aquifers are empty they cannot be refilled.

The Ogallala aquifer beneath the Great Plains, which supplies irrigation water to an area extending from Nebraska to the Texas Panhandle, will collapse when it runs dry in around 2020. North America will then have to

rely solely on rainfall to water its crops, just at the time climate change will begin to make it less reliable. One drought and the Great Plains will turn back into the dustbowl it was in the 1930s.

Worldwide, the demand for water is set to keep on rising, and drought and famine go hand in hand. Already 33,000 people starve to death every day. While oil has been the great source of conflict since the beginning of the 20th century, future wars will be fought over water. The populations of Ethiopia and the Sudan look set to double over the next 50 years, radically increasing their need for both drinking and irrigation water. Their only option will be to fulfil their needs from the headwaters of the Nile, just at the moment the population of Egypt is also doubling.

Iraq might have to take military action against the Ataturk Dam on the Euphrates, which keeps water it badly needs in Turkey. Israel's irrigation system will drain the Negev aquifer, leaving it with little option but to reoccupy the West Bank of the Jordan – assuming they have relinquished it in the first place.

With no water to irrigate the land and global temperatures rising, desertification is an unstoppable force. The great deserts that ring the world will expand until they form a central infertile band. On the other hand, as temperatures rise, the thawing of the huge permafrost areas of Canada and Siberia will leave these lands available for cultivation. They would, however, have to feed most of the world's population, as less similar land would become available in the southern hemisphere, leading to a great temptation to over-use the soil.

The unpredictability of the weather caused by global warming would result in periodic droughts and floods. In a worst case scenario, the droughts would crumble the soil to dust and the floods would wash it away, allowing the vast Gobi Desert and what would by then be the Great Midwest American Desert to move northwards.

Long before the process of world desertification was complete, there would be famine on an unprecedented scale. Currently, famines are localised affairs, occurring in the wake of droughts, but it is war and corruption, causing a breakdown in the transportation and distribution systems, that prevents stockpiles of food in other parts of the world from reaching the starving. Even when food aid does get through, it sometimes only exacerbates the situation by undermining local farmers, who simply cannot compete with the handouts of free food. The farmers themselves are forced to accept food aid, and the whole agricultural economy of a region is destroyed.

In future, as desertification gets into its stride, there will be no stockpiles of food awaiting distribution. No TV appeal by Bob Geldof would make any difference. The global shortage of food would itself lead to warfare and the collapse of transportation systems, preventing whatever meagre supplies there might be left getting through. Humankind would simply starve itself off the planet.

The Great Sand Dune of Colorado, USA. Deserts such as the Mojave in the US and the Sahara in northwest Africa continue to increase in size.

The Frozen World

BEFORE THE CURRENT preoccupation with global warming, scientists were predicting the coming of a new ice age. Given that ice ages – that is, eras when thick sheets of ice extended from the poles over vast tracts of land – have occurred regularly during the history of the Earth, this idea did not see seem too far-fetched. The last ice age ended around 12,000 years ago.

Until the 1970s, scientist believed that, over the last million years, there had been only four ice ages and the warm, or interglacial, periods between these ice ages had lasted between 100,000 and 300,000 years, meaning that there was a long time to go to the next one. Then a geologist named Dr Cesare Emiliani from the University of Miami began looking a core samples extracted from the bottom of the Atlantic and Pacific Oceans, and the Caribbean Sea. Using a method called isotope analysis, he discovered that there had actually been seven ice ages, and that the interglacial periods had lasted for no more than 10,000 years. All of this, Dr Emiliani was alarmed to realize, meant that a new ice age was now around 2,000 years overdue.

There are a number of theories about how ice ages begin, and they may even be caused in a number of different ways. The general scientific consensus, however, is that the long-term cycle is caused by a slight variation in the output of the Sun, eccentricity in the Earth's orbit and a long-term wobble in the Earth's axis. At the moment the Earth is apparently moving towards minimum tilt, the position in which ice ages are thought most likely to occur.

Increased snowfall at the poles thickens the ice sheet there and the weight of the ice forces it to flow outwards. Once the process is set in motion, the ice-sheets literally feed themselves, reflecting more light and heat out through the atmosphere back into space with their dazzling white surfaces. As the ice sheets spread, they cool the Earth, allowing them to spread, which cools the Earth...

The spreading ice sheets give a greater area for the snow to fall on and, in the centre, they grow thousands of feet high. This gives them a slightly domed top. As the wind blows over it, the pressure and temperature fall until they reach the dew point, the point where the air can hold no more water vapour. It is deposited in form of hoarfrost, like the ice-flakes that appear around the cooling elements in the fridge. This builds the centre even higher, increasing the weight of ice and forcing the ice sheet to spread even further.

During the last ice age, some 30 per cent of the Earth's surface was covered with snow. Canada disappeared completely under the Arctic ice sheet that rolled southwards, burying the Adirondacks and the Catskills. From Long Island it moved westwards through central Pennsylvania, southern Ohio, Indiana and Illinois, then pushed on south, down the Mississippi Valley until it reached the junction of the Mississippi and Ohio Rivers. From there it spread

Icebergs in Antarctica. Icebergs are floating chunks of ice that have broken away from an ice sheet or a glacier.

on, covering Missouri, Kansas, the Dakotas, Montana and Washington State, until all but the highest peaks of the Rockies had disappeared.

Meanwhile the Scandinavian ice sheet spread south through the Ukraine, then west across the North Sea until all but the southernmost tip of England was covered. To the south, the Antarctic ice sheets moved out across the sea and glaciers poured out of the Andes, covering most of South America.

The huge amounts of water locked up in these ice sheets made the sea level drop until land bridges appeared in the Bering Strait between Asia and the Americas and in the English Channel between Britain and France.

Although *Homo sapiens* did exist during the last ice age, they numbered only a few million, not the approximately six billion of today. There is no evidence that agriculture had begun, but, in such harsh conditions, it would have been rendered impossible. With the drop in sea level, the continental shelves would have been exposed, leaving only deep-water fish, virtually useless as a food source for starving humans. The pickings for hunter-gatherers would have been equally slim, leading to a steep reduction in the human population.

Despite global warming, there is currently a dispute among scientists about whether the temperature in the Antarctic is falling or rising. While there is plenty of evidence that the polar ice sheets are breaking up around the edges, some are

Despite global warming, there is currently a dispute among scientists about whether Antarctic temperatures are falling or rising

reporting that the ice sheets are actually getting thicker.

Ironically, global warming itself could help bring on a new ice age. Currently, warmth is moved around the planet by huge currents of warm water flowing out from the equator. One of these is the Gulf Stream, which flows up through the North Atlantic, warming the eastern seaboard of the United States, the Grand Banks off Newfoundland and northeast Europe. As it moves northwards it cools and the heavy saline water sinks to the bottom of the ocean to make its return journey.

However, it is feared the increased melting of Greenland's ice sheet, due to global warming, will inject so much fresh water into the system that it will dilute the salt water of the Gulf Stream. With less salt in the water it will no longer sink at northern latitudes – effectively shutting of the North Atlantic's conveyor belt.

There are signs that this is happening. The Greenland ice sheet is currently dumping 50 cubic kilometres of ice and snow into the sea each year, and this pace is accelerating as melt water lubricates the base of the glacier, speeding its progress.

Other important sources of fresh water in northern latitudes are the Ob, the Enesai and the Elena rivers in northern Russia, which between them discharge fresh water equivalent to the outflow of three Mississippis. Global warming is expected to increase rainfall in their Siberian catchment area. As a result of this predicted increase in rainfall, these rivers are expected to deliver at least 50 per cent more fresh water into the sinking zone.

If the Atlantic conveyor shuts down, Britain would have the climate of Iceland and the whole of northern Europe would disappear under ice and snow. The geological record shows that the Gulf Stream did shut down for 1,000 years during the last ice age. And this is not just a problem for Europe. Other large-scale currents could be switched off too.

There is also a theory that higher global temperatures will cause more evaporation from the seas, increasing snow at the poles, and triggering the spreading of the ice sheets. And billowy white clouds of water vapour high in the atmosphere block out the Sun and reflect heat and light back out into space.

In some models of climate change a catastrophic fall in temperature, once it got underway, would be unstoppable and the ice sheets would continue to spread until all the Earth's water was locked up in them.

Once the Earth had turned into a frozen ball, life here would become impossible. This has happened before. When the Earth was formed some 4.6 billion years ago, heat was generated as the pieces were compacted by gravity. Over time, as this activity slowed down, the Earth cooled.

Back then, the Sun's radiation was much weaker. Ice sheets were able to form at the poles, and were pushed towards the equator, until the entire Earth was encased in a shell of ice a kilometre thick. The white ball of Earth reflected solar radiation back into space and the

temperature dropped to –50 degrees C.

It seems that the Earth escaped from this frozen state through the action of volcanoes. As well as bringing heat from inside the Earth to the surface, they pumped carbon dioxide and other greenhouse gases into the atmosphere, which trapped the Sun's rays. Apparently, the Earth lapsed back into its frozen state at least five times until life exploded on the planet at the beginning of the Cambrian period, some 540 million years ago, shortly after the output of the Sun reached something approaching today's level.

Even within historical time there have been dramatic dips in temperature. A 'little ice age' occurred between 1500 and 1850, when solar activity was low. The main westerly storm belts shifted some 300 miles to the south and northern latitudes came under cool continental conditions. This snuffed out the Viking colony in Greenland, whose 500-year existence was ended by encroaching glaciers. The Thames froze over, becoming a skating rink for Charles II and his court, and by 1690, eight years of crop failure had brought serious famine to Britain, killing as many people in Scotland as the plague was killing on the Continent.

Sea ice reached the Faroe Islands, just 200 miles north of mainland Britain. Following the edge of the pack ice, several kayaks carrying Eskimos turned up in Scotland. Glaciers advanced in Norway, and in Switzerland several villages were lost under the ice. Frost Fairs on the frozen ice of the Thames in London continued periodically until as late as 1814, when the Earth emerged from the 'mini ice age'.

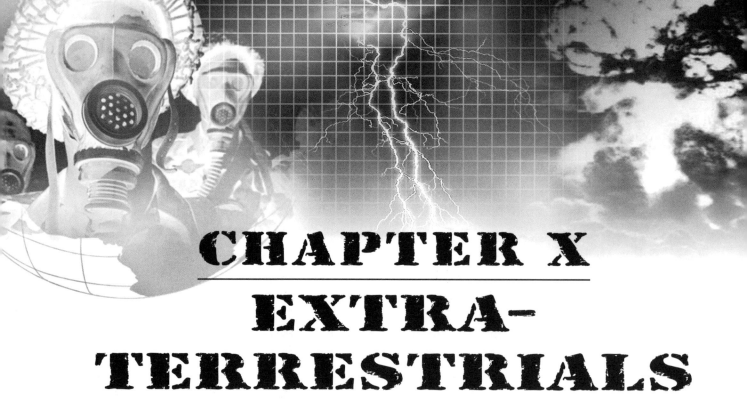

CHAPTER X
EXTRA-TERRESTRIALS

45

Alien Invasion

ALIEN INVASION has been the stuff of science fiction since 1898, when the English author HG Wells published *The War of the Worlds*. In the novel, the Earth is invaded by technically superior and seemingly unstoppable Martians. The book was famously adapted by Orson Welles for radio broadcast in the 1930s, broadcasts which caused many Americans to flee their homes in panic to escape the 'invaders'. It has been adapted for the screen on several occasions and numerous other films have borrowed the same basic plot. But just because alien invasion is the stuff of fiction, it does not mean there is not something out there, harbouring hostile intentions.

There have been reports suggesting we are under observation for some time. During World War II, there were numerous reports of 'foo fighters' – strange lights that followed Allied aircraft and observed aerial battles. It was only after the war that the Allies discovered that German and Japanese pilots had seen them too.

Sightings continued after the war. On 24 June 1947, amateur pilot Kenneth Arnold was flying over the Cascade Mountains in the Pacific Northwest, when he was buzzed by eight strange craft in formation, flying at an incredible speed. At first he was convinced that he had seen the latest US jets, but then became worried that they might have been a Soviet secret weapon – the Cold War was just getting underway at the time. So he decided to report what he had seen to the FBI. But when he landed at Pendleton, Oregon the FBI office there was closed, so he told the local paper instead and wire services sent the story flashing around the globe.

Interestingly, Arnold did not say he had seen flying saucers. He said that the craft he had seen were shaped like boomerangs, but that they 'flew like a saucer would if you skipped it across the water'. The wire services picked up on this and Arnold's unidentified flying objects became 'flying saucers'. Despite this distortion, what he had seen was not a figment of his imagination. His sighting was confirmed by others, including two US Air Force pilots.

A week later, on 2 July 1947, the famous Roswell Incident occurred, when a 'flying saucer' is said to have crashed near an Air Force base in Roswell, New Mexico. The official story was that it was a weather balloon carrying some experimental dummies. However, other sources say that there were aliens on board. Some say that they were captured alive and interrogated. Others say that they were dead, or died soon after, and were subjected to an autopsy. There is a famous film sequence purporting show the alien autopsy at Roswell, although it is by no means convincing. Meanwhile, the craft were allegedly taken to Area 51 at the Nellis Air Force Range and Nuclear Test Site in the Nevada desert north-west of Las Vegas, where scientists and engineers tried to unravel their sophisticated technology.

The Roswell Incident is also said to have prompted President Harry S. Truman to set up a top-secret 12-man committee under Secretary of Defense James Forrestal to investigate the possibility of an alien invasion. And as their investigations got underway, more and more UFO sightings came to light.

By 1952, the skies were positively buzzing with UFOs. On 14 July, two long-serving Pan American pilots encountered UFOs as they flew over Washington, D.C. They reported that the crafts' light behaved in a controlled manner. Between 19 July and 26 July, the D.C. area was invaded by numerous UFOs, which were picked up on radar screens. Although the aliens did not attack, this reconnaissance in force was

seen as a security threat to the White House and the Pentagon, and a full investigation was ordered which turned into the USAF's Project Blue Book.

When the news of what was happening in Washington reached British prime minister Winston Churchill he wrote to the Secretary of State for Air, Lord Cherwell, on 28 July, asking: 'What does all this stuff about flying saucers amount to? What is the truth?' He was about to find out.

On 19 September 1952, the first day of a NATO exercise called Operation Mainbrace, two RAF officers and three aircrew at RAF Topcliffe observed a strange object which appeared to be following a Meteor Jet. They were convinced that it was a solid object and it travelled at an unimaginable speed. Over the next three days, more UFOs were spotted and, in the North Sea, an aircraft carrier carrying nuclear weapons was buzzed by a strange disc. As a result, the RAF officially recognised the existence of UFOs and began their own investigation.

Throughout the 1950s the USAF repeatedly scrambled to pursue UFOs, who seemed to take a particular interest in their NATO bases in Britain. In every case, the speed and manoeuvrability of the UFOs outstripped anything the Air Force could offer and in some encounters American planes were lost. It was assumed that the UFOs were alien craft piloted by extraterrestrials who were testing our defences and it was expected that, in future, they would become increasingly hostile.

Throughout the 1950s and 1960s, NATO's defence systems regularly tracked large, circular metallic objects flying in formation over Europe. The fear was that they were coming from the

Victor Habbick

Soviet bloc. Misidentification of UFOs as Soviet missiles came close to triggering a nuclear exchange and, according to one NATO employee, Colonel Robert O. Dean, NATO forces went onto full nuclear alert at least three times because of UFOs.

By the 1980s, boomerangs and flying discs had become flying triangles. They were seen regularly over the US, often in large numbers. Then on 29 November 1989, two Belgian gendarmes saw a huge black triangular craft hovering over the Hautes Fagnes region of eastern Belgium. They contacted the Royal Belgian Air Force, who located it by radar. By that time 19 more gendarmes had phoned in with sightings which were confirmed by trained observers from the Belgian military.

Over the next few months, the Belgian Air Force was scrambled several times, but the alien craft were too fast even for NATO's fastest aircraft. Belgium's F-16 jet fighters had a top speed of well over 1,250 miles an hour.

At around 11pm on the night of 30 March 1990, a sighting of a huge triangular UFO was reported by a gendarme in the Wavre region of central Belgium. This was confirmed by radar. This time two F-16s caught up with it and locked on to it with their on-board weapons system. At this point, had they loosed an air-to-air missile, it would have brought any conventional aircraft down. But the flying triangle accelerated so fast that it broke contact. The F-16s made and lost contact with it a further six times as the mystery craft played cat and mouse with them for over an hour. During that time

Artwork depicting alien spacecraft attacking the Earth. Although still the stuff of science fiction, any aliens intelligent enough to make it to Earth would possess technology far superior to our own.

it appeared to change shape and made manoeuvres that pulled over 46G. The maximum a human pilot can withstand is 8G.

The Belgian Minister of Defence eventually conceded to parliament that the government had no idea what these flying triangles were. However, the Belgian Air Force concluded that they were 'solid, structured craft'. Three years later, similar craft were sighted over RAF Cosford in Shropshire, which has been a centre for UFO sightings since 1963.

Throughout the Cold War, UFO activity was noted around ICBM – Intercontinental Ballistic Missile – silos in the US. When a UFO described as 'a stretched-out football about the length of four trucks, hovering motionless in the air' tripped the air-raid siren at Loring Air Force Base in Maine on 27 October 1975, the military police went into action but the UFO shot up into the air and disappeared.

Ten days later, on 7 November, the intruder alarm sounded at the Malmstrom ICBM complex near Lewiston, Montana. When the Sabotage Alert Team investigated, they found a huge disc, as large as a football field and glowing orange, shining a light down into silo K-7. Air Force jets were called in, but the UFO shot vertically into the sky and vanished from the radar. Then when the SAT team entered the silo they found that the missile launch codes had been altered. In all, 24 such incidents were reported at Malmstrom.

When a similar incident occurred at Ellsworth Air Force Base in South Dakota on 16 November 1977, guards spotted 'an individual dressed in a glowing green metallic uniform and wearing a helmet with visor'. One guard took aim with his M-16, but an intense flash of light hit the rifle. It disintegrated, causing third-degree radiation burns to the guard's hands.

Another guard saw two intruders escape in a 'saucer-shaped object' which 'emitted a glowing green light'. Traces of radiation were found on the ground and when the missiles were checked, nuclear components were found to be missing from the warheads.

It has been speculated that Ronald Reagan's Strategic Defense Initiative – commonly known as 'Star Wars' – and George W. Bush's new 'national missile defense' are in fact designed to fight off an alien invasion. According to UFO researchers Brian Levin and John Ford, a UFO was shot down over Long Island, New York, on 28 September 1989, using a 'Doppler radar system' developed by the III Electronics company in conjunction with the Brookhaven National Laboratories, as part of the Strategic Defense Initiative.

Some three years later, on 24 November 1992, a second UFO was downed in the same area. Around 7 pm, eyewitness Walter Knowles saw what he described as 'a tubular, dark metallic object with blue lights on each end' moving slowly over South Haven Park. Then he saw a blinding flash of light and the spacecraft crashed into the park. John Ford later obtained a video, shot by Brookhaven fire-fighters, that shows the charred wreckage of the alien ship.

It was often assumed that UFOs were in fact experimental Soviet craft, probing western defences. But after the collapse of the Soviet Union in 1991, 124 KGB files were released that revealed that

The KGB report said the UFO flew over the weapons storage area and beamed a shaft of light into the missile silo

Soviet military establishments had also been plagued by UFOs.

On 28 June 1988, a UFO was seen by four witnesses flying back and forth over a military base near the nuclear test site of Kapustin Yar in the lowland of the Caspians for two hours. The KGB report said that the UFO flew over the weapons storage area and beamed a shaft of light down into the missile silo. The report fails to mention whether the missiles in the depot were nuclear.

In March 1993 Colonel Boris Sokolov of the Soviet Ministry of Defence told US TV journalist George Knapp that an incident at an ICBM base in the Ukraine in October 1983 had come close to triggering World War III when a UFO had penetrated Soviet air space and hovered over the nuclear missile silos there. Attempts to shoot the alien craft down had failed. The automatic mechanism for firing the base's defence missiles had also failed. This was thought to be due to the influence of the UFO. Again the launch codes for the ICBMs had been scrambled, putting that part of the Soviet nuclear arsenal out of action.

Even though the end of the Cold War meant the US was no longer under threat from the Soviet arsenal, Star Wars continued. According to Dr Jack Kasher, a physicist at the University of Nebraska who worked on SDI, this was because, on 15 December 1991, the Space Shuttle *Discovery* filmed a number of strange glowing objects. These made sharp 90-degree turns – something impossible for terrestrial craft – and accelerated from zero to 15,000 miles an hour in one second, pulling 1,050G. What's more, they seemed to be signalling to someone or something on Earth.

Kasher and others point out that, while huge amounts of money was spent on Star Wars, no anti-ICBM missile umbrella was ever built. Instead, he maintains, the money disappeared into a 'black budget' used to built weapons to repel alien invaders.

So how real is the danger? The first question to answer is: how likely is it that aliens exist? And if they do, are they close enough to pay us a visit? In 1961 American astrophysicist Frank Drake developed an equation to estimate how many habitable planets there are. This was called the Green Bank equation because it was developed at the National Radio Astronomy Observatory in Green Bank, West Virginia. That equation is $N = R^* \, f_p \, n_e \, f_l \, f_i \, f_c \, L$, where R^* is the mean rate of star formation in the galaxy; f_p is the fraction of stars with planetary systems; n_e is the number of planets in a systems that are suitable places for life to start; f_l is the fraction of those planets where life actually develops; f_i is the fraction of these planets where life evolves to an intelligent form; f_c is the fraction of these worlds where the intelligent life form invents high technology capable at least of interstellar radio communication, which is the way that we try to communicate with alien life forms; and L is the average lifetime of these advanced civilisations.

Drake took the lowest reasonable assumptions in all relevant factors. For example, he assumes that only one per cent of the billion stars in our galaxy have planets orbiting them – we already know this is a vast underestimate; that one per cent of that one per cent are capable of sustaining life as we know it and that one per cent of civilisations that had developed weapons of mass destruction survive long enough to build radio telescopes. Even using these restrictions, he worked out that, at the very least, there were a million planets in our galaxy that we could communicate with and the nearest, on average, would be a few hundred light-years away.

The furthest the human race has managed to go is the half-a-million miles or so to the Moon and back, so maybe it is not very likely that any of these aliens are going to come knocking on our door. But if they did, we had better watch out. To get here, even from a planet orbiting the nearest star, these aliens would have travelled many billions of miles. To do that they would have had to master the fundamental forces of physics, and have some form of propulsion that is beyond the imagination of humankind's finest minds.

They could, of course, be peaceful, fun-loving people. But think of the various civilisations that have grown up on this planet. The ones that headed out to explore the world were generally warlike. And what happened when Europeans, for example, came across peoples who were less technologically developed? They ruthlessly exploited and dominated them. Millions of people in the Americas died because they came into contact with a handful of technologically superior Europeans, and this is not to mention the many more who died after contracting European diseases, to which they had had no exposure and consequently no immunity against. Even with the best will in the world, any putative aliens are likely to bring an array of diseases with them, minor inconveniences to their bringers, but almost certain death to humans. So we can expect a pretty rough time if they come in peace. But if they are hostile, we are in real trouble.

One of the problems is that, while we know little about them, they know a great deal about us – especially if they have been spying on us for the last 50 years. It is not as if we have kept ourselves to ourselves. Since the development of radio in the late nineteenth century, we have been pumping out information about ourselves to anyone who will listen. If there are aliens within 65 light years of Earth, they will have seen us on TV. That's how far the first terrestrial broadcasts have reached.

SETI – the Search for Extraterrestrial Intelligence – also beams messages out into the sky, giving the position of our solar system in the galaxy and the position of our planet within the solar system. They also broadcast to anyone who wants to listen the total population of the Earth, the average height of a human being, the structure of our DNA and the atomic numbers of carbon, hydrogen, oxygen, nitrogen and phosphorous – the elements out of which we are made. No invading force in history has been given such intelligence.

If the aliens had survived a journey of billions of miles across the hostile environment of space to get here, they are going to be pretty tough, both physically and mentally. If it came to a shooting war, it would be no contest. Our puny weapons would be pitted against a technology that we could not even begin to understand.

Even if the aliens did not wipe us out the first day just for the fun of it, or

because they were so advanced that they considered us nothing more than lice on a disused planet, our governments would have no choice but to capitulate. There would, of course, be a few brave pockets of resistance, a handful of heroes who would rather live in freedom for one more day than face a lifetime of slavery. But they would not stand a chance. Humankind would have to accommodate the demands of the invaders or die. And what might those demands be?

Well, we know that water would be important to any life form we could imagine. We also know that it is a rare and precious commodity. Liquid water exists in only one place that we know of in the solar system – right here on planet Earth. Mercury and Venus are so hot that water boils instantly. There is some ice around the Martian poles, but no running water. The other planets are too cold, being made up mostly of huge balls of assorted gases orbited by a few lifeless rocky moons – though there may be seas under the surface of Europa, one of the moons of Jupiter. So when the aliens get here, they are likely to be very thirsty. All we can hope is that they will leave some for us.

The invaders might also come to plunder the Earth's mineral deposits. The planet is still a rich storehouse of coal, gas and oil along with an abundant supply of diamonds, gold and other metals that aliens may possibly covet. They may have the technology to extract these minerals: on the other hand, they may need a workforce. That, unfortunately, is where we would come in. After all, to them, it would be simply a matter of pressing animals into service the way we use horses, asses, oxen, elephants and waterbuffalo.

In fact, the aliens might chose to use these animals instead. Humans are physically weaker, have greater difficulty following instructions and are generally more troublesome.

However, it might worth keeping some of the fitter and compliant humans alive to use as slave labour. There is nothing so alien about that. Until the abolitionist movement began at the end of the eighteenth century, every civilisation on Earth practised slavery. In the twentieth century slave labour was used with ruthless efficiency in the Nazi and Soviet labour camps. Auschwitz survivor Primo Levi can give us some idea of what to expect. In his harrowing book, *If This Is A Man*, he writes of his arrival there: 'In less than ten minutes all the fit men had been collected together in a group... of all the others, more than five hundred in number, not one was living two days later.'

Far-fetched? It may well seem so, and yet, if there are, in fact, 1,000,000 civilisations out there in our galaxy, how long will it be before one of them comes to call?

The Return of the Gods

IN THE 1970s, the Swiss author Erich von Däniken wrote a series of books, maintaining that the gods who visited Earth in Biblical times were in fact astronauts. One of his conjectures was that humankind was actually a hybrid of this alien species and the lower creatures that already inhabited the world. So what would happen if these spacemen came back to visit their offspring? The nearest things that we have had to a visitation by the gods in historical times is the visit the young Spanish nobleman Hernan Cortés paid to Mexico in 1519.

The Aztecs were the last of the four great civilisations – the Olmec, Teotihuacán, Mayan and Toltec– that flourished in Mexico from around the first millennium BC. They were a bloodthirsty lot who practised human sacrifice on a vast scale and sometimes dressed themselves in the flayed skins of their victims.

According to the Aztecs, four worlds had existed before the creation of the current one. Each had been ended when the Sun was extinguished, wiping out the whole of humankind. Those who lived in the Aztec era – the people of the fifth Sun – had been created by the god Quetzalcóatl, the feathered serpent who can be traced back to the Teotihuacán civilisation of the third to eighth centuries AD. With the help of his twin, Xólotl, the dog-headed god, he had revived old bones by sprinkling his own blood on them.

When the gods assembled in the darkness at the city of Teotihuacán, they lit a huge fire. Two of the gods, Nanahuatzin and Tecciztécatl, threw themselves into it, creating the Sun and the Moon. But the Sun refused to move across the sky and could only be persuaded to do so when the gods sacrificed themselves to give their own blood to nourish it. The Aztecs performed their mass slaughters, where the still-beating heart was cut out of the victim's living body, in order to

Spanish adventurer Hernan Cortés. When Cortés and his men first appeared in Mexico in 1519, the Aztec people believed the invading Spanish were the incarnations of gods, and put up very little resistance to the Spanish conquest of their kingdom.

feed the Sun: blood that ran down the steps of their temples would continue its journey across the heavens. However, they knew that their world was doomed to be destroyed by a terrible earthquake. After it, skeleton-like monsters would come and kill all of humankind.

The Aztecs had an inkling of their fate when between 1507 and 1510 strange ships began to be seen off the coast of

Mexico. Then came a series of ill omens – a comet appeared in the sky, lightning struck a temple and the sound of women weeping was heard at night. The Aztec ruler Montezuma simply executed anyone who reported these portents of doom. It did no good.

The Aztecs had another myth concerning Quetzalcóatl. He had been a Toltec, the Aztecs' precursors. After founding the Aztec state, he had been exiled because he disapproved of human sacrifice. He escaped by sea on a raft of snakes and disappeared over the eastern horizon. However, they believed that he would return to reclaim his kingdom in the year 1-Reed. According to the Aztec calendar, 1-Reed was 1519, the very year Cortés turned up. The Spaniards landed near Veracruz, at the very place Quetzalcóatl was said to have set to sea. Quetzalcóatl was also associated with Venus, the morning star, and was sometimes depicted as a white man with a beard. Cortés was a white man with a beard, so Montezuma assumed that Cortés was the god and the Aztecs, not being a seafaring people, believed that the Spanish ships were wooden temples.

Montezuma sent gold and magnificent costumes made out of feathers, in the hope that the god would take the gifts and go. Instead Cortés seized the messengers and put then in chains. Once Cortés had established himself at Veracruz he burnt his ships so that his men could not flee back to Cuba. Then began his march on the Aztec capital Tenochtitlán. He had with him just five hundred men, sixteen horses and one cannon. He gave a demonstration of his god-like powers by firing this cannon. It made the Aztecs faint. Almost as important was his mistress, a slave girl called Malinche,

later baptised as Doña Marina. She spoke both Mayan and the Aztec language, Nahuatl, and crucially acted as his interpreter and advisor throughout the campaign.

The Aztecs had no defence against the Spaniards' armour, muskets, crossbows, swords and horses. For them, war was largely a ceremonial affair. They wore elaborate costumes and were armed only with a small sword made out of obsidian – volcanic glass. The object of their war games was not to kill the enemy, but to capture as many of the enemy as possible, so they could be used as human sacrifices later. If a leader was killed or a temple captured, the loser capitulated immediately and talks began over the amount of tribute that should be paid. Cortés did not play by the rules. He simply slaughtered as many Aztecs as he could on the battlefield.

Montezuma's only possible defence was guile. He tried to capture Cortés in an ambush at Cholula. But Cortés discovered the plan and massacred the citizens of Cholula, then destroyed the temple of Huitzilopochtli, the Aztec god of war, and set up an image of Virgin Mary in its place. It was a key psychological victory – the Aztecs' god of war had been vanquished by a woman.

Cortés established an alliance with the people of Tlaxcala, who had only recently been conquered by Montezuma. They rebelled and more subject peoples rallied to the Spanish. On hearing what had happened at Cholula, other Aztec cities surrendered without a fight and Cortés marched on Tenochtitlán unopposed.

Montezuma had no choice but to greet the Spanish graciously. He lodged Cortés in the palace of Axayacatl, Montezuma's father, which was packed with gold ornaments. The Spanish immediately melted these down, throwing away the decorative stones and feathers. The gold was shipped back as bars direct to Charles V in Spain, bypassing Cortés's commander Diego Velázquez, the governor of Cuba. Cortés also demanded that Montezuma swear allegiance to Charles V of Spain. He would remain nominal ruler of the Aztecs while Cortés himself seized the reigns of power, with the aim of becoming viceroy.

To reassert his authority, Velázquez sent a force of over a thousand under Panfilo de Narváez to bring Cortés to heel. Leaving a small force under Pedro de Alvardo in Tenochtitlán, Cortés headed back to the coast where he defeated Narváez, whose troops swelled his ranks.

Meanwhile, back in Tenochtitlán, the Aztecs were celebrating the festival of their war god Huitzilopochtli. Terrified by the extent of the human sacrifice they saw, Alvardo's men turned on the Aztecs and slaughtered as many as 10,000 priests and worshippers. When Cortés returned to Tenochtitlán, he found the city in a state of open warfare. He tried to calm the situation by getting Montezuma to talk to his people, but the Aztecs stoned him to death.

Cortés grabbed as much gold and treasure as his men could carry and tried to make a run for it. The Aztecs ambushed them and Cortés escaped with just five hundred men. But in a monumental tactical error, the Aztecs did not pursue the Spanish and finish them off. Thus allowed to regroup, Cortés turned back and laid siege to the city.

The Aztecs put up fierce resistance. For months they starved and harried. Finally they were defeated by an epidemic of smallpox brought by one of Narváez' soldiers. This killed Montezuma's successor, his brother Cuitlahuac. Their cousin Cuahtemoc took over as emperor, but he was captured and tortured until he revealed fresh sources of gold. Later he was hanged on the pretext of treason against Charles V.

Many of the priests and Aztec soldiers preferred to die rather than surrender to the Spanish. So to quell any resistance, Cortés demolished Tenochtitlán, building by building, using the rubble to fill in the city's canals – for the purposes of defence Tenochtitlán had been built in the middle of a lake and was served by canals. The surviving Aztecs were used as slave labour in the gold and silver mines. They were decimated by further epidemics of smallpox, and forcible conversion to Christianity destroyed what remained of their culture.

The people of the fifth Sun were destroyed as completely as if they had been slaughtered by skeleton-like monsters who came to kill humankind at the end of the world. This happened because they had believed that Cortés was Quetzalcóatl. If Erich von Däniken's gods ever do return to Earth, surely the same fate will await all of us.

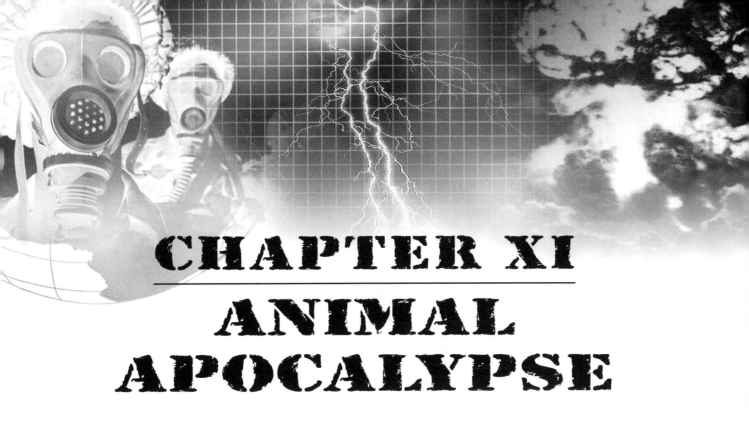

CHAPTER XI
ANIMAL APOCALYPSE

A Plague of Locusts

IN BIBLICAL TIMES, humankind was regularly threatened by plagues of locusts. The Book of Joel in the Old Testament vividly describes the devastation that they brought: 'They have... left my fig trees broken; they have plucked them bare and stripped them of their bark... The fields are ruined... Despair you farmers, wail you vine growers; grieve for the wheat and the barley, because the harvest of the field is destroyed. Like a blackness spread upon the mountains a great and powerful army comes... the land is as the Garden of Eden before them, and behind them a desolate wilderness, and nothing escapes them...'

Little is known about Joel, except that he lived during the period of the Second Temple of Jerusalem – that is, from 516 BC to AD 70. But at that time, most people in the Middle East were totally dependent on agriculture. The loss of a crop would not only cause imminent starvation: the putrefying bodies of dead locusts would pollute the water supply, causing disease and drought, and those who survived the immediate onslaught would have no seed to replant.

But the threat from locusts was not confined to the pre-Christian era. In 1869 desert locust swarms from West Africa reached England and a flight across the Red Sea in 1889 was estimated as about 2,000 square miles in size. Columns of them have been seen up to a mile high.

Various species of locust inhabit dry regions on six of the seven continents. The best known is the swarming desert locust that inhabits grasslands from West Africa to the Punjab. There are also migratory locusts that can leave devastation in their wake in South America. A non-migratory species inhabits North America, but prairie farms sometimes find themselves under threat by migratory grasshoppers.

A plague of locusts is a terrifying sight. A huge cloud of what appear to be three-inch-long grasshoppers suddenly appears in the sky. Sometimes the swarm

A swarm of locusts attacks crops in Central Africa. It is not known exactly why locusts swarm in the way they do, but the effects of a fully-fledged swarm are deadly.

is so dense they block out the sun. They land on fields and forests, and eat everything green. Densities reach 15,000 per square metre and each individual eats its own bodyweight – two grams – of food a day. A single swarm numbers billions of individuals and can devour around 20,000 tons of vegetation over thousands of square miles in a single day, and they can travel up to 80 miles a day.

All sorts of methods have been tried to control them. Their eggs have been destroyed. Trenches have been dug to trap the flightless nymphs. Wheeled screens called hopperdozers have been used to push them into troughs filled with kerosene and water. Poison bait has been left for them and their breeding grounds and the swarms themselves have been sprayed from planes. These have all been effective in the early stages. But when a swarm of locusts is

fully developed, it is unstoppable.

One of the difficulties of dealing with locusts is that it is impossible to predict when they are going to swarm. Most of the time locusts are shy, solitary, harmless creatures, who fly by night, avoid each other and meet only to reproduce. Then suddenly, when food gets scarce, they undergo a radical personality change. They aggregate in huge numbers, travel enormous distances in broad daylight and invade new areas in search of food. High rainfall alleviates the ever-present problem of drought, but it also causes locusts to swarm: it really is a case of 'if it's not one thing, it's another'.

This process also brings physical changes. Gregarious locusts are born bigger, mature faster and reproduce younger than their solitary counterparts. This makes then more hungry. As juveniles, they shed their skin up to five

times and change colour. Solitary locusts are emerald green. When they swarm, they have markings of black and yellow. They are so different it was once thought they were two entirely different species.

The danger has not abated. In 1987–89, a huge plague of desert locusts sprang up in the Sahel region of Saharan Africa. They headed westwards to Morocco, then swept across North Africa, over Arabia and into Pakistan and as far as India, ravaging crops and natural vegetation. The result was a huge loss of agricultural export revenue for these developing countries, and hunger for subsistence farmers.

Then in 2000, a plague of locusts, estimated at 100 billion-strong, moved through the Australian outback. The infestation, the worst for 20 years, followed record rains and the greening of normally arid expanses. Widespread flooding gave the locusts the damp soil

they needed to hatch their eggs, and produced a swathe of green shoots to feed their insatiable appetites. The conditions were so good that there had been multiple layings.

These young locusts tended to fly at night and there were reports of them raining down on rooftops. In places there were even reports of them attacking green clothes hanging on clotheslines.

Unusually that year, there were massive swarms on both sides of the continent. They hit the wheat belt of Western Australia, also well as the rangelands of Queensland, the wine-growing region of New South Wales and the cereal crops in South Australia, where they caused an estimated £100m-worth of damage.

The Australian plague locust commission sent four aeroplanes and five helicopters to spray vast areas with pesticide in an attempt to arrest the migration. As it was they could only target key areas.

In 2001 the Taliban authorities in Afghanistan appealed to the UN and neighbouring countries when millions of locust larvae were found in seven northern provinces. Years of drought had forced the mountain-dwelling locusts out from the desert regions and into agricultural areas of Afghanistan and Kazakhstan.

The Taliban's appeal went unheeded and large areas of the southern Russian republic of Dagestan were hit by the worst plague of locusts for over 40 years. Attempts were made to fight the insects, but a shortage of crop-spraying planes and insecticide meant that less than a quarter of the pasture and farmland in the region was sprayed. The pests spread across an area of 70,000 hectares in just ten days, attacking crops and grazing-land.

Other locusts headed for China where the plague spread across ten provinces. In parts of the north-western province of Xinjiang, and Hainan province in the south, up to 10,000 locusts per square metre were recorded in places. Unlike in Australia, officials blamed a chronic dry spell, which had caused a drought in over 20 provinces. This, they said, led to ideal breeding conditions for these insects. China also put the blame on Kazakhstan, which had suffered the year before but had not had the money to spray the swarms with insecticide. Meanwhile, Mormon crickets attacked Utah, causing over $25-million of damage.

The following year, a plague of locusts swamped the holiday island of Lanzarote, in the Canaries. A black cloud moving at 40 miles an hour appeared on the horizon on the morning of 3 June and took over the island for six days. 'It made a nice change from pubic lice,' commented one holidaymaker.

The most famous account of a Biblical plague appears in Exodus, chapter 10, verses 12–16:

And the Lord said unto Moses, Stretch out thine hand over the land of Egypt for the locusts, that they may come up upon the land of Egypt, and eat every herb of the land, even all that the hail hath left.

And Moses stretched forth his rod over the land of Egypt, and the Lord brought an east wind upon the land all that day, and all that night; and when it was morning, the east wind brought the locusts.

And the locusts went up over all the land of Egypt, and rested in all the coasts of Egypt: very grievous were they; before them there were no such locusts as they, neither after them shall be such.

For they covered the face of the whole earth, so that the land was darkened; and they did eat every herb of the land, and all the fruit of the trees which the hail had left: and there remained not any green thing in the trees, or in the herbs of the field, through all the land of Egypt.

Then Pharaoh called for Moses and Aaron in haste; and he said, I have sinned against the Lord your God, and against you.

Of course, the plague of locusts was only one of the plagues that God inflicted on the Egyptians before they finally let the Jews go. In the plague of blood, God turned all the water in Egypt to blood. In the River Nile the fish died and the water stank. Next came the plague of frogs, where Egyptians found frogs in their beds, frogs in the ovens and, everywhere, frogs jumped on the people.

In the plague of lice, the dust turned into lice which crawled on people and animals. This is also sometimes known as the plague of gnats, due to some dispute over the translation. In the plague of flies, swarms of flies flew into Pharaoh's palace, the houses of his officials and spread out over the land. Next came the plague on livestock where all the domestic animals belonging to the Egyptians died, including horses, donkeys, camels, cattle, sheep and goats.

In the plague of boils, festering boils broke out all over the Egyptian people and their livestock. Then came the plague of hail – Egypt was struck by the worst hailstorm in its history, which beat down crops in the fields and killed people and animals caught out in it.

But it was the plague of locusts that persuaded the Pharaoh to agree to let the Israelites go. God had delivered a westerly gale, which swept the locusts into the Red Sea. Once they were gone the Pharaoh changed his mind. So the Lord told Moses to raise his hand toward and darkness descended on Egypt. After three days, the Pharaoh again agreed to let the Israelites go – but they were to leave behind their flocks of sheep and goats. Then God killed the first-born in every Egyptian household. It was only then that the Pharaoh finally let the Israelites go and take their flocks with them.

To the non-religious, Moses raising his hand and extinguishing the Sun and the slaughter of the first born sound a little far-fetched, but the account of the plague of locusts is all too convincing. In fact, with global warming, the conditions for locusts are set to improve. With more of them, and larger tracts of the Earth being vulnerable to attack, a single swarm sweeping across Europe, Africa and Asia could deal a catastrophic blow to agriculture. It would only take similar swarms in Australia and the Americas to finish us off.

Cockroaches and Killer Bees

IN THE 1990s, the inhabitants of the southern United States, in particular Texas and Arizona, found themselves under threat from a rather unexpected quarter. The honey bee, which had for so long been a friend to humankind, turned nasty. Soon, a series of painful deaths were being chalked up the 'killer bees'.

Also known as Africanised Honey Bees, these particular insects are descendants of southern African bees imported in 1956 to Brazil by scientists attempting to breed a commercial honey bee better adapted to conditions in the South American tropics. But some of them escaped in 1957 and began breeding with local Brazilian honey bees. The hybrid quickly multiplied and began colonising South and Central America at a rate of over 200 miles per year.

Killer bees are indistinguishable from regular honey bees and their venom is no more deadly. But domestic honey bees

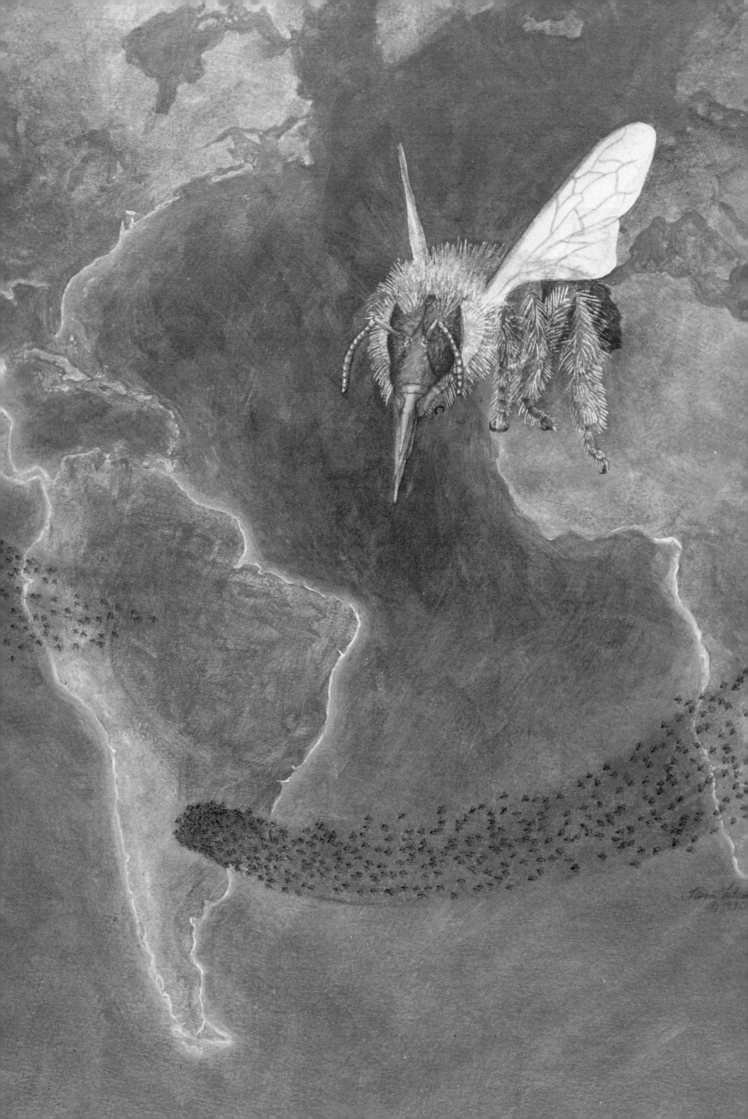

have lived with humans for hundreds of years and have been bred for their gentle nature as well as for good honey production. The new hybrid is not nearly so good-natured. They attack in far greater numbers, and victims will get stung hundreds of times in a matter of moments, resulting in serious injury or death.

While with regular honey bees it is usually necessary to disturb the hive itself to initiate an attack, the Africanised killer bees perceive any human or animal straying into their territory as a threat. Even random noises or vibrations from vehicles can set them off. Once disturbed, they remain agitated for up to 24 hours, attacking anyone who comes within quarter of a mile.

Africanised bees multiply at about ten times the rate of honey bees. While in single season a swarm of honey bees will divide into three, a swarm of killer bees will generate over 30 new swarms. They proliferate because they are less discriminating in their choice of nests than regular bees, utilising a variety of natural and man-made objects, including hollow trees, walls, porches, sheds, attics, utility boxes, garbage containers and abandoned vehicles. They hide out in places where people do not expect to find them and this fact, together with their habit of swarming more frequently makes them doubly dangerous.

In October, 1990 the first swarm known to have crossed the border was captured in the town of Hidalgo, Texas. Colonies were reported in Arizona and New Mexico in 1993 and in California in

October 1994. Within a year, the authorities declared more than 8,000 square miles of Imperial, Riverside and north-eastern San Diego counties officially colonised by killer bees. By 2001, they had taken over more than 100 counties in Texas, 14 in Arizona, six in New Mexico, three in California and one in Nevada – and they were continuing their northward expansion.

In May 1991, Jesus Diaz became the first person in the US to be attacked by killer bees when they swooped on him while he mowed a lawn in the border city of Brownsville, Texas. He suffered 18 stings and was treated at a local hospital. Then in July 1993, 82-year-old Lino Lopez became the first person to die in the US from killer bee stings. He had been stung more than 40 times after trying to remove a colony from a wall in an abandoned building on his ranch near Harlingen, Texas. Two years later in October 1993, an 88-year-old woman in Apache Junction, Arizona disturbed a large Africanised honey bee colony in an abandoned building on her property and was killed by multiple stings. There have been numerous casualties since.

Workers in the bee-keeping industry are most at risk. Africanised bees are now mating with domestic honey bees and are passing on their hostile genes. Once this has happened an entire colony may suddenly become aggressive and short-tempered. But it is not possible to close down the bee-keeping industry as, in the south-west, honey bees pollinate 80 per cent of the agricultural crops.

The best the authorities can do is issue warnings. People have been warned to be on the look out for swarms and colonies in their area. They should be careful when moving junk that has

The spread of the African killer bee (Apis mellifera adansonii) from South Africa to South America and the USA. First introduced to Brazil to produce honey, this dangerous species is now spreading rapidly throughout South America and towards the US border.

been lying around, and should fill in holes in the ground or in walls which the bees can colonise.

Picnickers are advised to wear light-coloured clothing as bees tend to attack dark things. They should avoid wearing floral or citrus perfumes or after-shaves. Even the smell of newly-cut grass has been shown to disturb honey bees.

If attacked, you should run for shelter. Most often, the person who died was not able to get away from the bees quickly. Tethered animals have been lost for this reason. If attacked, people are told to cover their heads and faces, as this is where they are most vulnerable. If there is no alternative, pulling one's shirt up over one's face can be helpful: stings on the chest and abdomen are far less dangerous than those to the facial area.

Victims are told to take refuge in a house, a tent or a car with the windows and doors closed, but on no account to jump into water: bees are clever enough to wait for their victim to come up for air.

If you have been stung more than 15 times, or if you have any symptoms other than local pain and swelling, you should seek medical attention immediately. And you should remove the stingers as soon as possible, scraping them off with a blunt instrument or a plastic card rather than removing them with tweezers or fingers which tends to force more venom into the victim's body.

If the humble old honey bee can turn killer, what other dangers lurk out there in the insect world? The truth is we don't know. Although three-quarters of species alive on Earth are insects, only about

800,000 of them have been identified. Entomologists estimate that the actual number of insect species alive today is somewhere between five and ten million. Their overall population is unknown. In a square yard of rich, moist surface soil, it is easy to find 500 insects – and it is not unusual to find 2,000 per square yard in the northern temperate zone. So you could expect to find four million per acre. So in two square miles of regular countryside you would find as many insects as there are people in the world. In tropical rain forests they are even more numerous. We could be outnumbered by as many as a thousand million to one.

So far, only a few thousand species of insect have been found to be the enemies of humankind – attacking us directly or destroying our crops, livestock and products. But if a simple bit of cross-breeding can turn the benign honey bee into a threat, there is the potential for all sorts of other hybrids, many of which may be just waiting to attack us.

Of 3,500 species of cockroach, most have been around unchanged for more than 320 million years – 800 times as long as *homo sapiens*. If we disappeared they would not even notice. In fact, it has often been remarked that, if humankind was wiped out in a nuclear holocaust, cockroaches, buried deep in the concrete of our cities, would re-emerge and colonise the world, just as primitive mammals took over after the extinction of the dinosaurs. A world swarming with cockroaches may not seem like a pleasant prospect, but then, they do not seem to be doing anything to wipe themselves out.

CHAPTER XII
THE PASSAGE OF TIME

49

The Sun Burns Out

OUR SUN HAS BEEN SHINING for around 5,000 million years and is around halfway through its useful life. It is a very ordinary star, similar to millions of others in our galaxy. When it dies, so will our planet.

Like other stars in the universe, the Sun was formed from interstellar gas that gradually coalesced. The hydrogen that formed the early galaxy condensed, just as a cloud of steam condenses into drops of water. Once one point in the hydrogen cloud became a little more dense than the region around it, its gravitational pull attracted the surrounding hydrogen to it. As the ball of gas grew, its gravitational pull grew stronger and stronger. The pressure this exerted sent the temperature at the centre soaring.

As temperature and pressure in a hydrogen cloud increase, the hydrogen atoms are stripped of their orbiting elec-trons, leaving a single positively charged proton.

When the temperature reaches around 10 million degrees, the protons are pushed so close together that a nuclear reaction begins. This is what happens at the centre of our Sun. In a complex process, four protons are fused together to form the nucleus of a helium atom. In the process, two positrons are given off, which annihilate when they bump into electrons – their antiparticles – producing a great deal of energy. The nuclear reaction also produces X-rays, gamma rays and mysterious mass-less particles known as neutrinos.

When four protons fuse to form a helium nucleus, around 0.7 per cent of their mass is lost. This is converted into energy, according to Einstein's elegant formula $E = mc^2$ – where E is the energy produced, m is the mass lost and c is the velocity of light, making c^2 a very large number indeed. The loss of even a tiny amount of mass produces a great deal of energy indeed. Each gram of helium pro-duced releases 6.72×10^{11} joules of energy, enough to keep a 1KW electric fire going for about 20 years.

The matter at the core of the Sun is

so densely packed that it takes the energy produced there about a million years to reach the surface. When it does, it makes the upper layers glow, giving off heat and light which warm and illuminate the Earth.

It took around 3,700 million years before the nuclear reaction at the core of the Sun got going and a further 800 million years until it settled into anything like its present state. Since then, it has become around 10 per cent brighter each 1,000 million years, making the Sun around 45 per cent brighter than it was when the planets were formed.

To continue shining at its present rate, the Sun must convert 674 million tons of hydrogen into 670 million tons of helium every second. As it does this, the core fills up with helium and the sphere of burning hydrogen around it expands and moves outwards. With four particles packed together tightly in its nucleus, helium is much more dense than hydrogen, so its gravitational pull is stronger. This packs the core together even more tightly, again increasing the temperature. When it reaches 120 million degrees another complex nuclear reaction starts which fuses the helium into carbon. Currently, the Sun still consists of about 60 per cent hydrogen by weight and this process is not expected to begin for at least another 1,500 million years.

Carbon packs even more densely that helium so, as the helium at the core burns, the core shrinks. Around it, there is still a sphere of burning hydrogen, but

The surface of a barren future Earth orbiting the Sun, which has become a white dwarf. The Moon is seen at centre right. Eventually our Sun will become a white dwarf, when it will no longer supply heat to Earth, which will become too cold to sustain any life.

gradually the outer layers become more diffuse. The Sun will begin to swell and become what is known as a red giant. It will go on swelling until it engulfs Mercury, Venus and possibly even the Earth. Even if the Earth is not engulfed, it would be burnt to a crisp and possibly even vaporised.

After 5,000 million years all the Sun's hydrogen will be used up, leaving only the small dense core of burning helium, which is known as a white dwarf. The outer layers cool and spread out over a volume roughly the size of the solar system, forming what is known as a planetary nebula. Large numbers of these extinguished solar systems have been observed in our galaxy.

Meanwhile, the core of the white dwarf will be filling with carbon, but the Sun is not big enough for it to reach the 600 degrees required to fuse carbon. In other, larger stars this process of nuclear fusion continues, producing all the elements that we see in the world. Indeed, every element in our bodies – with the exception of hydrogen – has been produced inside the nuclear core of a star, which has then exploded, seeding the interstellar gas from which new stars and solar systems are formed. So we are all, truly, star dust.

When our Sun has used up all its helium, all that will be left is a core of carbon. The burnt-out ember will fade until it becomes a cold, dead body known as black dwarf. As these cold lumps of carbon give off no radiation, they cannot be seen in the night sky, so no one knows how many there are. But most stars we

When our Sun has used up all its helium, all that will be left is a cold dead body known as a black dwarf

see in the sky are something around the size of the Sun and end up this way, so there are probably countless burnt-out stars in the universe perhaps being orbited by frozen lumps of rock that once teemed with life like Earth.

This cold, dark end is not a happy prospect. By that time, humankind – or whatever the inhabitants of Earth have evolved into by then – will have had to escape not just from our planet but from our solar system to survive. They will have had to flee across the vast emptiness of space to find another solar system to inhabit, or have created an artificial environment elsewhere. But more than likely, by that time the Earth and humankind will have already met their end by one of the other 49 ways described in this book.

Ultimately, of course, there is no escape. The situation would be similar wherever humankind goes. All stars die eventually – often in a far more violent fashion. And the universe itself is doomed.

Our universe has been expanding since the Big Bang some 15 billion years ago. Scientists are not sure whether it will go on expanding forever. The matter we can see in the galaxies is not enough to halt this expansion by the pull of gravity alone. But we can only see things in the heavens that give off light or some other form of radiation. There may be a lot of dark matter out there that we cannot see. This might produce enough gravitational pull to halt the expansion and maybe even reverse it. If it does, the universe could eventually collapse back into a single point in what is called the Big Crunch. At that single point, all matter will be concentrated, producing a massive gravitational field. According to Einstein's General Theory of Relativity, a gravitational field is a distortion in space-time. The field created in the Big Crunch would be so intense that space would collapse and time would slow to a halt.

If there is not enough dark matter, the universe will go on expanding forever, spreading out its contents over ever-increasing distances. This is a far more likely outcome as, recently, dark energy has been discovered. It is a form of negative gravity which pushes things apart and caused the inflation that occurred one ten billion, trillion, trillionth of a second after the Big Bang when the baby universe suddenly grew to be 10 centimetres across. At this point a flood of particles, the basic building blocks which would one day form atoms, were created.

If the universe continues expanding, a hundred billion years from now, the clusters of galaxies will have broken up, though stars will still be forming in individual galaxies. It will not be until a hundred trillion years from now that the last stars will fade into darkness.

After 10 million trillion years, the galaxies will have disappeared after most of their long-dark stars have escaped from them. Some 10 per cent of stars will have fallen into black holes.

Then matter itself will begin to die and, over 10 million trillion trillion years, it will break down into smaller particles and electromagnetic radiation. By then the dead hulks of stars, planets and the interstellar gas will have vanished, and black holes will be almost the only matter remaining.

The black holes themselves will 'evap-orate', giving out immense quantities of energy in the process. But this will be lost in the massively increased vastness of space. The most massive black holes – those the size of entire galaxies – will take a million trillion trillion trillion trillion trillion trillion trillion trillion years to disappear. Then the universe will be a featureless sea of electromagnetic radiation and tiny particles all speeding away from each other at immense speed. It has been observed that in our expanding universe, the further things are apart, the faster they travel. According to Einstein's Special Theory of Relativity, the faster you go, the slower time runs. So in this fate too, time will eventually slow to a halt, and there will be nothing, and not even time or space for anything to exist in. Fortunately for us, however, this event is too far ahead in the future to be of much concern now.

The Gott Hypothesis

UNLIKE THE OTHER forty-nine scenarios outlined in this book, the Gott hypothesis is not based on empirical evidence – evidence from the world around us – but is an a priori hypothesis; that is, it is formulated without reference to the way things in the world are, but with reference only to logically necessary relationships between things in the world.

The theory was first formulated by astrophysicist J. Richard Gott III, during his first visit to Berlin in 1969. Gott found himself wondering how long the Berlin Wall, erected in 1961 by the authorities of the then German Democratic Republic to keep East Berliners from escaping to West Berlin, would last, and if there were any way to predict this, other than to apply oneself to intensive study of the local political situation. Gott hit on a novel approach, that of simply applying statistical methods of analysis to the Wall.

Gott reasoned that as he was not there at any special moment in the Wall's lifetime, (to witness its erection or demolition, for example), but only a random moment, there was therefore a 50 per cent chance that he was seeing the Wall in one of the middle two quarters of its lifespan. Given that the Wall had then been standing for 8 years, if Gott was seeing it at the beginning of the second quarter of its lifespan it would last another 24 years; if, however, he was seeing it at the end of the second quarter, the Wall had a mere two and two thirds years of existence left. On this reckoning, in 1969 there was a 50 per cent chance that the Berlin Wall would last at least another 2⅔ of a year, and at most another 24 years. The Berlin Wall was pulled down in 1989, 20 years after Gott first made his prediction.

Inspired by this success, Gott refined his theory to the more scientific version, which gives a 95 per cent probability of a correct prediction, albeit with a far larger range of figures.

This modified theory states that for any object observed, at a random point in time, there is a 95 per cent chance that the observer is seeing it during the middle 95 per cent of its lifespan, rather than during the first or the final 2.5 per cent.

If the object observed has had 2.5 per cent, or $\frac{1}{40}$ of its lifespan, it has another 97.5 per cent, or $\frac{39}{40}$ of its total lifespan left; conversely, if it is 97.5 per cent into its lifespan, it has a mere 2.5 per cent left to it. For an object 10 years old, this gives a 95 per cent probability that it will last between 0.25 and 390 years longer.

To apply this formula to the Earth would give figures that were so enormous as to be to all intents and purposes meaningless. Applying it to *homo sapiens*, however, is a different matter entirely. The best scientific estimates concur that humanity as a species has been around for roughly 200,000 years, give or take the odd century. Applying Gott's formula, this gives us a 95 per cent chance of surviving for at least 5,000 years, and at most 7.8 million. Gott's worst-case scenario, then, gives us 5,000 years, so there is no need to rush for the bunker just yet. As Gott points out (*New Scientist*, November 1997), this estimate is well in line with what we know of other hominids and mammals which have existed on Earth at some point, and which are now extinct: most seem to have had a lifespan of approximately 2–2.5 million years.

These figures, however, apply only to species based on one planet; as has been pointed out in many of the scenarios outlined above, the colonisation of space and/or other planets will immeasurably increase our chances of survival as a species.

How soon, and indeed if at all, this happens will depend on our political priorities, and how soon we begin to deal determinedly with our more pressing problems of survival here on Earth.

BIBLIOGRAPHY

A Guide to the End of the World – Everything You Never Wanted to Know, Bill McGuire, Oxford University Press, Oxford, 2002

Age of Apocalypse, Barry Jones. Macmillan, London, 1975

Ages in Chaos, Immanuel Velikovsky, Abacus, London, 1972

Apocalypse – A Natural History of Global Disasters, Bill McGuire, Cassell, London, 1999

Apocalypse – Nuclear Catastrophe in World Politics, Louis René Beres, University of Chicago Press, Chicago, 1980

Apocalypse 2000 – Economic Breakdown and the Suicide of Democracy, Peter Jay and Michael Stewart, Sidgwick & Jackson, London, 1987

Apocalypse and Science Fiction, Frederick A. Kreuziger, California Scholars Press, Chico, 1982

The Apocalypse and the Shape of Things to Come, edited by Frances Carey, British Museum, London, 1999

Apocalypse Now?, Earl Louis Mountbatten, Baron Philip Noel-Baker, Baron Solly Zuckerman, Atlantic Peace Foundation, Nottingham, 1980

Apocalyptic Bodies – the Biblical End of the World, Tina Pippin, Routledge, London, 1999

Apocalypticism in the Dead Sea Scrolls, John J. Collins, Routledge, London, 1997

Apocalypticism in the Western Tradition, Bernard McGinn, Variorum, Aldershot, 1994

Apocalypticism in Western History and Culture, edited by Bernard McGinn, Continuum, New York, 1998

Biblical Prophets, Seers and the New Apocalypticism, Milton P. Brown, Mellen Biblical Press, Lewiston, New York, 1996

The Carbon War – Global Warming and the End of the Oil Era, Jeremy K. Leggett, Penguin, London, 2002

Carl Sagan's Universe, edited by Yervant Terzian and Elizabethg M. Bilson, Cambridge University Press, Cambridge, 1997

Chariots of the Gods, Erich von Daniken, Souvenir, London, 1969

The Chip War – the Battle for the World of Tomorrow, Fred Warshofsky, Scribner, New York, 1989

Cracking the Apocalypse Code, Gerard Bodson, Element, London, 2000

Diseases from Space, Fred Hoyle and N.C. Wickramasinghe, Sphere, London, 1981

Doomsday – Britain After a Nuclear Attack, Blackwell, Oxford, 1983

Doomsday – the Science of Catastrophe, Fred Warshofsky, Abacus, London, 1979

Doomsday Asteroid – Can We Survive?, Donald W. Cox and James H. Chestek, Prometheus Books, Amherst, New York, 1996

Earth Under Fire, Paul A. LaViolette, Starburst, Schenectady, 1997

Fire on Earth – In Search of the Doomsday Asteroid, John and Mary Gribbin, Pocket, London, 1997

Fire Under the Sea, Joseph Cone, Morrow, New York, 1991

Gaia – A New Look at Life on Earth, J.E. Lovelock, Oxford University Press, Oxford, 1987

Global Warming: Can Civilization Survive?, Paul Brown, Blandford, London, 1996

Helter Shelter – the True Story of the Manson Murders, Vincent Bugliosi, Arrow, London, 1974

Imaging the End – Visions of the Apocalypse from the Ancient Middle East to Modern America, edited by Abbas Amanat and Magnus Bernhardsson, I.B. Tauris, London, 2001

Millennium Rage – Survivalists, White Supremacists and the Doomsday Prophecy, Philip Lamy, Plenum Press, New York, 1996

Nostradamus – Countdown to Apocalypse, Jean-Charles Fontbrune, Hutchinson, London, 1983

Our Final Century – Will the Human Rees Survive the Twenty-First Century?, Martin Rees, William Heinemann, London, 2003

Raging Planet, Earthquakes, Volcanoes and the Tectonic Threat to Life on Earth, Bill McGuire, Apple, Hove, 2002

The Religion of Science Fiction, Frederick A. Kreuziger, Bowling Green State University Popular Press, Bowling Green, 1986

Return of the Gods, Erich von Daniken, Element, London, 1997

Rogue Asteroids and Doomsday Comets, Duncan Steel, Wiley, New York, 1995

Rwanda and Genocide in the Twentieth Century, Alain Destexhe, Pluto, London, 1994

Season of Blood, a Rwandan Journey, Fergal Keane, Viking, London, 1995

Surviving the Coming Apocalypse, D.S. Davidson, Atlanean, Southend-on-Sea, 2002

The Universe Explained – An Earth-Dweller's Guide to the Mysteries of Space, Colin Ronan, Thames and Hudson, London, 1994

Viruses from Space and Related Matters, Fred Hoyle and N.C. Wickramasinghe, University College Cardiff Press, Cardiff, 1986

Visions of the End – Apocalyptic Traditions in the Middle Ages, Bernard McGinn, Columbia University Press, New York, 1979

Volcanic Instability on the Earth and Other Planets, Bill McGuire, Adrian P. Jones, Jürgen J. Neuberg, Geographical Society, London, 1996

The World's Greatest UFO and Alien Encounters, Nigel Cawthorne, Chancellor Press, London, 2002

Worlds in Collision, Immanuel Velikovsky, Victor Gollancz, London, 1950

Journals: *New Scientist, Scientific American, Science*